Sharing Water
The Church of All Worlds
Member Handbook
4th Edition, 2024

Oberon Zell, Editor

Church of All Worlds
Nebo, North Carolina, USA, Earth

Sharing Water: The Church of All Worlds Member Handbook
4th Edition, 2024
Design and layout by Oberon Zell, Editor

ISBN: 979-8-3304-4565-3

Published by Church of All Worlds
PO Box 1359
Nebo, NC 28761 US

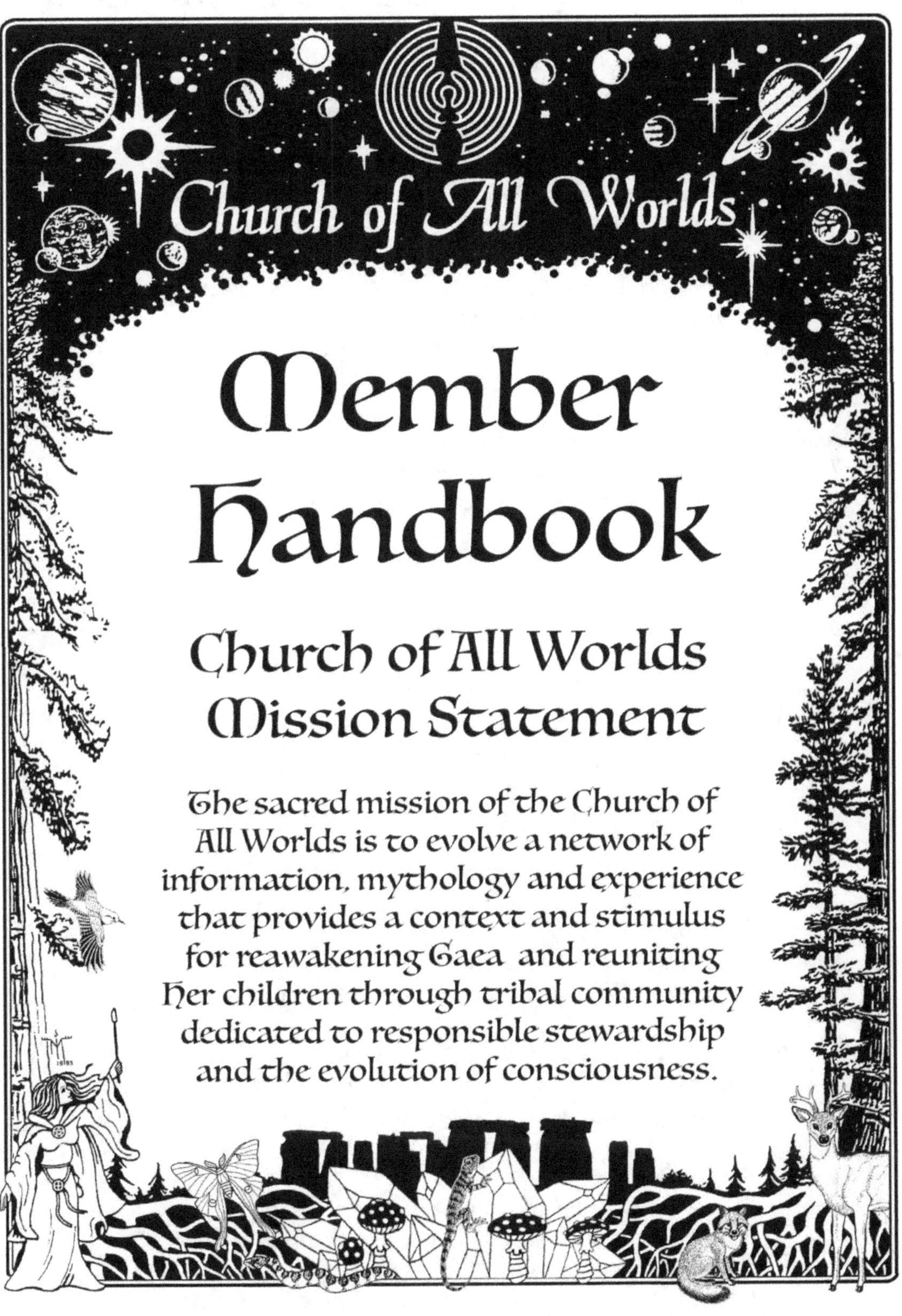

Member Handbook

Church of All Worlds Mission Statement

The sacred mission of the Church of All Worlds is to evolve a network of information, mythology and experience that provides a context and stimulus for reawakening Gaea and reuniting Her children through tribal community dedicated to responsible stewardship and the evolution of consciousness.

The Galloping Garrulous Grok-Flock

(Verses by Oberon Zell)
(Chorus by Adam Walks Between Worlds)

Chorus: *Oh we're nifty and keen; our religion is green*
And we're proud of our planet out in space (out in space!)
And you won't see us grovel 'cause we're from a sci-fi novel;
We're the Galloping Garrulous Grok-Flock in your face!

Well, the saga started in 1961
When a man named Heinlein began the fun
When he wrote a sci-fi book about another man

The man was Valentine Michael Smith
And he was born on a one-way trip
To the planet Mars where they crashed the ship
And all the men and women in the crew were killed.

But the baby was saved by the Martian race,
The wisest beings in outer space
And they brought him up to think and grok like them.

Twenty-five years later another ship
Arrives on Mars on a second trip
And they find our boy and bring him back to Earth

And he views our world with alien eyes,
And through him we have a big surprise
As we find that all we take for granted just ain't so.

Sex and love and politics,
Religion especially needed a fix;
So Mike creates the Church of All Worlds to make a go.

Now two college boys thought it would be a joy
To try an' start living like Martians in their dorm
So they shared a glass of water and they did what they oughter
And the Galloping Garrulous Grok-Flock was born!

Chorus: *Oh we're nifty and keen; our religion is green*
And we're proud of our planet out in space (out in space!)
And you won't see us grovel 'cause we're from a sci-fi novel;
We're the Galloping Garrulous Grok-Flock in your face!

The Atlan water-brotherhood
Stayed underground and all was good
'Til in '67 we went public in a major way

The Church of All Worlds was incorporated
And people asked just how we rated
Our trad—were we Christian, Buddhist, Hindu or what?

And we said "We're Pagans," which raised a fuss
'Cause no one had ever said "Pagans are us!"
And a whole lotta people showed up and said "Me too!"

Thou art God and Thou art Goddess—Immanent Divinity
Sharing Water, sharing Life; Priestesses along with Priests
Worshipping Nature through the turning Wheel
With naked rites and sacred sex, our mission is a world to heal.

So we published a zine we called Green Egg
For all the Pagans of every peg
And we made a sandbox big enough for all to play.

Then we found the Goddess and She found us
And folks all over got on the bus
And that's how the global Pagan movement was born!

Now sixty years have come and gone
And there's just no stopping this magickal song
You can join the chorus and sing along
For the Age of Aquarius has come and we're still here!

Chorus: *Oh we're nifty and keen; our religion is green*
And we're proud of our planet out in space (out in space!)
And you won't see us grovel 'cause we're from a sci-fi novel;
We're the Galloping Garrulous Grok-Flock in your face!

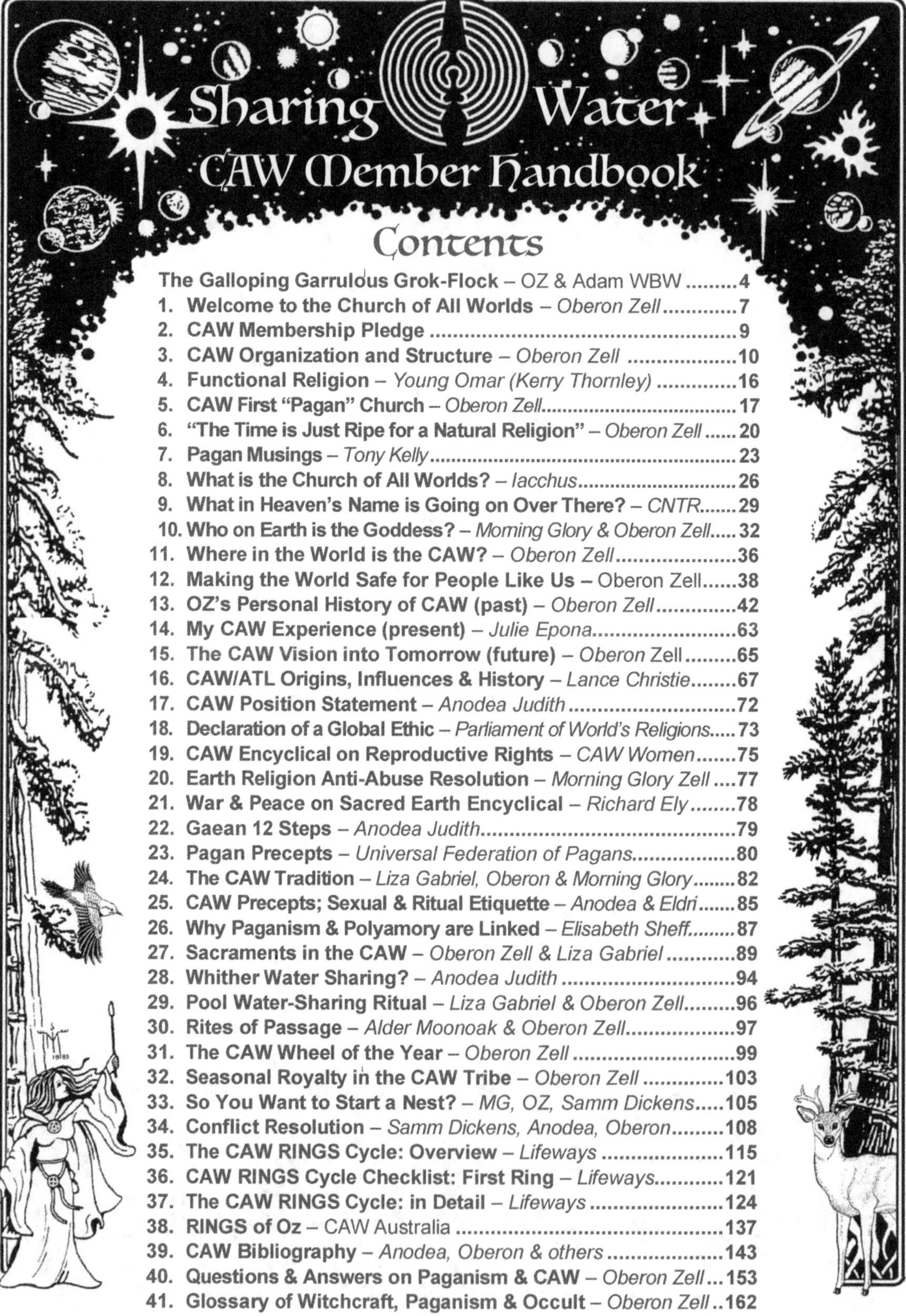

Sharing Water
CAW Member Handbook

Contents

The Galloping Garrulous Grok-Flock – OZ & Adam WBW 4
1. Welcome to the Church of All Worlds – Oberon Zell 7
2. CAW Membership Pledge 9
3. CAW Organization and Structure – Oberon Zell 10
4. Functional Religion – Young Omar (Kerry Thornley) 16
5. CAW First "Pagan" Church – Oberon Zell........17
6. "The Time is Just Ripe for a Natural Religion" – Oberon Zell 20
7. Pagan Musings – Tony Kelly 23
8. What is the Church of All Worlds? – Iacchus........26
9. What in Heaven's Name is Going on Over There? – CNTR........29
10. Who on Earth is the Goddess? – Morning Glory & Oberon Zell.....32
11. Where in the World is the CAW? – Oberon Zell.................36
12. Making the World Safe for People Like Us – Oberon Zell.......38
13. OZ's Personal History of CAW (past) – Oberon Zell 42
14. My CAW Experience (present) – Julie Epona.................63
15. The CAW Vision into Tomorrow (future) – Oberon Zell 65
16. CAW/ATL Origins, Influences & History – Lance Christie........67
17. CAW Position Statement – Anodea Judith 72
18. Declaration of a Global Ethic – Parliament of World's Religions.....73
19. CAW Encyclical on Reproductive Rights – CAW Women.......75
20. Earth Religion Anti-Abuse Resolution – Morning Glory Zell 77
21. War & Peace on Sacred Earth Encyclical – Richard Ely 78
22. Gaean 12 Steps – Anodea Judith.................79
23. Pagan Precepts – Universal Federation of Pagans.................80
24. The CAW Tradition – Liza Gabriel, Oberon & Morning Glory........82
25. CAW Precepts; Sexual & Ritual Etiquette – Anodea & Eldri.......85
26. Why Paganism & Polyamory are Linked – Elisabeth Sheff.........87
27. Sacraments in the CAW – Oberon Zell & Liza Gabriel 89
28. Whither Water Sharing? – Anodea Judith 94
29. Pool Water-Sharing Ritual – Liza Gabriel & Oberon Zell.........96
30. Rites of Passage – Alder Moonoak & Oberon Zell.................97
31. The CAW Wheel of the Year – Oberon Zell 99
32. Seasonal Royalty in the CAW Tribe – Oberon Zell 103
33. So You Want to Start a Nest? – MG, OZ, Samm Dickens.....105
34. Conflict Resolution – Samm Dickens, Anodea, Oberon.........108
35. The CAW RINGS Cycle: Overview – Lifeways 115
36. CAW RINGS Cycle Checklist: First Ring – Lifeways.............121
37. The CAW RINGS Cycle: in Detail – Lifeways 124
38. RINGS of Oz – CAW Australia 137
39. CAW Bibliography – Anodea, Oberon & others 143
40. Questions & Answers on Paganism & CAW – Oberon Zell...153
41. Glossary of Witchcraft, Paganism & Occult – Oberon Zell ..162

Church of All Worlds

PO Box 1359, Nebo, NC 28761 USA

www.CAW.org

Welcome to the Church of All Worlds

by Oberon Zell, Primate

Dear new Waterkin,

Welcome to the Church of All Worlds! By signing your membership pledge and application you have declared your support of a philosophy and way of life that is aimed at living in harmony with the life forces and rhythms of our Mother Planet, our Holy Mother Earth. The CAW is organized as a support network, a spiritual touchstone and a catalyst for the building of Pagan community. Our various branches and activities are intended to offer choices for participation by members in ways that are in harmony with their personal and philosophical being to foster growth, learning and action in the service of the Goddess Who is our Mother.

With this, the 3rd reincarnation of CAW, we have become a Phoenix of the Digital Age, and we are working diligently to make all of our membership materials and networking resources available electronically. Going digital has allowed us to lower our operational costs, and by extension to lower the cost of membership, but it also means that we no longer automatically send out print copies of most materials. So if you do not have Internet access and need print copies of anything, please contact CAW Central at www.CAW.org and we will happily make physical copies available to you on a "Print on Demand" basis for a moderate and reasonable cost.

As you begin your journey with us, we would like to give you a basic introduction to the Vision of the Church of All Worlds, and the many ways that are available for participation. We recommend that you explore our web site www.CAW.org, where you will find a number of essays and articles that offer explanations of the basic concepts of Neo-Paganism and the position of CAW within the greater Neo-Pagan context.

You will also find information which addresses the historical, organizational and liturgical aspects of CAW; our RINGS Cycle training program; our bibliography (which is constantly expanding) and many items meant to give you a sense of CAW 's identity. Please remember that the web site is always a project in process, and that we are continually reorganizing, so revisit it often.

The Best Way to participate in CAW Communities is to join our Forums and Group discussion groups if you have not already done so. The forums are set up to allow Waterkin easy web access to participate in as many aspects of our organization as possible, from social discussions to participation in CAW's tribal government form, the Curia. Information on the CAW Websites, Mailing Lists and Social Media Links may be found on the CAW.org website at this link: https://caw.org/community/

Use these resources to help you "get your bearings" about who to go to for more information and how to find the activity or involvement that is right for you, such as establishing a local Nest or Branch in your area. We also recommend that you consider reading books on the bibliography to expand your knowledge of CAW and Neo-Paganism.

The Church of All Worlds is an organization founded to promote—with proper respect for diversity—a particular world vision. From our new and radical tribal government structure, which we believe incorporates the best of Pagan decision-making processes—the wisdom of leadership by our most respected Elders, an open people's forum inspired by the ancient Curia intended to provide open communication, and maximum participation from our membership at all levels, to our newly-redesigned RINGs program, which has been both broadened to permit more diversity and to more effectively achieve its stated goals, everything has been re-thought and revised.

Please note our "nondiscrimination clause:" Paragraph 3.8 of our CAW Canons states that:

> This church shall hold no regard for a person's race, color, gender, sexual orientation or preference, relationship style, nationality, religion, or socioeconomic class.

The Church of All Worlds is an integral organization within the global Neo-Pagan movement, but it is by no means the only one. We consider ourselves unique in that we try to creatively understand and incorporate practices from many Pagan cultures that seem to fit our overall vision. We also strongly recommend that you consider completing at least the 2nd Circle of our training program, as a way to begin working on your own personal growth and to begin to more fully understand our vision.

Most specifically, we feel that it is important, if you have not already done so, to read the books required for 2nd Circle, as these books will tell you much about us. In ***Stranger in a Strange Land*** you will find much of the philosophy which was seminal in our birth; the chapter on CAW in ***Drawing Down the Moon*** will give you a synopsis of our early history; ***Radiant Circles,*** by Alder Moonoak, is a brilliant exposition of CAW philosophy and teachings;

GaeaGenesis: Conception and Birth of the Living Earth, is the comprehensive presentation of our Gaean thealogy; and ***Creating Circles & Ceremonies*** provides an extensive compilation of CAW rituals, liturgy and theology, along with information on our sacraments, including our central sacrament, water sharing. These are not dogma, but form the basis for our creative ritual and magickal practices and a deeper understanding of who we are.

We hope these resources will help you get started and feel involved with the vision of the Church of All Worlds wherever you may live on our green and lovely planet. I hope it is the beginning of a lifelong adventure for you as the CAW has been for us. And I would like to personally welcome you onto this path of adventure, growth and reverence.

May you never thirst!

Oberon Zell

Oberon Zell, Primate
August 12, 2024

Sharing Water, by Nybor, 1997.

Church of All Worlds

Membership Pledge

In dedication to the celebration of Life in its many forms, I hereby declare my commitment to a way of life that is ethical, benevolent, humanistic, life-affirming, ecstatic and ecologically sane. I subscribe to means and methods that are creative rather than destructive, tolerant rather than authoritarian, gentle rather than violent, inclusive rather than exclusive. I pledge myself to harmonious eco-psychic awareness with the total biosphere of Holy Mother Earth.

Like an ancient tree, I would have my roots deep in the Earth and my branches reaching for the stars.

I acknowledge my personal responsibility for myself, to my fellow humans, and to the whole of Nature; and I recognize this total responsibility, in each of us, as the source of our infinite freedom to become who we are and do what we will. I dedicate myself to my own inner growth and development that I may be of greater service to myself and the world around me. For these reasons I recognize Divinity both within and without, and I say to myself and others: THOU ART GODDESS; THOU ART GOD!

I wish to unite with others upon a spiritual path that encompasses both the Heavens and the Earth, and hereby make application to join the membership of the Church of All Worlds, in order that we may learn together and teach each other ways to bring about these ends.

I understand that this association does not require the severing of any other religious ties.

Signature_____________________________________Date___________

CAW Organization & Structure

By Oberon Zell, Primate

THE CHURCH OF ALL WORLDS WAS FOUNDED AT WESTMINSTER COLLEGE ON April 7, 1962 by Tim (Otter/Oberon) Zell and Richard Lance Christie after reading and being inspired by Robert Heinlein's 1961 science-fiction novel, *Stranger in A Strange Land.* Incorporating in Missouri in 1968, **CAW** became the first of the Neo-Pagan Earth Religions to obtain full Federal recognition, and was best known during the 1970s for publishing *Green Egg,* the foremost Neo-Pagan journal at the time. In 1978, CAW relocated our headquarters to NorCalifia, where we continued our growth and chartered a number of Subordinate Organizations. For further details of our history, read *Drawing Down the Moon,* Beacon Press (1987 edition), by Margot Adler.

The CAW is an organization of individuals who regard the Earth and all life on it as sacred. We consider living in harmony and understanding with life's myriad forms a religious act While we prescribe no particular dogma or creed, our commonality lies in our reverence and connection with Nature and with Mother Earth, seeing Her as a living entity. We are not only Her children, but evolving cells in Her vast, organic body. We embrace philosophical concepts of immanent divinity and emergent evolution. We are essentially "Neo-Pagan," implying an eclectic reconstruction of ancient Nature religions, and combining archetypes of many cultures with other mystic, environmental and spiritual disciplines. But we are not trying to recreate a Paradise Lost; we are actively involved in helping to save the present world from ecological ruin as well as working to actualize a visionary future. We envision our roots deep in the Earth and the past. With our branches reaching towards the stars and the future, we evoke and create myths not only of a Golden Age long past, but also of one yet to come. More than this philosophical attitude, we have created a new Tribalism, where we relate to each other as members of a tribe, with interconnecting clans and families. And in turn, we are one of the Nations of Earth Religions, bound together by our common love and reverence for our Mother, the Living Earth. Our sacred mission is:

"...to evolve a network of information, mythology and experience to awaken the divine within and to provide a context and stimulus for reawakening Gaea and reuniting Her children through tribal community dedicated to responsible stewardship and the evolution of consciousness."

We offer philosophical alternatives to "life-negating" paradigms which have produced war, profiteering, racism, sexism, exploitation and desecration of our natural resources. As the literal meaning of *"religion"* is "re-linking," we are dedicated to healing the separations between mind and body, men and women, civilization and Nature, Heaven and Earth. Some of our individual paths include Shamanism, Witchcraft, Vodoun, Buddhism, Hinduism and Sufism, as well as science fiction, transpersonal psychology, bodywork, Transcendental Meditation, artistic expression and paths of service.

Sacred Lands

We see ourselves as Stewards, not owners of these lands, and we work hard to protect and restore them:

Annwfn is a 55-acre parcel of wooded land in northern Califia, which is our Heart and Sanctuary. We hold many of our festivals, retreats, ceremonies, workshops and staff meetings there. Annwfn has a small pond, organic herb and vegetable garden, a small orchard, seasonal streams, a two-story Temple and two houses. Annwfn is semi-forested with oak, Douglas fir, redwood, madrone, manzanita, bay laurel, and introduced cedar. Access is questionable at certain times of the year. Email caretakers @annwfn.org for additional information.

Nests and Branches

Individual congregations of CAW are known as Branches and/or Nests. A Branch is a regional grouping (i.e. Bay Area Branch, Southern Iowa Branch, etc.) which provides open meetings for interested people and a "Door" into CAW. A Branch may comprise one or more Nests. A Branch's focus is primarily outward. A Nest is a smaller, more intimate congregation of members who are not required to hold open meetings. We recommend that Nests limit themselves to a dozen or so participants but each Nest determines this themselves. Any new "Nestmates" must be accepted by all existing Nest members. A Nest's focus is primarily inward.

Subordinate Organizations

Over the years, the Church of All Worlds has chartered a number of subsidiary Orders and branch organizations through which we practice and teach our religion. Participation in CAW activities has often been through one or more of these branches, though the main body of the Church has sponsored a number of open festivals as well as other occasional events throughout the year. Individual local Nests also hold regular meetings on a more frequent basis. Our subsidiaries are listed below:

Green Egg Magazine

https://greeneggmagazine.com/
Our "Journal of the Awakening Earth" is published quarterly as a downloadable PDF and runs 40-60 pages with a four-color cover. *GE* features articles, fiction, interviews, poetry, book reviews, comics, and columns, with an auxiliary online "Readers' Forum" on Facebook.

GE was the 1992, 1994 and 1995 winner of the Wiccan/ Pagan Press Alliance Gold Award for "Readers' Choice" and the 1992 Dragonfest Publishers Awards for "Best Graphics" and "Best Humor & Cartoons." The first issue of *GE* was published in St Louis on Ostara, 1968, and 80 issues were produced over the next decade. After a ten-year hiatus, *GE* resumed publication on Beltane, 1988. Another 56 printed issues were published (to #136); then it went online in 2007, where it has been ever since. At the time of this writing (Sept. 23, 2024), 187 issues have been published over 55 years. *Green Egg* is the longest-running magickal publication ever!

Nemeton

Founded in 1972 by Gwydion Pendderwen and Alison Harlow, Nemeton is the fundraising and publishing branch of the Church. We publish records, tapes, religious and philosophical tracts, songbooks, coloring books, other books and posters.

Forever Forests

Founded in 1977 by Gwydion Pendderwen, this is our ecological branch, through which we work for the planet in the form of tree planting festivals and information dissemination about forestry issues. We have planted thousands of trees on logged-over land in Northern Califia since 1977. At other times of the year we plant fruit and nut trees, practice organic gardening, do erosion control and occasionally lead tree plantings for other groups. Our tree plantings are combined with ritual healing ceremonies, organic cooking, music and entertainment, hot tubs and a yearly forum. Our purpose is to bridge the ecological and the spiritual.

Ecosophical Research Association (ERA)

Founded in 1977 by Oberon & Morning Glory Zell, this was the research and exploratory branch of the Church. The ERA was dedicated to exploring the origins and actualizations of myths and legends that are pertinent to the evolution and destiny of life on this planet. After Tim Zell (now Oberon) formulated the original Gaea Thesis in the early 1970s, we felt a need for a subordinate organization which was primarily concerned with mythological research.

The first official ERA project was the resurrection of the Living Unicorns in 1980. The ERA supported research in history, mythology and the natural sciences for better understanding of the intricate web of life in which we live.

ERA members have gone: on a diving expedition to Papua New Guinea in search of mermaids; trekking into the Himalayas after the yeti; pilgrimages to Machu Picchu in Peru and Delphi and Eleusus in Greece. ERA explorers have also visited various archaeological sites throughout the world to probe the ancient mysteries of oracles, ruined temples, painted caves and lost civilizations. The ERA has also maintained a library, museum and collection of mythic sculptures and Goddess figurines.

Much of the research and journals from various ERA projects and expeditions has subsequently been published in Oberon's books, with more in process: *A Wizard's Bestiary, 2007; That Undiscover'd Country, 2021; GaeaGenesis, 2022; Barsoom, 2022; Hystory's Mysteries, 2024; The Hunting of the Ri, 2025.*

Holy Order of Mother Earth (HOME)

Founded in 1978 by Morning Glory and Oberon Zell and Alison Harlow, HOME was originally chartered "for the purpose of establishing and maintaining a wilderness sanctuary and religious retreat/training center." HOME became a CAW magickal working Tradition, which formed the basis of our "Magic 101" course, as developed by Anodea Judith for Lifeways. HOME created and conducted CAW and public rituals, ceremonies and festivals. A three-volume looseleaf grimoire called *HOME Cooking: Rites and Rituals of the CAW* was compiled to make this material available and to help Nests create their own rituals. All this material was eventually published as a single book: *Creating Circles & Ceremonies* (New Page 2006).
NO LONGER ACTIVE.

Peaceful Order of the Earth Mother (POEM)

Founded in 1988 by Willowoak lstarwood, POEM was dedicated to children and child nurturing. Its purpose was to inspire our young people with activities, projects and teachings which will build competence, confidence, tribal and global consciousness and an understanding of the rhythms of Nature. POEM provided enriching activities for children at gatherings.
NO LONGER ACTIVE.

International Order of the Red Pentacle

Founded in 1995 by Avilynn Pwyll, this Healer's Guild was a service network akin to the Red Cross and Red Crescent. The purposes of the IORP were to: 1) provide community access to a body of healers of every kind, and of any beings; 2) be a source of networking in which these healers can empower each other in their practices; 3) actively weave spirituality into services consistent with Pagan principles. Qualifications for Apprentice, Journier and Expert would be determined by each network. Annual IORP membership included membership card, button, newsletter, and enrollment in the network of your choice.
NO LONGER ACTIVE

The Nine Million Fund

Founded in 1995 by Night AnFey, this was a charitable institution developed for the Pagan community. The purpose was to create a better life on Gaia while at the same time developing the reputation of Paganism as a worthwhile and serving spirituality. We did this through raising funds for community-based projects, done in the name of Paganism, such as scholarships, legal assistance, community help such as housing for the elderly and assistance for the physically and mentally challenged, and generating projects committed to causing a difference.
NO LONGER ACTIVE.

Lifeways

Lifeways was founded by Anodea Judith in 1984. Its original incarnation was as the teaching branch of CAW. This was accomplished by means of the R.I.N.G.S. system. Over the years, the initial teaching materials became scattered and dated. The RINGS system eventually became its own organization in CAW and Lifeways' mission changed. (See chapters 30-33.)

Anodea went on personally to develop a teaching program called Sacred Centers, which became Sacred Centers Academy, which is mostly chakra-based teachings: www.sacredcentersacademy.com/
NO LONGER ACTIVE.

Membership

Membership in the Church of All Worlds is based on a nine-Circle system of progressive involvement which falls into three concentric bodies (Rings)—1st Ring, Seekers, 2nd Ring, Scions and 3rd Ring, Beacons. Each Ring comprises 3 Circles. The first Circle (in the 1st Ring) consists of anyone who attends our activities or explores in any way our path. Second Circle are people who actually join CAW and Third Circle are people who wish to make a stronger commitment and become more involved.

The three Circles of the **Second Ring (Scions)** are made up of those who have made a deeper commitment to CAW and help run the Church and the subsidiary branches and who are actively embarked on a personal program of self-development and training, usually but not always leading to ordination as a Priest or Priestess or investiture as a Minister.

The **Third Ring (Beacons)** is made up of longtime members of the Church who have worked as Scions, undergone personal development and religious training, shown leadership qualities and may even have completed the CAW's requirements for ordination.

The Church is governed by a Board of Directors with elected members from all three Rings.

Basic membership, which places you in the First Ring Second Circle, is $30/year. We also now offer lifetime memberships! These include a lifetime subscription to *Green Egg*.

CAW members ("Waterkin") receive a Membership Certificate and welcome letter and are automatically enrolled in the CAW RINGS System which allows the member to advance through the Circles; Members will also receive this *Membership Handbook;* any mailings we put out during the year; all information and calendars from the subsidiary branches; and an annual free trip around the Sun!

Members are encouraged to donate whatever else they feel they can afford, as the costs of running this "Three Ring Circus" increase every year. Your financial support empowers a religious body that is aligned with your beliefs. The money goes toward Annwfn sanctuary maintenance, printing and mailing costs, and other reasonable Church expenses.

CAW Australia

The Church of All Worlds Australia Inc. (CAW Oz) is an autonomous daughter Church primarily located on the east coast of Australia. We came into creation originally as a Nest founded by Fiona Judge and Tony Nomchong; later as an incorporated church and recognised charity.

On Nov. 20, 1992, the Church of All Worlds Australia Inc. became the first legally-incorporated non-Abrahamic church in Australia, and in 1994 Fiona Judge became our first ordained Clergy (Priestess). Starting with the summer 1993 issue, *The Emerald Egg of Oz* newsletter was a quarterly insert in *Green Egg* magazine for many years.

CAW Oz was responsible for the *Pagan Summer Gathering / Pagan Seasonal Gathering* which ran continuously as an annual residential event from 1992 to 2020. PSG fell into hiatus with COVID19 restrictions and was replaced with online members moots which ran fortnightly for a couple of years. This then combined with the Crow's Nest moots on Zoom hosted by Brahn th' Blessed which continue to run fortnightly and are open to all like minds across the globe.

CAW members are also invited to our *Sacred Connections* events a few times each year. These are members-only residential weekends that occur on an *ad hoc* basis at the properties of some of our members. Conducted on a shoestring budget, these weekends are primarily to promote a sense of tribe and to share in the company of like-minded individuals.

Many other things have happened over the past three decades, but few have survived the acceptance of Pagan as a household name. This was something many fabulous people fought long and hard for in Australia. We advocated for acceptance and have achieved it.

CAW Australia holds to the same ideals and philosophies as out parent church. We continue to consider ourselves a tribe, share water, hold ritual, and honour the God/Goddess in each of us. Our Clergy, Scions, and Scholar's Guild are ready to support and guide you in your exploration of the numinous and liminal. You can also be supported through the RING system if you are seeking recognition of personal growth within the CAW tradition.

In 2024, we have a single tier membership of $30 per annum but offer family and concession discounts. We welcome soul-kin to join us as new members and see if we fit your idea of an inclusive religious group.

Membership dues and donations go towards maintaining our presence in Australia and subsidising our events. For more information, or to get in touch, see www.caw.org.au.

CAW Alliances

The Church of All Worlds has many friends and allies in the global Pagan Community. We have taken these relationships one step further by creating formal alliances with several organizations. Thus we may cooperate more fully by joint sponsoring of events, including those held on Sacred Lands belonging to our respective groups; by mutual participation in Regional Councils; by offering the services of our respected Elders as mediators in local disputes; issuing joint statements to the media on various position issues; and in countless other ways that we will discover in the coming years.

We offer space to include materials relating to allied groups' principles and activities in our legendary journal, the *Green Egg,* and access to our Sacred Lands in NorCalifia and Australia (and other potential sites as well) for use in retreats, festivals, and such other events as may be agreed upon. We see such alliances as public declarations of mutual love, trust, and respect.

Declaration of Alliance

To establish and increase the amity between our peoples, [GROUP] and the **Church of All Worlds** hereby declare and establish an Alliance of mutual trust, recognition and support. Mutual promotion and co-sponsorship of various events shall be undertaken in a spirit of respect, honor and appreciation. In accordance, Waterkin friendship is hereby pledged between [GROUP HEAD] of [GROUP] and Oberon Zell, Primate of the Church of All Worlds.

Furthermore, let it be understood that this Alliance is based upon the tenets of Perfect Love and Perfect Trust, and upon the awareness of Deity within all, wherein we acknowledge our Divine Unity. May none so allied be rent asunder, for in our Union we are stronger than in our division. In the names of the Goddess and the God, may this Alliance bring forth the greater light of Wisdom and Understanding between all of our Peoples.

So Mote It Be.

Allied Organizations:

Keltic Orthodox Church of the Order of the Royal Oak. Andy "Thorne" Phillips thorne_crossroads@yahoo.com (1989)

Church of the Iron Oak, Lady Belladonna Galadriel Temperance Elensaar scribe@ironoak.org (1995)

Feraferia. Jo Carson jocarsonvisualfx@earthlink.net 11/30/20

Church of the Eternal Source (CES). Michael Poe Imhotep3100@gmail.com 11/30/20

Venusian Church. Nirav Pannama/Ron Petersen venusianchurch@yahoo.com 8/19/20

Aquarian Tabernacle Church (ATC). Belladona Laveau belladonnalaveau@gmail.com 11/30/20

Southern Delta Church of Wicca. Terry Riley terryriley1954@yahoo.com 12/3/20

Forest Moon Grove. Eric & Issy Cooper medicyne_eagle@yahoo.com 12/5/20

Tribe of the Oak. Ellen Evert Hopman saille333@mindspring.com 12/18/20

Mannaheim Heathen Hearth. Burt Johns bjohns@cox.net 12/21/20

The Wisdom School & Temple of Sophia. Lady Tiana Sophia Mirapae ladytiana@verizon.net 1/9/21

Weald Workers of Lamar County. Donovan Yarbrough donovanyarbrough29@gmail.com 4/6/21

Wite Rayvn Metaphysical Church. Alfred Willowhawk alfred.willowhawk@outlook.com 12/23/20

Buckland Museum of Magick. Steven Intermill bucklandmuseum@gmail.com 12/23/20

Oak Spirit Sanctuary. Kerry Lynn info@oakspiritsanctuary.org 12/23/20

Vegas Vortex/Mystery School. Jeff McBride jeffmcbride93@gmail.com 11/30/20

GaiaStar Temple. Mitch & Lori Stargrove mitch@dancingdna.com 12/23/20

Ár nDraíocht Féin (ADF). Ian Corrigan tredara@gmail.com 11/30/20

Council of Magickal Arts (CMA). Candyce Eskew help@magickal-arts.org 11/30/20

Corellian Nativist Church. Don Lewis DonLewisHP@aol.com 12/23/20

EarthSpirit. Andras Corban-Arthen andras@earthspirit.com 11/30/20

Isis Oasis Sanctuary/Temple of Isis. deTraci Regula tregula@msn.com 11/30/20

Rhinoceros Lodge (Hellenic). Jon DeCles/Pyrokanthos rhinoceroslodge@pon.net 12/23/20

The Troth. Diana Paxson diana@westria.org 12/23/20

Temple of Witchcraft. Christopher Penzack christopherpenczak@gmail.com 12/23/20

Foxwood Temple of the Old Religion; House of Brigh Faery Seership Institute. Orion Foxwood faeryseer@gmail.com 12/23/20

Temple of the Nine Wells. Gypsy Ravish wlpssp@comcast.net 12/23/20

Ardantane. Amber K amberk1@aol.com 12/23/20

Cerren Ered. Andy Thorne Phillips thorne_crossroads@yahoo.com 12/23/20

Serpentstone family Grove, Rhiannon Zell rhiannonofss@gmail.com 5/14/24

Church of All Worlds

PO Box 488, Laytonville, CA 95454 USA
(707) 984-7013 • FAX 707-984-7063
e-mail: cawnemeton@aol.com

Organizational Flow Chart

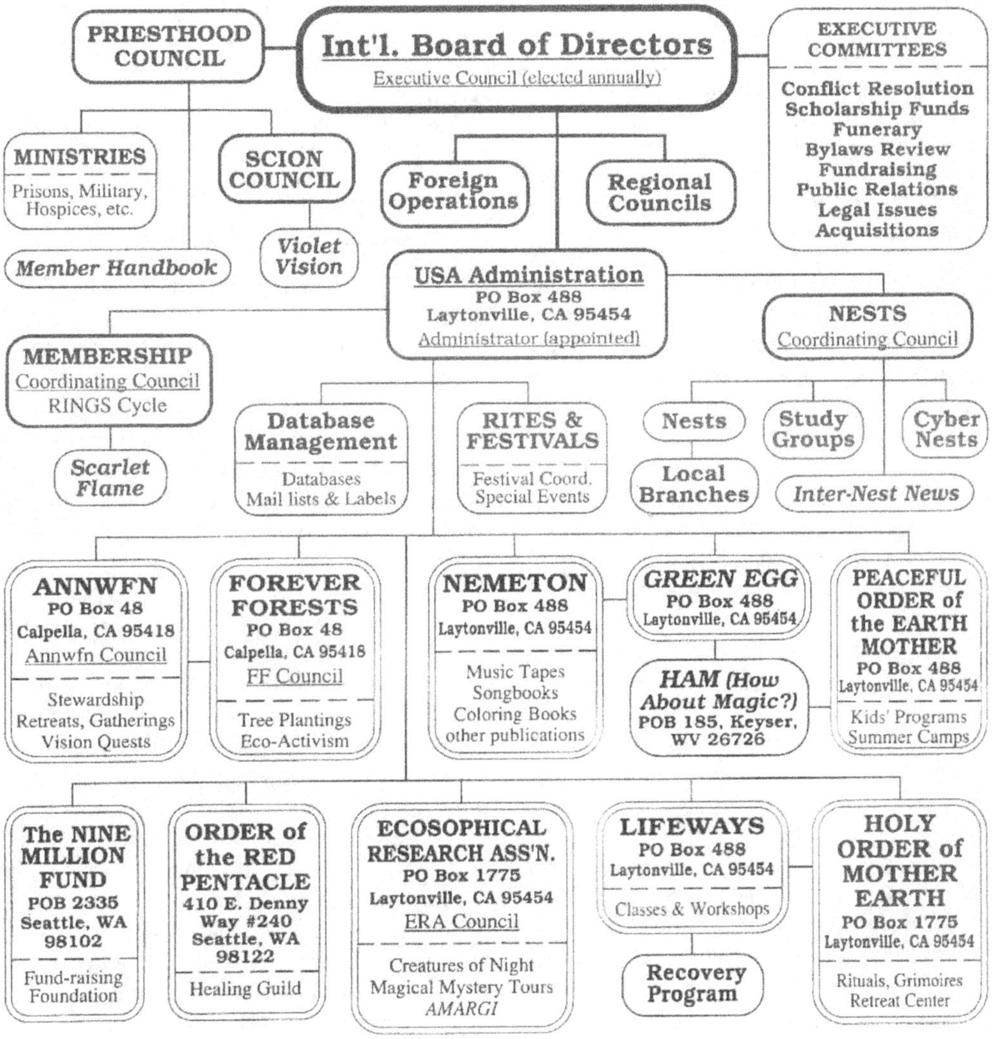

This CAW Organization Flow Chart was printed on the back of the *CAW Membership Handbook,* 3rd Edition, 1997. It is reprinted here for historical reference only, as virtually everything about it is now obsolete—especially all the addresses. Do not consider it a representation of the present Church! Still, this chart does give an interesting perspective of how CAW was structured in the 1990s. And perhaps it may serve as an inspiration for our once-and-future Church in years to come... ~OZ

Functional Religion

by Young Omar (Kerry Thornley)
Kerista's Erotic Ethic & Etc., Sept. 4, 1966, Kerista Press, Los Angeles

Introduction by OZ: *I first came upon this prophetic little article in 1967, just at the time our original Atlan water-brotherhood (founded in 1962) was deciding to create a public face and establish the Church of All Worlds as a legal religious entity. As soon as we began to present ourselves as a church, people wanted to know what religious category we were. Were we some kind of Christians? Hindus? Buddhists? We knew we were none of those, but we hadn't actually considered what we were, as opposed to what we weren't. Kerry's article proposed such an identification, and we immediately adopted the term "Pagan," promoting it widely, through the vehicle of the early* Green Egg, *to other newly-emerging groups of "Old Religionists" we encountered. The term caught on, unifying many disparate little groups into the foundations of the modern Pagan Movement.*

Ironically, Kerista itself, the utopian polyfidelity organization for whom this article was written, rejected the appellation if "Pagan." As Kerista's founding prophet, Brother Jud, told me a decade later, "I am an authentic Hebrew prophet, not a Pagan!" Sadly, after a remarkable 30-year run, Kerista disbanded in 1991. But CAW continues, and modern Paganism is thriving.

All religions have social functions or they soon die out. Christianity is in crisis today precisely because it has lived beyond most of its functions. Once it was more or less the propaganda bureau for the kings. Then came the separation of Church and State. Once it was the explainer of all the natural mysteries. Then came science to prove it wrong. Today the liberal theologians are still trying to restore to Christianity these functions, changing only masters, not techniques.

Liberal Christians now try to put their church to work as a propaganda agent for reform. And the theologians seek to explain the greatest mystery of them all-why they cling to the Judea-Christian format in the face of scientific advancement. But the masses do not listen. They continue to go to church though they dimly realize their minister is reactionary, their scriptures are bullshit, and, to boot, their church—indeed their religion—is ugly. The dead hand of habit and the live prod of fear— these are their motives. Who would be cruel enough to deprive them of such pathetic solace? Let us forget them. Instead, let us look at the jobs of the far less intellectual, but far more constructively functional, religions of old. These were the "Pagan" religions-the religions that survive to this day in England and the United States as "Witchcraft." These are the Rosicrucians, as well, and the many occult traditions that have remained under- ground since with tongue in cheek and sword in hand the Christian conquerors attempted the most prolonged and massive brainwashing in the history of Europe.

Speaking of the primitive religions, B.Z. Goldberg in his great book *The Sacred Fire* wrote: "What was forbidden at large in the bush not only was permitted, but, in fact, became a duty in the temple of the gods." The main function, then, of these religions was NOT to aid and abet the State, nor was it to re-enforce the strictures of the society-it was to provide refuge and relief; it was to temporarily or in a limited space lift the taboos of the tribe, of the collective. It was to give the individual a means of restoring or maintaining his sanity.

Thus "Pagan" religions were generally functional in a worthwhile sense, in a social sense that was positive. At once they both stabilized and overthrew the social structure, much as does the "black market" today in nations where the ruling class unwisely attempts to regulate the economy by law.

The positive social function of providing an excuse for the lifting of taboos has recently been re-introduced into modern society by the psychotherapeutic schools in the forms of existential games, ego dancing, and sensory perception workshops. So while science contradicts the function of Christianity as an explainer of mysteries, it confirms that of Paganism as an institutionalized cultural countertrend—and paves the way for the return of Paganism as a legitimate social force, for the advent of Liberal Paganism, of a New Theology of Paganism, and of Pagan Reductionism.

Keristan movements comprise the Unitarian-Universalist Church of the Pagan Resurgence!

God is dead. Christianity is dying.

Long live Kerista! Long live Paganism!

CAW First "Pagan" Church

By Oberon Zell

Sunday 12/2/2018

> It is crucial to stress right from the start that until the 20th century, people did not call themselves pagans to describe the religion they practised. The notion of paganism, as it is generally understood today, was created by the early Christian Church. It was a label that Christians applied to others, one of the antitheses that were central to the process of Christian self-definition. As such, throughout history it was generally used in a derogatory sense.
>
> ~ Davies, Owen (2011). *Paganism: A Very Short Introduction.* NY: Oxford University Press. p. 1

I'M OFTEN CHALLENGED FOR claiming that in 1967 the Church of All Worlds was the first church *ever* to specifically self-identify as *"Pagan."* My detractors insist that we weren't. So I want to know: who else before us ever claimed that identity? It would be great to be able to prove that our history as Pagans has additional antecedents so identifying.

So I put this question to the many religious scholars and academics I know, asking them if they could cite examples of any religious groups, organizations, or individuals declaring themselves as "Pagan" prior to 1967. A number gave references to the intermittent use of the term over the centuries, but very few of people actually identifying themselves as "Pagan," and *none* for any church or religious group.

Sam Webster referenced *Gemistos Plethon* (1428) and Giordano Bruno (1600), but I could find no mention of their Paganism in their Wikipedia bios.

Jordan Gruber says: "Sam Webster tends to know his stuff, but Wikipedia is hardly authoritative for anything." So, for what it's worth, this site states that "Bruno was prosecuted mainly for *paganism,* heresy and blasphemy." See https://news.slashdot.org/.../giordano-bruno-after-400-years

And this site says, "Bruno's philosophy was an unusual one, to say the least. *Pagan* at its core, he drew on a mix of ancient knowledge, including the works of Lucretius, Pythagoras, and the Hermetic tradition, as revived by the Italian humanist Marsilio Ficino and the philosopher Giovanni Pico della Mirandola." See http://www.academia.edu/ /Giordano_Bruno_Magic_Theology

And here we learn that "[Bruno] was intoxicated by the teaching of the church: its great libraries filled with *pagan* and Christian learning..."

So, while Bruno probably didn't overtly identify as a Pagan, or start a Pagan religions movement, he was probably quite aware that he was studying and championing Pagan ideas. https://www.thenation.com/.../hungry-mind-giordano-bruno.../

In 1807, William Wordsworth proclaimed:

I'd rather be a Pagan suckled in a creed outworn;
So might I, standing on this pleasant lea,
Have glimpses that would make me less forlorn;
Have sight of Proteus rising from the sea;
Or hear old Triton blow his wreathèd horn.

(~William Wordsworth, "The World Is Too Much With Us")

Linda Woodhead said:

There were certainly people using the word pagan positively in relation to religious sensibility from the late 19th century on. In Tess of the D'Urbervilles (1891), for example, Hardly discusses how theologically repelled Angel's father would have been by his son's *"pagan pleasure in natural life and lush womanhood."*

In 1914 Aleister Crowley wrote to C.S. Jones of the North American O∴T∴O∴ exhorting him to "be the founder of *a new and greater Pagan cult."*

And Benjamin Zeller wrote:

H.P. Lovecraft also referred to his religious interests as Pagan at one point in his early life, though he later embraced non-theism, or what he called "Unfaith." He wrote this in a 1922 essay for a Freethought magazine:

> "When about seven or eight *I was a genuine pagan,* so intoxicated with the beauty of Greece that I acquired a half-sincere belief in the old gods and Nature-spirits. I have in literal truth built altars to Pan, Apollo, Diana, and Athena and have watched for dryads and satyrs in the woods and fields at dusk. Once I firmly thought I beheld some of these sylvan creatures dancing under autumnal oaks; a kind of 'religious experience' as true in its way as the subjective ecstasies of any Christian."
>
>   ~ H.P. Lovecraft

But none of these references claimed Paganism as anyone's actual stated religion, and none mentioned any organized church so self-identified prior to my claiming that identity for myself and the Church of All Worlds on Sept. 7, 1967. The most definitive responses were from Dr. Ronald Hutton and Rev. Patrick McCollum:

From: Ronald Hutton
Sent: Saturday, December 1, 2018 4:55 AM

I think that there are two different issues mixed up together here. One is whether members of a self-conscious modern Pagan movement used the capital letter for themselves before Oberon did. The other is the usage of 'pagan' and 'Pagan' in the previous two hundred years.

The first is the simpler. In Britain at least, and those American movements in contact with it, *I can find no trace of people whom we can identify as practitioners of a modern Pagan movement calling themselves either 'pagans' or 'Pagans' between 1950 and 1967.* They called themselves 'witches' or 'Wiccans' or by other tradition-specific names. *The term 'Pagan' emerges rapidly around 1970, embodied in 'The Pagan Front,' 'The Pagan Way,' 'The Pagan Movement,' etc., and that may have been due to Oberon's influence. Nor can I find an example of the use of 'Neo-Pagan' by such people in the years 1960-67, so that does look like Oberon's work.*

The other issue is a semantic quagmire. Between 1830 and 1950 the term 'pagan' was freely used in Britain (and I presume other English-speaking lands), not just to mean pre-Christian religions but in association with a bundle of qualities vaguely associated with libertarian thoughts and lifestyles, religious scepticism, raunchiness, and Puritan-baiting ('He was very pagan at heart, believing only in himself,' 'She has pagan eyes, full of temptation,' etc). To complicate matters further, between 1700 and 1830, writers would often freely capitalise Words of Special Significance within Sentences. So, when Byron gives 'Pagan' a capital, it reflects this custom, and does not endow the word with any special meaning that 'pagan' did not have.

On the other hand, some individuals between 1700 and 1900 were pagans in a religious sense, of venerating classical deities, such as Shelley and Swinburne. As a further blurring of the picture, the term 'neo-pagan' appeared in England in the 1890s, to describe people who opposed prevalent hidebound morality, often inspired by the ancient world. This was sometimes capitalised, so that the young Rupert Brooke and his set in Edwardian England called themselves the 'Neo-Pagans', without any religious connotation, to indicate that they were free spirits.

So, I think that on present evidence, *Oberon could well deserve the credit that he has taken,* but the linguistic background is very complicated.

With every good wish to all,
Ronald Hutton
(Professor, Department of Historical Studies, Oxford University; *Triumph of the Moon: A History of Modern Pagan Witchcraft,* 2000)

From: Patrick McCollum
Sent: Fri, Nov 30, 2018 at 9:51 AM

I can only speak back to 1965 when I was first initiated, but *no one that I had ever met in those days used the term Pagan as a spiritual identification, and no one in our group which arrived in the US in 1954 or '55 ever used the term.* In those early days, I had the opportunity to travel extensively across the United States and Canada, and *I personally never heard one single person use the term Pagan to identify themselves.*

I remember the complex process of various terms being thrown on us as the community began to grow, mostly by outsiders. And I *clearly remember Oberon throwing out the term Pagan, and then later Neo-Pagan,* as we as a community tried to self-identify rather than succumb to the labels being attached to us by others.

I think it's always impossible to pin any surety on the origin of any terms, but what I do see as important here is that *Oberon played a key role in the term becoming what it is today.*

I have often observed that as new generations enter the conversations, it often seems important to them to lessen the contributions or observations of those who came before them. I have lots of thoughts as to why that is, but that's another fun discussion.

There are very few still alive who were actively present when these shifts first started. But I would assume that their faded memories have far more credibility than that of those who come later who are trying to figure it all out and get it written down as history.

After all, I was just at the American Academy of Religion last week, and something like 8,000 scholars are still trying to sort out the beginnings of Christianity!

I would simply say as one who was actually there as it happened, that *Oberon threw out the term, and that once he did, the term stuck!*

Blessings, Patrick McCollum (Director of Public Chaplaincy, Cherry Hill Seminary; Chaplaincy Liaison, American Academy of Religion; Minority Faith Chair, American Correctional Chaplains Association; Executive Director, National Correctional Chaplaincy Directors Association; President, Patrick McCollum Foundation; Religion Advisor, United States Commission on Civil Rights; Recipient, Mahatma Gandhi Award for the Advancement of Pluralism; publications: *California Department of Corrections Wiccan Chaplains Manual,* 1998; *Courting the Lady,* 2000; *Religious Accommodation in American Jails,* 2013)

"Oberon Zell was the first person to conceive and publish the biological and metaphysical foundations of what has become known as the "Gaia Theory"—the unified body and emergent soul of the living Earth. Oberon's profound reconciliation of science, mythology and spirituality inspired and infused a worldwide neo-Pagan, panentheistic movement. For 48 years he has been writing and lecturing on Gaian consciousness! His visionary sculpture of the 'Millennial Gaia' is a three-dimensional revelation, an artistic masterpiece that fuses evolutionary biology with sculptural elegance."

~Ralph Metzner, Ph.D.
Founder-President, The Green Earth Foundation; Professor Emeritus, California Institute of Integral Studies

"In March of 1968, the *Green Egg* appeared. From its inauspicious beginnings as a one-page ditto sheet, it grew over 80 issues into a 60-page journal, becoming *the most significant periodical in the Pagan movement during the 1970s and made Tim [Oberon] Zell, its editor, a major force in Neo-Paganism (a term which Zell coined)."
~Rev. Dr. J. Gordon Melton
Encyclopedia of American Religions
Director, Institute for the Study of American Religions

"Oberon Zell-Ravenheart is not only *one of the founders of contemporary Neo-Paganism* but remains one of its most respected spokesmen."
~Patricia Monaghan
Author, *The Book of Goddesses & Heroines*

ADDENDUM by OZ: Capitalizing "Pagan"

Whenever I read an article or interview in the print media about Pagans and Paganism, I note the common and infuriating phenomenon that while "Christian" and "Christianity" are always capitalized (they are, after all, proper nouns and adjectives denoting a religion), "paganism" and "pagan," however, are invariably written in lower case—even though these, too, are proper nouns and adjectives denoting a religion. What is the proposed justification for this?

Terms such as "Pagan," "Paganism," "Witch" and "Witchcraft"—when used to denote modern Pagan religion and spirituality—are proper nouns designating the names of religions and their practitioners, and should therefore always be capitalized, just like Christian, Christianity, Jew, Judaism, Moslem, Islam, Hindu and Hinduism. Journalists rarely capitalize Pagan/Wiccan terms, however, because dictionaries and style sheets generally indicate the words as lowercase. Modern practitioners consider this refusal to capitalize the names of our religions to be a gross insult—as would the members of any other religion.

"The Time is Just Ripe for a Natural Religion"

By Oberon Zell

NOTORIOUS MAGICIAN ALEISTER Crowley advocated the use of lunar, solar, and seasonal Nature-based rituals. In 1914 he wrote to C.S. Jones of the North American O∴T∴O∴ about a ritual of Isis that his Lodge had performed:

> I hope you will arrange to repeat this all the time, say every new moon or every full moon, so as to build up a regular force. You should also have a solar ritual to balance it, to be done at each time the Sun enters a new sign, with special festivity at the Equinoxes and Solstices.
>
> In this way you can establish a regular cult; and if you do them in a truly magical manner, you create a vortex of force which will suck in all the people you want. *The time is just ripe for a natural religion.* People like rites and ceremonies, and they are tired of hypothetical gods. Insist on the real benefits of the Sun, the Mother-force, the Father-force, and so on, and show that by celebrating these benefits worthily the worshippers unite themselves more fully with the current of life. Let the religion be Joy, but with a worthy and dignified sorrow in death itself, and treat death as an ordeal, an initiation… In short, be the founder of *a new and greater Pagan cult.*

While C.S. Jones did not do anything with this mandate, others did. Particularly one Gerald Gardner, who met "The Great Beast" briefly just before Crowley's death in 1947.

The modern Pagan community can be dated from various germinal events in the mid-20th century—one of these was the publication of Gardner's *Witchcraft Today* in 1954, which resulted in the first generation of self-identified modern Witches. However, "Wiccan" Witchcraft was generally unknown outside of the UK until 1962, when Gardner assigned Raymond and Rosemary Buckland to bring the Craft to the US.

The exponential growth of modern Witchcraft and Neo-Paganism over the past 70 years has shown that Crowley's vision of the revival of *"natural religion"—"a new and greater Pagan cult"*—was prophetic. Gerald Gardner had that same vision and applied it successfully to his "Wiccan" religion, inducting his first initiate in 1950. But Gardner's early Wiccans never thought of themselves as *Pagans,* and some (such as Maxine Sanders) still do not.

The emergence and evolution of this *"new and greater Pagan cult"* can be briefly summarized in decades, as follows:

1900s-1910s *60-year cultural renaissance:* **"The Golden Dawn."**
Magickal societies, arcane lodges, and esoteric fraternities. Rosicrucians. O∴T∴O∴ Crowley. Creating mystic rites & rituals.

1920s-'30s Academics and folklorists spawn romantic writings and secret societies hearkening to old pagan ideals. Gleb Botkin's Church of Aphrodite (1938).

1940s Foundational scholarly books of folklore and anthropology; earliest covens form. Margaret Murray, Gerald Gardner.

1950s British Tradition Witchcraft (BTW) becomes established and spreads, with considerable media attention. Alex Sanders.

1960s *60-year cultural renaissance:* **"The New Age."**
Founding of various non-Wiccan "Old Religion" groups; from 1967, all eventually claiming identity of "Pagan:" Druids, Hellenes, Khemetics, Heathens. CAW. Zell.

1970s Pagan councils, alliances, and associations; early Pagan newsletters. Gaea Thesis unites Pagan community with common thealogy. First Pagan festivals and conventions: Starwood, PSG. *Green Egg.* Starhawk.

1980s Pagan festivals proliferate; with home computers, explosive proliferation of Pagan publications. Many books on Paganism published—especially by Llewellyn.

1990s   Pagan festivals become huge; major high-quality newsstand magazines; early Internet, BBCs, etc. CAW. *Green Egg.*

2000s   Pagan businesses and Pagan Pride events proliferate; with rise of Amazon.com, newsstand magazines disappear or go digital; Paganism goes Internet.

2010s   Pagan stores & festivals flourish; Facebook, Twitter, Instagram & YouTube; Pagan numbers increase exponentially into the millions; modern Paganism is recognized as the 2nd largest "faith group" in America, and the fastest-growing.

2020s   *60-year cultural renaissance:* "The Awakening."
In the great COVID pandemic, Pagan festivals go virtual and global via Zoom, etc. Paganism becomes recognized as a significant world religion, and a major player in Earth healing and restoration.

Lance Christie and I met in Sept. of 1961 at the very start of our college years. Inspired by Robert Heinlein's latest sci-fi novel, *Stranger in a Strange Land,* we shared water on April 7, 1962, founding a "water-brotherhood" we called "Atl"—an Aztec word meaning "water." Our initial Mission Statement was "to make the world safe for people like us."

Over the next five years, our esoteric "aqua-fraternity" grew to more than 100 people before undergoing an amiable mitosis which resulted in two parallel sister branches: the public Church of All Worlds (CAW) and the more private Atlan Foundation. It was at that juncture (Sept. 7, 1967), in a talk at a local Beatnik coffeehouse, that I first claimed the term "Pagan" as a religious identity for myself and the CAW.

Prior to then, the appellation *"pagan"* was used most commonly by Christians as a derogatory slur for "primitive savages" and other nonbelievers whom missionaries were supposed to go out and convert to Jesus. It was always *"those* pagans," never *"us* Pagans."

Six months later (March 4, 1968), the Church of Worlds was legally incorporated, and the first issue of *Green Egg* was printed that Ostara. My promoting the identity of "Pagan" through *Green Egg* inspired other early groups seeking to reclaim their pre-Christian spiritual heritage to adopt the designation as well.

And thus a movement of "Green Religion" was launched, embracing Nature worship, pantheism, polytheism, Goddesses, Priestesses, the Gaea Thesis, the Wheel of the Year, common liturgy, magick, sacred sex, sexual and gender diversity, polyamory, and many other features rejected by the mainstream religions. Foundations were laid, memes were established, and a legacy was created.

Lance and I were both avid students of comparative religion and the history of Christianity. When we decided to go public with the Church of All Worlds, we were keenly aware of the profound responsibility we were taking on in the founding of a new religion.

Nearly 2,000 years before our time, a gentle rabbi of Nazareth had preached a simple reformist doctrine of love, compassion, inclusivity and non-judgmentalism while railing against hypocrites and exhorting the rich to give to the poor; preaching that "you are gods" and "the Kingdom of Heaven is within you." A thousand years later, intent on world dominion under a single Emperor/Pope, his followers were waging brutal crusades and holy wars (an oxymoron…) and burning people at the stake for heresy—all in his name.

We debated this matter at great length: what had gone wrong? And more to the point, what foundations could we lay in *our* lifetimes for *our* new religion to ensure that a thousand years from now, *our* descendants would not be perpetuating atrocities in our name?

In our analysis, we concluded that Jesus' teachings (and those of the early Church) had several fatal flaws which eventually and inevitably led to the Spanish Inquisition (bet he didn't expect *that!*). And we conceived of "antidotal" memes to each of these, as follows:

1. **"Monothesisism:"** the idea that there is but One-True-Right-and-Only-Way (OTROW). As Isaac Bonewitz once said, "Monotheism, monarchy, monopoly, monogamy, monotony…" This meme inevitably implies that all other ways are *wrong,* and thereby *evil,* and must be repudiated, punished and eradicated. Distain and condemnation of "infidels," "heretics," "apostates," "nonbelievers" and "godless pagans." "Holy wars," crusades, jihads, and genocide. Like the Daleks of *Doctor Who,* monothesists hate everything that isn't them.

    Antidotal meme: "Infinite Diversity in Infinite Combinations" (Vulcan IDIC): different strokes for different folks.

2. **Monotheism** (only one God): Divinity as not only singular, but transcendent, eternal, omnipotent, omniscient, and solely masculine—"Our Father in Heaven."

    Antidotal meme: Polytheism; multiple Gods as well as Goddesses; Divine Feminine; Mother Earth; immanent Divinity ("Thou Art God/dess").

3. **Exclusivity:** the idea of "the Chosen People" as a righteous elite Divinely favored above all others. All others are outsiders.

    Antidotal meme: Inclusivity: "We have a place set for you at our table;" all are welcome who choose to be here and play nice; we are all children of the same Mother; and a mother loves *all* her children.

4. **Evangelism,** proselytizing, missionaries, and conversion ("proselytution").

    Antidotal meme: No missionaries or proselytution: those who would join us must seek us out on their own initiative.

5. **Uniformity**: that all people must believe and behave the same.

    Antidotal meme: Uniqueness: embracing and cherishing diversity.

6. **Heaven and Hell** as eternal reward or punishment in the Afterlife.

    Antidotal meme: Multiple afterlife options, including reincarnation for those who want to return. But no Hell!

7. **Patriarchalism:** disempowerment of women; clergy could only be men (Priests).

    Antidotal meme: Feminism: empowerment of women; ordination of Priestesses (only Pagan religions have Priestesses).

8. **Unsanctioned sexual relationships**—indeed, sex itself—as vile, profane, and "sinful."

    Antidotal meme: Sacred sexuality: "All acts of love and pleasure are My rituals."

9. **Body shame and modesty taboos** ("They knew they were naked, and they were ashamed.")

    Antidotal meme: Holy nakedness: ritual and social nudity ("skyclad").

10. **Heterosexual monogamy** (one man and one woman) as the only acceptable form of love and marriage.

    Antidotal meme: Polyamory: sanctioning and celebrating *all* consensual loving relationships, regardless of sex, gender, or number. LBGTQ+

11. **Nature regarded as inanimate**; a "creation" made by God to be exploited by Man.

    Antidotal meme: Emergent evolution. "The Gaea Thesis," "Mother Earth," "Mother Nature," animism. Nature as sacred, alive, and sentient.

12. **"Original sin"** as disobedience and insubordination; required submission to "authority."

    Antidotal meme: "Harm none" and "Be excellent to each other" as our only Commandments; otherwise, "Do what thou wilt."

13. **Dogma** in the form of immutable scriptures, doctrines, creeds, catechisms and "articles of faith," carved in stone and required for "true believers."

    Antidotal meme: Many myths and legends of the past and future; visons, songs, and poetry, constantly evolving and being reinterpreted for each new generation in literature, art, media, and rituals.

14. **"Heresy"** as disbelief in the official proclaimed doctrines, to be punished severely.

    Antidotal meme: No required beliefs or dogmas; question everything and everyone.

15. **"The Holy Roman Empire;"** a universal empire holding dominion over all peoples under a single ruler: "One King to rule them all." The Divine Right of Kings. Christian Dominionism. Sharia Law.

    Antidotal meme: "The United Federation of Planets" (Star Trek); "The Rebel Alliance" (Star Wars); decentralized coalitions, councils, networks, and alliances of free and sovereign peoples.

16. And perhaps most importantly, **a short-sighted failure** of the founding prophet to write down his teachings, leaving it to others decades and centuries later to make it all up to suit themselves—and the agenda of Empire.

    Antidote: Writing it all down while the founders are still alive!

Through the publication of *Green Egg,* and our ever-expanding Pagan network of alliances and councils, we embedded these antidotal themes deeply into the growing Pagan movement. And thus, began what we came to call "The Ultimate Conspiracy" (because by the time you know enough to grok what we are all about, it's too late—you are already one of us!).

Pagan Musings

By Tony Kelly

[Tony Kelly of the Selene Community in Wales wrote this piece in 1970. It was published in 1971 in the British edition of The Waxing Moon *under the title "Pagan Movement." Under the title "Pagan Musings" it has passed from hand to hand and group to group all over the United States. Tony Kelly was one of the founders of the Pagan Movement in the British Isles, which, with the Pagan Way in the United States, began as a single group of researchers into ancient goddess cults. They later divided, agreeing that each country required a different approach in bringing back Paganism.]*

WE'RE OF THE OLD RELIGION, SIRED of Time, and born of our beloved Earth Mother. For too long the people have trodden a stony path that goes only onward beneath a sky that goes only upwards. The Horned God plays in a lonely glade for the people are scattered in this barren age and the winds carry his plaintive notes over deserted heaths and reedy moors and into the lonely grasses. who know now the ancient tongue of the Moon? And who speaks still with the Goddess? The magic of the land of Lirien and the old Pagan gods have withered in the dragons breath; the old ways of magic have slipped into the well of the past, and only the rocks now remember what the moon told us long ago, and what we learned from the trees, and the voices of grasses and the scents of flowers.

We're Pagans and we worship the Pagan gods, and among the people there are Witches yet who speak with the moon and dance with the Horned One. But a Witch is a rare Pagan in these days, deep and inscrutable, recognizable only by her own kind, by the light in her eyes and the love in her breast, by the magic in her hands and the lilt of her tongue and by her knowledge of the real. But the Wiccan way is one way. There are many; there are Pagans the world over who worship the Earth Mother and the Sky Father, the Rain God and the Rainbow Goddess, the Dark One and the Hag on the mountain, the Moon Goddess and the Little People in the mists on the other side of the veil. A Pagan is one who worships the goddesses and gods of nature, whether by observation or by study, whether by love or admiration, or whether in their sacred rites with the Moon, or the great festivals of the Sun.

Many suns ago, as the pale dawn of reason crept across the Pagan sky, man grew out of believing in the gods. He has yet to grow out disbelieving in them. He who splits the Goddess on an existence-nonexistence dichotomy will earn himself only paradoxes, for the gods are not so divided and nor the magic lands of the Brother of Time. Does a mind exist? Ask her and she will tell you yes, but seek her out, and she'll elude you. She is in every place, and in no place, and you'll see her works in all places, but herself in none. Existence was the second-born from the Mother's womb and contains neither the first-born, nor the unborn. Show us your mind, and we'll show you the gods! No matter that you can't, for we can't show you the gods. But come with us and the Goddess herself will be our love and the God will call the tune. But a brass penny for your reason; for logic is a closed ring, and the child doesn't validate the Mother, nor the dream the dreamer. And what matter the wars of opposites to she who has fallen in love with a whirlwind or to the lover of the arching rainbow.

But tell us of your Goddess as you love her, and the gods that guide your works, and we'll listen with wonder, for to do less would be arrogant. but we'll do more, for the heart of man is aching for memories only half forgotten, and the Old Ones only half unseen. We'll write the old myths as they were always written and we'll read them on the rocks and in the caves and in the deep of the greenwood's shade, and we'll hear them in the rippling mountain streams and in the rustling of the leaves, and we'll see them in the storm clouds, and in the evening mists. We've no wish to create a new religion for our religion is as old as the hills and older, and we've no wish to bring differences together. Differences are like different flowers in a meadow, and we are all one in the Mother.

What need is there for a Pagan movement since our religion has no teachings and we hear it in the wind and feel it in the stones and the Moon will dance with us as she will? There is a need. For long the Divider has been among our people and the tribes of man are no more. The sons of the Sky Father have all but conquered nature, but they have poisoned her breast and the Mother is sad for the butterflies are dying and the night draws on. A curse on the conqueror! But not of us, for they curse themselves for they are Nature too. They have stolen our magic and sold it to the mindbenders and the mindbenders tramp a maze that has no outlet for they fear the real for the One who guards the path.

Where are the Pagan shrines? And where do the people gather? Where is the magic made? And where are the Goddess and the Old Ones? Our shrines are in the fields and on the mountains, in the stars and in the wind, deep in the greenwood and on the algal rocks where two streams meet. but the shrines are deserted, and if we gathered in the arms of the Moon for our ancient rites to be with our gods as we were of old, we would be stopped by the dead who now rule the Mother's land and claim rights of ownership on the Mother's breast, and make laws of division and frustration for us. We can no longer gather with our gods in a public place and the old rites of communion have been driven from the towns and cities ever deeper into the heath where barely a handful of heathens have remained to guard the old secrets and enact the old rites. there is magic in the heath far from the cold grey society, and there are islands of magic hidden in the entrails of the metropolis behind closed doors, but the people are few, and the barriers between us are formidable. The old religion has become a dark way, obscure, and hidden in the protective bosom of the night. Thin fingers turn the pages of a book of shadows while the sunshine seeks in vain his worshippers in his leafy glades.

Here, then, is the basic reason for a Pagan Movement; we must create a Pagan society wherein everyone shall be free to worship the goddesses and gods of nature, and the relationship between a worshipper and her gods shall be sacred and inviolable, provided only that in her love of her own gods, she doesn't curse the names of the gods of others.

It's not yet our business to press the lawmakers with undivided endeavor to unmake the laws of repression and, with the Mother's love, it may never become our business for the stifling tides of dogmatism are at last already in ebb. Our first work, and our greatest wish, is to come together, to be with each other in our tribes for we haven't yet grown from the Mother's breast to the stature of the gods. We're of the earth, and sibs to all the children of wild nature, born long ago in the warm mud of the ocean floor; we were together then, and we were together in the rain forests long before that dark day when, beguiled by the pride of the Sky Father, and forgetful of the Mother's love, we killed her earlier-born children and impoverished the old genetic pool. The Red child lives yet in America; the Black Child has not forsaken the gods; the old Australians are still with their nature gods; the Old Ones still live deep in the heart of Mother India, and the White Child has still a foot on the old Wiccan way, but Neanderthaler is no more and her magic faded as the Lli and the Archan burst their banks and the ocean flowed in to divide the Isle of Erin from the land of the White Goddess.

Man looked with one eye on a two-faced god when he reached for the heavens and scorned the Earth which alone is our life and our provider and the bosom to which we have ever returned since the dawn of Time. He who looks only to reason to plum the unfathomable is a fool, for logic is an echo already implicit i the question, and it has no voice of its own; but he is no greater fool than he who scorns logic or derides its impotence from afar, but fears to engage in fair combat when he stands on his opponent's threshold. don't turn your back on Reason, for his thrust is deadly; but confound him and he'll yield for his code of combat is honorable. so here is more of the work of the Pagan Movement. Our lore has become encrusted over the ages with occult trivia and the empty vapourings of the lost. The occult arts are in a state of extreme decadence, astrology is in a state of disrepute and fears to confront the statistician's sword; alien creeds oust our native arts and, being as little understood as our own forgotten arts, are just as futile for their lack of understanding, and more so for their unfamiliarity. Misunderstanding is rife. Disbelief is black on every horizon, and vampires abound on the blood of the credulous. Our work is to reject the trivial, the irrelevant and the erroneous, and to bring the lost children of the Earth Mother again into the court of the Sky Father where reason alone will avail. Belief is the deceit of the credulous; it has no place in the heart of a Pagan.

But while we are sad for those who are bemused by Reason, we are deadened by those who see no further than his syllogisms as he turns the eternal wheel of the Great Tautology. We were not fashioned in the mathematician's computations, and we were old when the first alchemist was a child. We have walked in the magic forest, bewitched in the old Green Thinks; we have seen the cauldron and the one become many and the many in the one; we know the Silver Maid of the moonlight and the sounds of the cloven feet. We have heard the pipes on the twilight ferns, and we've seen the spells of the enchantress, and Time be stilled. We've been into eternal darkness where the Night Mare rides and rode her to the edge of the Abyss, and beyond, and we know the dark face of the Rising Sun. spin a spell or words and make a magic knot; spin it on the magic loom and spin it with the gods. Say it in the old chant and say it to the Goddess, and in her name. Say it to a dark well and breathe it on a stone. There are no signposts on the untrod way, but we'll make our rituals together and bring them as our gifts to the Goddess and her God in the great rites. Here, then, is our work in the Pagan Movement; to make magic in the name of our gods, to share our magic where the gods would wish it, and to come together in our ancient festivals of birth, and life, of death and of change in the old rhythm. We'll print the rituals that can be shared in the written work; we'll do all in our power to bring the people together, to teach those who would learn, and to learn from those who can teach. We will initiate groups, bring people to groups, and groups to other groups in our common devotion to the goddess and gods of nature. We will not storm the secrets of any coven, nor profane the tools, the magic, and still less, the gods of another.

We'll collect the myths of the ages, of our people and of the Pagans of other lands, and we'll study the books of the wise and we'll talk to the very young. And whatever the Pagan needs in her study, or her worship, then it is our concern, and the Movement's business to do everything possible to help each other in our worship of the gods we love.

We are committed with the lone Pagan on the seashore, with he who worships in the fastness of a mountain range or she who sings the old chant in a lost valley far from the metalloid road. We are committed with the wanderer, and equally with the prisoner, disinherited from the Mother's milk in the darkness of the industrial webs. We are committed too with the coven, with the circular dance in the light of the full moon, with the great festivals of the sun, and with the gatherings of the people. We are committed to build our temples in the towns and in the wilderness, to buy the lands and the streams from the landowners and give them to the Goddess for her children's use, and we'll replant the greenwood as it was of old for love of the dryad stillness, and for love of our children's children.

When the streams flow clear and the winds blow pure, and the sun never more rises unrenowned nor the moon ride in the skies unloved; when the stones tell of the Horned God and the greenwood grows deep to call back her own ones, then our work will be ended and the Pagan Movement will return to the beloved womb of our old religion, to the Nature goddesses and gods of Paganism.

What is the Church of All Worlds?

by Iacchus, CAW Priest *(retired)*

THE CHURCH OF ALL WORLDS IS one of the oldest incorporated Neo-Pagan churches in the United States, and among its members are people of various faiths including Abrahamic traditions. It has an international membership, board of directors, an ordained Priesthood of women and men, a consecrated membership dedicated to the service of the Church called Scions, a process of personal development of 9 circles (stages) and various subsidiary organizations and Nests. CAW promotes lifestyles that support personal freedom and responsibility, environmental stewardship, progressive and cooperative social order and pluralistic democracy.

CAW evolved from a group of friends and lovers who were in part inspired by the science fiction novel *Stranger in a Strange Land* by Robert Heinlein back in 1962. This book suggested a spiritual and social way of life and was a metaphor expressing the awakening social consciousness of the times. Inspired by this awakening of consciousness and the book, *Stranger in a Strange Land,* this group grew, evolved, became "water-kin" and created a religious organization that was recognized as a church by the federal government of the United States on March 4, 1968. They named this religious organization the Church of All Worlds after the church founded by the hero in the book. The Church's organizing spiritual and social concepts and values include; a belief in immanent Divinity, a pluralistic perspective towards religion, living in harmony with Nature, self-actualization, deep friendship and positive sexuality. In time the church's spiritual and social concepts and values became recognized as Neo-Pagan. As CAW continued to develop, it both influenced and was affected by the growing Neo-Pagan movement.

CAW believes that the nature of our universe and planet is a manifestation of Divine Being. As such the nature of human being is an expression of Divine being. In recognition of this we greet and honor one another with the phrase "Thou art God" or "Thou art Goddess."

A fundamental rite of CAW is a communion of souls called Water-sharing. In this rite one shares water with at least one other and recognizes within another the Divine Being with the phrase "Thou art God" or "Thou art Goddess" and "May you never thirst." This similar to the Hindu greeting of "Namaste" which means the "Divine in me greets the Divine in you." Since water is essential to all known life on this planet and so is seen as very precious, CAW envisions Water-sharing as a way of honoring this preciousness in a symbolic act that also recognizes one believes Divine Being is a living experience in all Humanity. The phrase "never thirst" serves as a reminder of one's conscious connection with living as an experience of Divine being.

CAW's vision is rooted in a shared value system whose core values are accepted by its members regardless of belief. CAW does not ask or require members to give up their religious affiliation or beliefs, as long as they share CAW's common values. One of these core values is a pluralistic attitude toward life and religion. A pluralistic attitude is essential to CAW's identity as a Church. CAW sees this attitude as reflecting a valuing of diversity with harmony in Humanity and nature as expressions of Divinity. It believes a pluralistic acceptance of a diversity of belief systems fosters religious freedom and peace within humanity. As a result the religious/spiritual orientations of CAW members may include animistic, polytheistic, monotheistic and monastic concepts.

CAW's diversity of beliefs about Divinity is expressed through a variety of religious practices or worship. These various religious practices seek to bring humanity into conscious harmony with Nature and Divinity within it. Many within CAW follow the Neo-Pagan ritual observance of what is commonly called the "Wheel of the Year." It has 8 Holy days, the solstices and equinoxes days and the cross-quarter days. Many members ritually observe each month, the Full and/or New Moon. CAW believes the ritual observation of the "Wheel of the Year" and cycles of the Moon can bring about a communion with Divinity through attunement of one's life with the waxing and waning of Nature. Some believers see in the changing seasons, the waxing and waning of darkness and light, an expression of the life cycle of Divinity that includes birth, love, death and rebirth.

CAW encourages its members to create and re-create rituals and myths that attune their life with Nature, bring honor to and communion with Divinity, reflect its values and build community. One such myth is the vision that our planet is an individual living system, a Goddess, variously named Mother Earth or Gaia. Many members believe themselves to be children of this Goddess. This myth expresses the basic CAW tenets that our planet and life on it are sacred, and responsible stewardship of life and its environment is an act of worship.

CAW believes that humanity needs to be in harmony with its Self, for the Self is seen as a manifestation of Divine immanence in Nature. It sees the human Self as the seed pattern and potential of the human Soul. As such the Soul is a system of becoming that seeks to actualize its potential – the Self. The human Self is a potential wholeness where there is a unity of behaviors and experiences, such as mind with body, consciousness with unconsciousness, spirit with nature, instinct with culture, self with other, community with individuality, humanity with environment and being with becoming. CAW sees conscious actualization of human wholeness and the gaining of experiential knowledge of the nature of Self as an essential religious endeavor. Self-knowledge and actualization make it possible for the Self-conscious creation of harmony between humanity and Nature. This harmony is part of the human potential and is a primary religious goal and quest for CAW.

CAW envisions the religious and psychological development of the Soul as embryonic. In recognition of this, CAW members will often refer to themselves as "Eggs." CAW seeks to foster, through contemplation, ritual, integrative behavior and lifestyle, this embryonic journey of self-knowledge and actualization. CAW recognizes that altered states of consciousness can be ways of becoming aware of and knowing unconscious aspects of the Self. Altered states of consciousness are enthusiastic, ecstatic and celebratory aspects of this embryonic journey and include such techniques as drumming, fasting, chanting and magic.

Some members of CAW envision the human Self as the image or archetypal pattern of Divinity that is immanent in Nature. For them the phrase "Thou Art Goddess" or "Thou Art God" and the actualization of Self has additional religious emphasis. For them, the individuation and actualization of Self is a process that grows out of instinctively determined life and ethics into a more comprehensive way of being. This state being is envisioned as a microcosmic Deity where instincts are in harmony with the self- conscious wholeness of soul.

In order to achieve the unity of instinct with culture, self with other, community with individuality, CAW believes friendship is essential. Friendship begins for a CAW member with the recognition that each human being, as a sovereign expression of Divinity, has the same rights as one's Self. This equality is seen as a sacred bond with all humanity and a fundamental quality of the relational interdependence of Self-actualization. CAW members are to give due respect and civility to the relationship of friendship. Members of CAW are friends or "dear ones" who love themselves but not only themselves, treating others with the same regard and respect that they would have others treat them with. Through friendship celebrated by the rite of Water-sharing the membership of CAW creates and grows what is termed as "Water-kin." This friendship is the value that weaves CAW members into a network of relational interdependence envisioned as a neo-pagan and post-modern tribe. Public Water-sharing by members expresses this friendship and is a rite of tribal confirmation.

CAW encourages deepening or increasing intimacy in friendship called "growing closer." Part of growing closer is the increasing ability to act interdependently with others and achieving or approximating "win-win" interpersonal outcomes. CAW believes that development of such interdependence is fundamental to the psychology of Self-actualization and increasing social good. When two or more people feel they have established a level of interdependence and a bond of trust that expresses kinship, then another stage of water sharing may occur. This stage is a rite of confirmation that a spiritual kinship, similar to the tribal feeling of being cousins, exists between the people sharing water. It is a stage that initiates openness to further 'growing closer'. Continued 'growing closer' is characterized by increasing affection, affiliation and intimacy.

When a state of being is established between Water-kin where those involved recognize that the other's happiness is essential to one's own, then another stage in growing closer may be acknowledged. Water sharing at this stage recognizes that communion of souls called love. In CAW, the water rituals that recognize the 'growing closer' stages of kinship or love may be intuitively given or experientially earned. CAW believes that the process of growing closer leads increasingly to a fuller understanding of, and communion with, immanent Divinity. Such understanding is connoted by the term "grok" and is also symbolized by the sharing of water.

To foster growing closer and the development of water-kin and tribe, CAW has religious communities called Nests. The Nest is the basic local organizational and congregational unit of CAW. A Nest is a group of 3 or more members who come together to learn, discuss, and creatively practice the values and purposes of the church. Just as a nest in nature provides life with a means and context for growth, so too is a CAW Nest to provide an individual member with a community and culture to foster self-actualization and communion with the Divine.

As a part of integrating instinct with culture, CAW believes our reproductive instinct needs to be stewarded as to maintain a sustainable human population upon our planet. CAW encourages responsible reproductive strategies and choices. Men and Women share the responsibility for pregnancy prevention and child rearing equally in CAW. Further, CAW supports the ancient tradition of mother right that women have the right to choose to give birth or not.

CAW believes that sexuality is an expression of the Divine. To honor this belief CAW values and encourages positive sexuality. Positive sexuality is the ethical affirmation of sexual behavior and the pleasure seeking instinct for the fostering of social bonding and communion with each other and Divine Being. Consent and peer-ship are the basis for ethical sexual behavior and positive sexuality. The expression of positive regard in human sexual behavior is essential for positive sexuality.

Positive sexuality includes sacred sexual behavior. For CAW, sacred sexuality requires an attitude wherein individuals affirm their essential worth, confirm the equality and essential self worth of others, and seek to act interdependently to mutually fulfill sexual desire and affection and affiliation needs. Sexual behavior that expresses or reflects this attitude is believed to be sacred by CAW in that such behavior honors and expresses immanent Divinity. The practice of sacred sexuality and sacred sexual rituals are encouraged by CAW. CAW believes that homoerotic and hetero-erotic sexuality can be expressions of sacred sexual behavior.

When nudity is a symbolic act that reflects an individual's affirmation of self worth, the beauty of sexuality, basic trust in others and a peaceful heart, then CAW believes nudity is a sacred sex practice that is an expression of Divinity within. CAW encourages nudity as a sacred sex practice for those who are called to do so, within the privacy of a nest, in a secluded natural environment or at 'clothing optional' gatherings, as an expression of sacred sexuality and a fostering of growing closer with others. Further, CAW believes if one chooses to be naked in one of its private rituals, it can be a sign that one is free.

CAW recognizes and blesses a variety of committed sacred sexual relationships as marriages. These marriages may or may not be sexually exclusive and may be monogamous, polygamous or polyamorous. This variety of committed relationships not only reflects the ethical freedoms that CAW supports, but also reflects the historical and anthropological facts showing that humanity has practiced a wide variety of committed sexual relationships called 'marriage'. CAW believes multiple forms of marriage are, in part, a reflection of humanity's diverse nature, which desires both social stability and sexual variety, and that there are many ways to satisfy these desires. The pluralistic approach of CAW to marriage is envisioned as an expression of the diversity of nature and Divinity within it. This approach, for CAW, is an essential religious concept and custom, in that it fosters humanity's harmony with nature and immanent Divinity through integration of instinct with culture.

CAW as a religion is a system of values, customs and ideas organized in an organic fashion. It will grow, develop and evolve in a way that brings about the best in humanity and honors Divinity.

What in Heaven's Name is Going on Over There?

Some factual information about Neo-Pagan religion

(Reprinted with permission from The Center for Non-Traditional Religion, Index, WA)

IT'S A LOGICAL QUESTION HEARD spoken often between neighbors. In this country we are gifted with the freedom to do pretty much as we wish on our own property, whether it's having a family reunion, a barbeque in the yard, or a private religious gathering in our own homes. Sometimes we may not fully understand what our neighbors may be doing, and lack of understanding can easily bring unease and sometimes even fear. Things that we don't understand or are foreign or "different" to us can easily raise those sorts of unintentional feelings. Often we just don't understand someone or something, and that's unsettling. It is such fears that motivate us to unconscious, often prejudicial behavior.

Since before the dawn of written his- tory, people have instinctively gathered together in groups for the feelings of comfort and security that come with socialization and fellowship. One of our basic drives is that of spirituality-the need for the comfort and security of group worship of the Al- mighty. One of the oldest religious artifacts ever found on Earth was a small limestone carving, a figurine of a plump female, an object of veneration found near Willendorf, Austria, and named "the Venus of Willendorf" by archaeological scholars. This goddess statue has been dated to 28,000 BC! Throughout northern Europe there are many archaeological evidences of early people's veneration of an Earth Mother figure, a Mother Goddess from whom all things come, including the miracle of birth, death and rebirth. The forces of Nature were full of the dual polarity of male and female which produced all Life. No wonder that early people envisioned the Almighty as female, a Mother figure!

The basic neolithic concept of deity being represented by an immanent or internal dual polarity, a God and a Goddess force contained within everything, was commonplace throughout northern Europe. Historically, this concept held firm throughout most of the world for thousands of years until the rise of the Judeo-Christian philosophy, which introduced the concept of a single, all-powerful and external or transcendent male God. In early Biblical translations, Genesis 1:26 first refers to deity as *Elohim,* which is a plural Hebrew word for god which includes *both* male and female genders. Later, in Genesis 2:7, the single male godform called *Yahweh* appears, to dominate the Old Testament and Judaism thenceforth. But in Gen. 1:26 we read that Elohim declaims the creation of *humanity—a population* of people, not just two. Later, in Gen. 2:7-9, Adam and Eve are created as a special, chosen people, special to Yahweh alone. Many people often overlook this small but telling detail. There were "other people," those who were not the "chosen people" of Yahweh in the Bible—the people of the land of Nod, east of Eden, from whence came Cain's wife, for example. These were the Pagans.

Prior to the rise of Judaism and Christianity, this nature-based form of worship we now call Paganism was almost universal throughout the world. Although each locale and people had their own names for their deities, they had no name for their religion because it was looked upon as universal and did not need differentiation from any other. Later, differentiation became necessary to distinguish the "old religion" from the newer religious movements. During the time of the spread of the Roman church throughout the urban population centers of early Europe, the Romans began calling the country people, who still practiced the old ways and worshiped the old gods, *pagani,* which meant "country dweller." In the British Isles, a stronghold of Paganism, the term *heathen* similarly meant the simple country folk who dwelt out on the heath or meadow- lands and still honored the old gods. Neither term was originally intended as a denigration. When describing the religions movement known as Paganism, the word should always be capitalized, as with Baptist, Jew, or any other proper name.

Let's take a look at the Pagan religious philosophy. Since Paganism doesn't have a formal structure and hierarchy such as we are accustomed to in more traditional Western religions, there are many relatively small groups. There are a few national and international federations of these small groups, such as the Covenant of the Goddess (USA), the Pagan Anti-Defamation League (UK), the Fellowship of Isis (Ireland), and the National Alliance of Pantheists (USA). But these do not possess the familiar authoritarian church hierarchy. There are many other loosely organized regional federations which annually sponsor over one hundred open and semi-open gatherings throughout the USA. Because of this small group autonomy, we can best define Pagan church groups by their similarities rather than by their differences. Remember, when Pagan- ism was the *only* religion in Europe, every- one had their own ideas about the details of the religion, yet they were bonded together by the similarities. So it is even now.

Today, most people who define themselves as Pagans use the word as a general term for "native and natural religions, usually polytheistic, and their members." In simple terms, it is a positive, nature-based religion, preaching brotherly love and harmony with and respect for all life forms. It is very similar to Native American Indian spirituality. Its origins are found in the early human development of religion: animist c deities gradually becoming redefined to become a main God or Goddess of all Nature. This God or Goddess-bearing different names at different times and in different places--can be found in nearly all of the world's historic religious systems. Paganism does not oppose nor deny any other religion. It is simply a pre-Christian faith.

Most Pagans seem to agree on many of these commonly held beliefs:

- Divinity is immanent or internal, as well as transcendent or external. This is oft expressed by the phrases 'Thou Art God" and "Thou Art Goddess."
- Divinity is just as likely to manifest itself as female. This has resulted in a large number of women being attracted to the faith and joining the clergy.

- A multiplicity of gods and goddesses, whether as individual deities or as faces of one or a few archetypes. This leads to multi-valued logic systems and increased tolerance towards other religions.
- Respect and love of Nature as divine in Her own right. This makes ecologic awareness and activity a religious duty.
- Dissatisfaction with monolithic religious organizations and distrust of would-be messiahs and gurus. This makes Pagans hard to organize, even "for their own good," and leads to constant mutation and growth in the movement.
- The conviction that human beings were meant to live lives filled with joy, love, pleasure and humor. The traditional Western concepts of sin, guilt and divine retribution are seen as misunderstanding of natural growth experiences.
- A simple set of ethics and morality base on the avoidance of harm to other people Some extend this to some or all living beings and the planet as a whole.
- The knowledge that with proper training and intent, human minds and hearts are fully capable of performing all of the magic and miracles they are ever likely t need, through the use of natural psychic powers which everyone possesses.
- The importance of acknowledging and celebrating the solar, lunar and other cycles of our lives. This has led to the investigation and revival of many ancient customs and the invention of some new ones.
- A minimum of dogma and a maximum of eclecticism. That is to say, Pagans are reluctant to accept any idea without personally investigating it, and are willing to adopt and use any concept they find useful, regardless of its origins.
- A strong faith in the ability of people to solve their own current problems on all levels, public and private. This leads to...
- A strong commitment to personal and universal growth, evolution and balance. Pagans are expected to be making continuous efforts in these directions.
- A belief that one can progress far towards achieving such growth, evolution and balance through the carefully planned alteration of one's consciousness, using both ancient and

modem methods of aiding concentration, meditation, reprogramming and ecstasy.

- The knowledge that human interdependence implies community cooperation. Pagans are encouraged to use their talents to actively help each other as well as the community at large.
- An awareness that if they are to achieve any of their goals, they must practice what they preach. This leads to a concern with making one's lifestyle consistent with one's proclaimed beliefs.

The group of people who may on occasion gather outdoors near your home, perhaps at a neighbor's place, and the people who have given you this pamphlet are followers of this pre-Christian religious faith. There is no need to fear them or their religion. They don't recruit or proselytize. They gather, often in robes, in serene, natural outdoor surroundings to be in contact with Nature during their services; otherwise you'd never know they were there. Their own children are encouraged to examine many other religions and make an informed personal choice of which to follow as they grow older. These people may call them- selves Neo-Pagans, Wiccans, or simply Pagans. They are neither evil nor weird. They hold Life in all its forms as sacred, and many are vegetarians. Few, if any, hunt wild animals for sport. They are simple, gentle people, people just like you and your friends, only different in that they hold to another view of spirituality than Christian, Moslem or Jew—one you just aren't very familiar with yet.

What does all of this mean? It should be obvious that Pagans are nothing to be feared, ridiculed or even singled out. Pagans are simply a little different in their approach to and acceptance of personal spirituality. Their religion is based on humanity's first stirrings to spirituality, of reverence toward the Earth as a living, breathing entity. They honor all living things, practice ecology, and are tolerant of those who follow a different path from their own. These are things everyone could benefit from studying.

The Center for Non-Traditional Religions, Dept XP, PO Box 409, Index, WA 98256. This pamphlet may be reproduced freely provided nothing whatsoever is changed. ©1989 CNT

Dancing the Maypole. Beltane at Annwfn, 2012. Photo by Richard Ely.

Who on Earth is the Goddess?

By Morning Glory Zell and Oberon Zell

(Originally published 1978 in the *Covenant of the Goddess Newsletter*; reprinted in *Green Egg* #88, 5/1/90; reprinted in *GaeaGenesis: Conception & Birth of the Living Earth*, 2022)

"Who is this All-Mother you're always talking about?"
"Why, you are, Edward. . . The All-Mother. You're the All-Mother, I'm the All-Mother, that little bird singing out there, it's the All-Mother. The All-Mother is everything. The All-Mother is life..."[1]

THE PRIMAL AND SUPREME DEITY of the ancient world—the oldest and most universally worshipped—was the Great Mother; Mother Earth, Mother Nature. Images of Her date back to Aurignacian Cro-Magnon peoples, from over 30,000 years ago, and are found all over the Eurasian continent from Spain to Siberia. For thousands of years before there were any male gods, there was The Goddess, and Her worship continued unabated clear up until its violent suppression by Iron Age patriarchy.

Women and Nature were held in esteem when and where worship of the Mother prevailed. The Chinese called Her Guanyin; the Egyptians knew Her as Isis; the Navajo call Her Changing Woman. To the Greeks She was Gaea, and to many black peoples She is Yemanja. She is Aphrodite—the Goddess of Love—and She says: *"All acts of love and pleasure are my rituals."* She is also the ancient Crone Hecate—who gives us both wisdom and death.

The Goddess is diversity. She represents both Darkness and Light and Her worship is the reconciliation of opposites. There can be no such thing as a "Good Goddess" or an "Evil Goddess." Death is part of the natural cycle as night follows day and we should accept it with grace as Her final gift. The search for Balance is the goal of Her people, and it is achieved by the acceptance of multiple paths and truths. Dion Fortune once commented that all goddesses are manifestations of the One Great Goddess whose identity is as the universal feminine Spirit of Nature.

The eldest and greatest aspect of the Goddess is as Great Mother Nature, the all-encompassing energy of Universal Life. Her womb is the Quasar—the white hole through which all energy pours into creation, and Her all-devouring mouth is the Black hole itself through which all matter is consumed to be reborn once again between Her thighs as the universe is squeezed from Spirit. Her energy then coalesces into Matter-Mater--the Mother of all forms. She ignites, becoming the Star Goddess: Nuit, whose galactic breast is our Milky way. Of Her are born star systems and planets including, of course, our very own Earth Mother, Gaea.

Because of the diversity of the Goddess, She is seen as manifesting in many distinct aspects. She is often called The Triple Goddess, which refers to Her link in the fertility cycle where She appears as Maiden, Mother and Crone. Some ancient cultures personified this Triplicity as the waxing, full, and waning Moon, and other three-faced Goddess aspects are familiar to us as the Fates, the Graces, the Furies, the Muses—or even as Faith, Hope, and Charity. Another familiar division of Her aspects is into Mother and Daughter (Demeter and Persephone), or as Sisters/Lovers (Fauna and Flora). Such polarities are also important in Her worship. Sometimes the polarity can exist with two distinct aspects of the Goddess representing both poles, but more commonly it is the great gender polarity, for the Goddess is a deity of sexual loving.

She is Ishtar or Aphrodite, the eternal Lover who awaits with eager arms the mortal man brave enough to risk Her immortal favor. Many men have worshipped Her as a lover, but she may never be possessed, for She belongs only to Herself. She is *Parthenos,* the eternal Virgin (in the pre-patriarchal meaning "of her own household"). She represents the Strong Woman—not dominant, but independent. Her lovers are not truly human but Divine. She has

---

[1] Mack Reynolds, *Of Godlike Power,* 1966, pp. 146-147

been the Beloved of many gods, and though jealous male gods eventually suppressed Her worship, She shared the co-rulership of Heaven and Earth for thousands of years of marital bliss. She is the inescapable Yin necessary for the cosmic balance of Yin and Yang. Symbols associated with Her (the Tree of Life, the Sacred Serpent, the Labyrinth) are found in all parts of the globe—at the heart of all the Mysteries and underlying all the later accretions of successive religions. The search for Her is the search for our deepest ancestral roots.

I am the star that rises from the twilight sea.
I bring men dreams to rule their destiny.
I am the eternal Woman; I am She!
The tides of all souls belong to me-
Touch of my hand confers polarity—
These are the moontides, these belong to me.[2]

Art by
Sarah Casby

Honor Thy Mother

In all the cultures where She is still worshipped, there is no confusion over Her identity —She is Nature, and She is the Earth. She is not an atavistic abstraction, not a mystical metaphor, not a construct of consciousness. Her body is of substance as material as our own, and we tread upon Her breast and are formed of Her flesh. "Walk lightly on the bosom of the Earth Mother," says Sun Bear, and Indigenous peoples agree. Cherokee shaman Rolling Thunder emphasizes that "It's very important for people to realize this: the Earth is a living organism, the body of a higher individual who has a will and wants to be well, who is at times less healthy or more healthy, physically and mentally."[3] Frank Waters, author of *Masked Gods* and *Book of the Hopi,* makes the same point:

> . . . To Indians the Earth is not inanimate. It is a living entity, the mother of all life, our Mother Earth. All Her children, everything in nature, is alive: the living stone, the great breathing mountains, trees, and plants, as well as birds, animals, and man. All are united in one harmonious whole.[4]

Renowned historian Arnold Toynbee, writing on "The Religious Background of the present Environmental Crisis," also observed that:

> For pre-monotheistic man, nature was not just a treasure-trove of "natural resources." Nature was, for him, a goddess, "Mother Earth," and the vegetation that sprang from the Earth, the animals that roamed, like man himself, over the Earth's surface, and the minerals hiding in the Earth's bowels, all partook of Nature's divinity.[5]

Before ever land was, before ever the sea,
Or soft hair of the grass, or fair limbs of the tree,
Or flesh-coloured fruit of my branches, I was –
And thy soul was in me.[6]

The Gaea Thesis

To understand the nature of the Earth Mother, we must first understand our own origins. Biologically, unisexual organisms are always considered to be female, since only the female brings forth life from her own body; in the act of reproduction single cells are referred to as mothers and their offspring as daughters. Each

---

[2] Dion Fortune, "Charge of the Moon Goddess"
[3] Doug Boyd, *Rolling Thunder,* 1974, p. 51.
[4] Frank Waters, "Lessons from the Indian Soul," *Psychology Today,* May 1973, p. 63

[5] Arnold Toynbee, "The Religious Background of the Present Environmental Crisis," *International Journal of Environmental Studies,* 1972, Vol. III
[6] Algernon Charles Swinburne, "Hertha"

of us began our individual life as a single fertilized cell, or zygote. In the process of its innumerable divisions and multiplications, that cell kept dividing up and redistributing the very same protoplasm. That protoplasm which now courses through all the several trillion cells of your adult body is the very same substance which once coursed through the body of that original zygote. For when a cell reproduces, the mother cell does not remain intact, but becomes the two new daughter cells. And therefore, no matter how many times cell fission occurs in the process of embryological development, all the daughter cells collectively continue to comprise but one single organism.

We may imagine that, should our cells have consciousness akin to our own, they may very well fancy themselves to be independent entities living and dying in a world that to them would seem to be merely an inanimate environment, blood cells racing along our arterial highways, but we know them to be in fact minute components of the far vaster living beings that we ourselves are.

Over three billion years ago, life on Earth began, as do we all, with a single living cell containing a replicating molecule of DNA. From that point on, that original cell, the first to develop the awesome capacity for reproduction, divided and redivided and subdivided its protoplasm into the myriads of plants and animals, including ourselves, which now inhabit this third planet from the Sun.

But no matter how many times cell fission occurs in the process of embryological development, all the daughter cells collectively continue to comprise but one single organism. All life on Earth comprises the body of a single vast living being—Mother Earth Herself. The Moon is Her radiant heart, and in the tides beats the pulse of Her blood. The protoplasm which coursed through the body of that first primeval ancestral cell is the very protoplasm which now courses through every cell of every living organism, plant, or animal, of our planet. And as in our own bodies, Earthly life was biologically female for the first 2½ billion years, before sexual reproduction, complete with males, evolved

around half a billion years ago. In evolutionary theory we say, "ontogeny recapitulates phylogeny" (the development of the individual repeats the development of the ancestry); ancient people anticipated such scientific ideas when they intuitively conceptualized our planetary Divinity, like that first single cell, as feminine: our Mother Earth. The soul of our planetary biosphere is She whom we call Goddess.[7]

First life on my sources first drifted and swam.
Out of me are the forces which save it or damn.
Out of me man and woman, and wild-beast and bird.
    Before God was, I am.[8]

"... Be the terror and the dread of all the wild beasts and all the birds of heaven, of everything that crawls on the ground and all the fish of the sea: they are handed over to you." (Gen. 9:2-3)

Since the time of the Exodus, 3,600 years ago, Western Civilization has been pursuing a course that has taken it farther and farther from the Mother. The three great monotheistic religions of the West—Judaism, Christianity, and Islam—have from their beginning actively suppressed the worship of the Goddess and have tortured and brutally murdered millions of Her people. Today, She is all but forgotten in the hearts of Her children, and Her body lies ravished in the wake of human progress. The Goddess is the concept of feminine Divinity incarnate. The denial of feminine Divinity results in the oppression of all women, including Mother Nature Herself. As Toynbee says:

> The thesis of the present essay is that some of the major maladies of the present-day world—for instance, the recklessly extravagant consumption of Nature's irreplaceable treasures, and the pollution of those of them that man has not already devoured—can be traced back in the last analysis to a religious cause, and that this cause is the rise of monotheism.[9]

---

[7] Algernon Charles Swinburne, "Hertha"
[8] Swinburne, *Ibid.*

[9] Toynbee, *Ibid.*

This is not to say that all non-monotheistic religions have a perfect track record for the treatment of women in those societies. Certainly, Hindu cultures revere various goddesses and yet are among the more sexist and female-suppressive societies in the modern world. Nevertheless, there is abundant archeological evidence to indicate that things were not always as they are now, especially in truly ancient societies like India.

Before the Aryan Indo-European invasion around 1,500 BCE many Neolithic and Bronze Age cultures, including the Harrapan culture of the Indus Valley and the Minoan people of Crete, had societies that appeared remarkably egalitarian. These societies were universally characterized by the worship of a powerful Great Mother whom the Hindu people still call Maha Devi Ma. She was later broken into a multiplicity of minor goddesses which were demoted to the position of wives or concubines of the gods.

By the time sacred writings were codified in the Vedas, the Primal Goddess Maha Devi in India had been divided into a triplicity of goddesses characterized as Creator, Preserver, and Destroyer: Saraswati, Laksmi, and Kali; respectively the consorts of Brahma, Vishnu, and Shiva. In Greece, a similar process led to Kore, Demeter, and Persephone (or Hecate) created from the original Cretan Rhea. Once the Great Mother had been married off, She became easier to control and the way was paved for Her dowry of natural wealth to be handed over to the financial control of Her divine consorts.

Whether this new mythical development was a simple mirror of the social diminishment of women's rights or whether it preceded diminishment and was invoked as a justification is a moot point. But the land, formerly tied to matrilineal territorial clans, passed into the hands of patriarchal kings and princes who began to treat it as their private property and to lay waste to the forests—to build vast temples and palaces to house their harems and other slaves.

The Goddess of Nature went from the position of being the body and soul of all that lives to that of a wife, mother, and household servant. Many traditions have given lip service to the so-called "Female Principle," either in the form of a divided identity like the Hindu Shakti or as a semi-divine emanation. But the power of the Goddess of Nature has gradually lost its ability to inspire the necessary respect and reverence once accorded to the Source and Bearer of Life.

Where are You, then, Mother,
Whose strength was before
All other powers? Your name
Is the only freedom.[10]

Pantheism is the view that everything in Nature is alive, and that all living is Divine. In that context, then, the simplest explanation of Divinity is as "an energy field created by all living things. It surrounds us, it penetrates us, it binds the galaxy together." (Star Wars: "The Force")

Thus, a pantheistic theology of Immanent Divinity ("Thou Art God/dess") contrasts sharply with the theology of Transcendent Divinity ("God is Out There") presented by most of "The World's Great Religions." Unlike the God worshipped by Christians, Muslims, and Jews, the Goddess is not an all-powerful, indestructible, non-physical being who created the world and exists apart from it. Though Mother Nature is Life on the universal scale, Gaea, the Earth Mother is the very Soul of this living planet, and She lives or dies as all life on this planet lives or dies. . .

Mother, not maker;
Born, and not made.
Though Her children forsake Her,
Allured or afraid,
Praying prayers to the God of their fashion,
She stirs not for all who have prayed.

O my children, too dutiful
Towards Gods not of me,
Was not I enough beautiful?
Was it hard to be free?
For, behold, I am with you,
am in you, and of you --
Look forth now and see![11]

---

[10] Ramprasad Sen, *Grace and Mercy in Her Wild Hair;* 18th Century Bengal.

[11] Swinburne, *Ibid.*

Where in the World is the CAW?

By Oberon Zell

THE CHURCH OF ALL WORLDS OFFERS a religious position uniquely suited to the educated, enlightened, inquiring modem mind. In harmony with the principles and conclusions of science, receptive to the values and wisdom of the ancients and the great religions of humanity, sensitive to the deep psychological and spiritual needs of all people, we aspire to be the kind of free, growing and unifying religion that today's and tomorrow's world so urgently needs.

The Church of All Worlds is Neo-Pagan: a modem Earth Religion—an orientation chosen because of its traditional associations with Life and the processes of Nature, which we consider an appropriate religious orientation for the emerging Aquarian Age. As western civilization has been to a great degree the product of the past two thousand years of Piscean Age Christianity, so do we envision a new whole-Earth culture of transformative religious ecology to become the product of the next epoch of Aquarian Age Neo-Paganism. In common with many other Neo-Pagan religions, CAW presents a life- affirming religious philosophy for the joyous unification of eros, ethos and ecos; of cult, culture and cultivation.

We consider the Church of All Worlds to be radically evolutionary in concept, rather than merely revolutionary. Our stated mission is:

> **"…to evolve a network of information, mythology and experience to awaken the Divine within and to provide a context and stimulus for reawakening Gaea and reuniting Her children through tribal community dedicated to responsible stewardship and the evolution of consciousness."**

We offer alternatives to the life-negating paradigms which produce war, profiteering, racism, sexism, exploitation and desecration of our natural resources. Instead, we work towards the restoration of the Whole, healing the separations between mind and body, men and women, civilization and Nature, the heavens and the Earth.

We see the evolution of Life on Earth as moving towards a point of actualization whereby the entire planet will come to share a single vast global consciousness. We see humanity as being instrumental in the course of that evolution. As humans seem to be the only creatures on the planet capable of disrupting entire ecosystems, it becomes our manifest responsibility through our unique freedom of choice to prevent such systems from being disrupted.

We are not anti-technology or science, for we recognize that certain scientific and technological advances, such as ecology, geology, astronomy, psychology, archaeology, cybernetics, astrophysics, communications and the technology of the bio-renaissance can be positively evolutionary and in harmony with the accelerating advance of planetary consciousness. What we oppose is the senseless use of industrial technology to wreak havoc with the planetary ecosystem, often in the name of the Biblical injunction that Man is to have "dominion over the Earth." We perceive our role not as dominion, but as responsible stewardship.

Applying evolutionary concepts to each individual, we agree with Erich Fromm that the purpose of life is "to become what we potentially are." We identify strongly with the concepts of human self-actualization identified by Abraham Maslow and found in transpersonal psychology and ethics.

On a personal level, we attempt to foster self-actualization. According to Maslow, in his *Motivation and Personality* (1954), that means: (1) embracing the facts and realities of the world (including ourselves) rather than denying or avoiding them; (2) being spontaneous in ideas and actions; (3) creativity; (4) interest in solving problems; (5) feeling a closeness to other people and generally appreciating life; (6) having a system of morality (ethics) that is fully internalized and independent of external authority; and (7) having discernment and ability to view all things in an objective manner.

Rejecting utterly concepts of predestination and inherent sin, we affirm the ultimate freedom and responsibility appropriate to conscious entities, which we express in the phrase "Thou Art God/dess," derived from Robert Heinlein's germinal 1961 science-fiction novel, *Stranger in a Strange Land.* This implies that each one of us must define our own specific purpose. There is no excuse; no shelter from the awesome responsibility of total freedom.

Recognizing that all life on Earth comprises a single vast living Entity, which has been intuitively conceptualized as a feminine Divinity from time immemorial, we are in harmony with our Pagan ancestors who worshipped The Goddess: Mother Earth, Mother Nature; or, as She was known to the ancient Greeks, Gaea. Thus we also affirm mystically and mythically the pantheistic conceptualization of immanent divinity inherent in all living entities, as synergic living Nature, for we define Divinity as the highest level of aware consciousness accessible to each living being, manifesting itself in the self-actualization of that being. Hence, "Thou Art God/dess" applies equally to a person, a tree, a grasshopper or a planet.

As Neo-Pagans, we are concerned, not with life after death, but with life after birth. We have no dogmas of immortality, considering that whatever one believes about an afterlife may very well be what one gets. We view death as an evolutionary prerequisite for the emergence of new life, and so we return the dead to the Earth, from which the elements of their energy and matter will eventually be recycled and reconstituted into the energy and matter of other life forms. Other than our ecological responsibility of returning to the Earth that which we have taken from Her, we are not concerned with dying, but with living.

We are deeply concerned with improving the quality of that life, to which end we agree with population ecologists that its quantity (in sheer numbers of people) must be drastically reduced. Thus we are strongly supportive of the various measures of birth control advocated by such agencies as Planned Parenthood, including full legalization of abortion. We greatly fear that if humanity does not choose to limit its numbers by reducing births, Nature will do it for us by increasing deaths.

Where we're going and how we hope to get there

The word *religion* means "re-linking." The basic commitment of the Church of Al Worlds is to the re-integration of people with themselves, their fellow humans, and wit the whole of living Nature. We are committed to developing an organic, vitalistic philosophy of life and its expression in a organic culture.

To this end, the CAW devotes itself to those who need or want the help and understanding of others through the processes of unlearning and learning. It is our aim to offer assistance through any personal expansion programs found to be effective. Further, we are committed to remain open-minded and receptive to new ideas, interests and goals and learn to live responsibly and responsively with each other.

We advocate involvement with every conceivable aspect of the emerging Aquarian Age culture, from religious service and mythology to family relations and child-rearing; from education to ecology; from psychic development to space travel; from the sensual to the sexual; from intentional communities to planetary government and world peace. "Nothing short of everything will ever really do." We are engaged in the eclectic reconstruction of ancient Nature religions, combining myths, customs, lore and archetypes of many cultures with other mystic and spiritual disciplines. But we are not trying to recreate a Paradise Lost; we are actively involved in helping to save the present world as well as working to actualize a visionary future. With roots deep in the Earth, the Past and with branches reaching towards the stars, the Future, we evoke and create myths not only of a Golden Age long past, but also of one yet to come...

The Earth, Our Mother is Sacred. Thus, all places, from a Sacred Grove in Ireland to downtown Manhattan, is Sacred Space and every activity can be considered essentially a religious activity. For us, recycling is as much a religious duty as prayer and meditation, as are composting our organic garbage, practicing birth control, using bio-degradable products, training and study, environmental activism and celebration of the sea- sons. We recognize that the essence of a religion is in the living of it. It is not so much the Path one chooses, but how well one keeps to it!

Making the World Safe for People Like Us...

By Oberon Zell

T THE END OF ROBERT HEINLEIN'S 1961 sci-fi novel, *Stranger in a Strange Land,* as you may recall, our messianic protagonist Valentine Michael Smith is dramatically martyred. He is now out of the picture. All his friends and followers, and those who had joined his "Church of All Worlds" were left to carry on as best they could. And by this time the readers of the story have become part of it, insofar as they end up considering themselves so. I did, and so did many others, both at the very beginning, and continuing.

For SISL only provided an origin myth, just as the four Gospels did for Christianity. The real saga begins *after* the origin, as all who have been touched by the messianic life portrayed in the original story are left to carry on from there. We have been doing this now for 62 years, and through all that time we've continued to evolve from those humble origins to become something far greater and more complex.

While this happened in a science-fiction universe still a ways into our future, and on a probability path that will never exist now, it happened in our own time as soon as each of us finished reading the book. For me, that was early 1962. Lance Christie and I—freshman students at Westminster College in Fulton, MO—read it, and shared water on April 7. We pledged our lives to the actualization of the precepts and principles found in that book, and began turning everybody we thought was cool onto it. And by sharing water with those who grokked the book, we created a water-brotherhood we called *Atl* (Aztec for "water").

Our initial mission-statement was *"To make the world safe for people like us."* But what did we mean by that, exactly? And what would it take to achieve?

Firstly, what does it mean to be "safe"? In SISL, Heinlein says: "There is no safety this side of the grave." I say safety means freedom from fear—to live our lives and raise our families freely without fear of persecution, discrimination, harassment, violence, rape, mugging, stoning, lynching, burning at the stake...

Freedom from angry mobs with torches and pitchforks—as has literally been the case throughout history.

Secondly, who are "people like us"? I say we are the ones who don't fit into the boxes of the normal and ordinary. We are the outsiders, the exceptions, the unusual, the extra-ordinary. The changelings, black sheep and ugly ducklings of whatever society we are born into. Nerds, Weirdos, Geniuses, Creatives, Mutants, Gays, Queers, Divergents, Hippies, Pagans...

In a personal letter to me dated 1/20/1972, Mr, Heinlein wrote:

> "I hope I have convinced you that STRANGER is dead serious...as questions. Serious, non-trivial questions, on which a man might spend a lifetime. (And I almost have.)
>
> "But anyone who takes that book as answers is cheating himself. It is an invitation to think—not to believe. Anyone who takes it as a license to screw as he pleases is taking a risk; Mrs. Grundy is not dead. Or any other sharp affront to the contemporary culture done publicly—there are stern warnings in it about the dangers involved. Certainly "Do as thou wilt is the whole of the Law" is correct when looked at properly—in fact it is a law of nature, not an injunction, nor a permission. But it is necessary to remember that it applies to everyone-including lynch mobs. The Universe is what It is, and It never forgives mistakes—not even ignorant ones."[12]

Consider the Gated Community analogy:

---

[12] Robert A. Heinlein to Tim Zell, 1/20/1972 (This entire letter, along with my initial letter to Mr. Heinlein, to which this was in reply, was printed in *Green Egg* Vol. XXI, No. 82; Lughnasadh, 1988)

If you want to live in a safe neighborhood, one way to do this is to create an isolated "safe" neighborhood and then keep all of the "unsafe" people out. This approach is so popular that we even have a name for it: the "Gated Community." In ancient times this was the principle of Medieval castles and walled cities—even the entire country of China, with its famous Great Wall. Think of Mycenae, Athens, Heraklion, Troy, Alexandria, Rome, Paris, London…

But there is another approach, and that is to try and create a world where all neighborhoods and thus all people are safe. Doing this means that you can be safe anywhere, not just in your own little Gated Community. This means that you have improved not only your own life, but the lives of your fellow citizens as well. For some people, being part of a safe, educated, inclusive nation *is* in their own self-interest.

So right from the start Lance and I recognized that it wouldn't be enough to just create our nice little Nest of Waterkin and hide out, meeting in secret, and hope that Mrs. Grundy doesn't find us. No, we would need to create a legal Church to give us protection under the 1st Amendment to the US Constitution: "Congress shall make no law regarding the establishment of religion; nor prohibiting the free exercise thereof."

> "…religion is a null area in the law. A church can do anything any organization can do—and has no restrictions. It pays no taxes, need not publish records, is effectively immune to search, inspection, or control—and a church is anything that calls itself a church. Attempts have been made to distinguish between 'real' religions entitled to immunities, and 'cults.' It can't be done, short of establishing a state religion…a cure worse than the disease. Both under what's left of the United States Constitution and under the Treaty of Federation, all churches are equally immune—especially if they swing a bloc of votes." ~Robert A. Heinlein, *Stranger in a Strange Land*

The value of having a legal church in America as an exempt vehicle to do pretty much whatever you want to do without governmental interference was irresistible. So we incorporated the Church of All Worlds in the state of Missouri on March 4, 1968, and received our 501(c)(3) exemption from the IRS on June 18, 1970.

But even establishing a legal church wouldn't be enough "to make the world safe for people like us" if we'd still be surrounded by a larger society that wants to destroy us. Creating the legal CAW in SISL didn't stop the angry populace from storming the temple with torches and pitchforks.

No, we would have to think bigger, and create an entire new religion, such as was proposed in a remarkable article by John Poppy in the Jan. 1970 issue of *Look* magazine (the final issue): "Why We Need a New Religion." And such a new religion would need a new identifying label.

So on Sept. 7, 1967, I invoked the ancient identity of "Pagan" (which traditionally encompasses all non-Abrahamic religions) as a category for CAW—and potentially an entire new religious movement. And on March 21, 1968, I produced the first issue of *Green Egg* magazine (initially just a single-page newsletter), referring to "The First *Pagan* Church of All Worlds," and began promoting the identity of "Pagan" to every new spiritual group I would hear about that seemed to fit the criteria I had in mind.

Like CAW, these mostly began as student study groups on college campuses, and included: Feraferia (Mycenaean) in Altadena, CA; Delphic Fellowship (Greek) in Los Angeles; Church of the Eternal Source (Egyptian) in Burbank; Ordo Templi Astartes (Canaanite) in Pasadena; the Neo-Dianic Faith in Los Angeles; The Discordian Society in Venice, CA; Reformed Druids of North America at Carlton College; and Witches of various Traditions around the country. I would send them a copy of *Green Egg,* and say: "You guys seem to be Pagans. So are we! Let's all be Pagans together!" And they all said, "Yes, we're all Pagans!" And in 1969 we formed the first Pagan ecumenical council—the Council of Themis. And thus was born a global religious movement.

Ben Franklin—political leader, inventor, bon vivant, philosopher—was once asked what he considered his greatest invention. He said "Americans." For he was the one who coined and popularized that umbrella term to include the many groups who had settled in the New World, but thought of themselves as separate: Puritans, Lutherans, English, French, New

Yorkers, Virginians... Franklin promoted the *inclusive* identity of *Americans* through his publications and writings, and it brought all those diverse factions together, making possible an *American* Revolution—though it still took a while for the wider identity to be embraced by all. In the words of Steve Zaffon and Dave Logan:

> Future-based language is responsible for historical moments becoming turning points. Benjamin Franklin is credited with inventing the word *American* and, in so doing, transforming thirteen warring colonies into a nation. His word displaced what most political analysts of the day predicted what was inevitable—that the colonies would never speak with one voice.[13]

And that is what the word *Pagan* did. It brought together Hellenics, Druids, Khemetics, Norse, Shamans, Witches, Minoans, Dianics, and CAW visionaries inspired by myths, fantasy, and science-fiction into a single broad religious coalition: *Pagans* (literally, "People of the Earth;" Ancient Ways, the Old Religion, Nature Religion, Green Religion…). We learned that what unites us is more important than what divides us, and Paganism became a Movement—now recognized as the fastest-growing and 2nd-largest "faith group" in America, with over four million people so-identifying as of 2021.

Of course, a new religion required a corresponding new theology and liturgy based on immanent Divinity and feminism. This I introduced with my 1970 vision of Gaea as the Soul of our living planet—literally, the superorganism comprising the entire planetary biosphere as a single organism conceived in the Cambrian Explosion half a billion years ago:

> In 1970 Tim [Oberon] Zell began writing about the planet Earth as Deity, as a single living organism, and this became the Church of All Worlds' central myth. Since 1971, the myth has been revised constantly and has become a unique eco-religious perception…
> ~**Margot Adler**, *Drawing Down the Moon,* 1979

> Oberon Zell was the first person to conceive and publish the biological and metaphysical foundations of what has become known as the 'Gaia Theory'—the unified body and emergent soul of the living Earth. Oberon's profound reconciliation of science, mythology and spirituality inspired and infused a worldwide neo-Pagan, panentheistic movement.   ~**Ralph Metzner, Ph.D.**, President, The Green Earth Foundation

And we created corresponding liturgy derived from ancient Pagan sources and contemporary reconstructions.

So once we had a legal church, and had started a global new religion to provide a larger context for it, we needed a centralized communications system that would reach everyone. A universal "watering hole," so to speak, where everyone would come to drink (literally "grok"). This I did with *Green Egg:*

> In March of [1968], the *Green Egg* appeared. From its inauspicious beginnings as a one-page ditto sheet, it grew into a 60-page journal over the next 80 issues, becoming the most significant periodical in the Pagan movement during the 1970s and made Tim Zell, its editor, a major force in Neo-Paganism (a term which Zell coined).
> ~ **Rev. J. Gordon Melton**, *The Encyclopedia of American Religions,* 1991
>
> Tim Zell, by using terms like *Pagan* and *Neo-Pagan* in referring to the emerging collectivity of new Earth religions, linked these groups, and *Green Egg* created a communications network among them.
> ~ **Margot Adler**, *Drawing Down the Moon,* 1979

By this time we were realizing that we needed to transform the entire dominant paradigm of Western Civilization from the exclusivist Judeo-Christian-Islamic monotheist paradigm to a broader and all-inclusive poly-pantheism. A new Paganism. Conjuring a genuine miracle would be sure to get people's attention. So in 1980 Morning Glory and I manifested "the Impossible Dream" and resurrected

---

[13] Zaffon, Steve & Logan, Dave, *The Three Laws of Performance,* Jossey-Bass, 2009.

authentic Living Unicorns. Real magick right out there in front of everyone!

Well, that worked pretty well, as our Unicorns soon became the star attractions of "The Greatest Show on Earth," so we looked around to see what else we would need to change. SISL had considered a revolutionary alternative approach to relationships—particularly sexual ones. Like "Pagan," this too needed a new word. So we came up with *polyamory* and *polyamorous*—launching another significant social movement. Today, polyamory is practiced by about 4-5% of the population of America. And according to Pew Research, 51% of adults under 30 in the US now think that open marriage is acceptable.

And finally, after having developed and presented viable alternative approaches to religion and sexuality, I turned my attention to the educational paradigm, and created a revolutionary school of "Esoteric Education," as well as a series of textbooks. The Grey School of Wizardry was incorporated on March 14, 2004, and is now the world's foremost academy of arcana.

Right about the time SISL came out, I articulated my lifetime "Mission Statement:" "To be a catalyst for the coalescence of consciousness." This has served me ever since. In my life, I have ever been a tosser of pebbles and a sower of seeds.

Stranger in a Strange Land became an icon of the 1960s counterculture, winning the prestigious Hugo Award for best novel in 1962. In 2012, it was included in a Library of Congress exhibition of "Books That Shaped America." SISL introduced us to pantheism, immanent divinity, water sharing, Pagan priestesses, psychic abilities, afterlife, communal living, ritual and social nudity, sacred sex, polyamory, and group marriages.

There were the descriptions of rituals, including Priestesses, and The Goddess, along with ritual nudity (none of these things were to be found anywhere else but in Pagan religions). So we have created and evolved rituals conducted by ordained Priestesses (CAW was the first legal church to ordain Priestesses!), to celebrate The Goddess and all the pantheons of the Old Gods. We have evolved new social and family structures, new subsidiary spinoffs, publications, music, literature, liturgy, statuary, jewelry, businesses, lifestyles...

In the novel—published in 1961 and set, remember, 25 years after the first human mission to Mars, which still has not occurred, so we are still looking decades into the future—the mainstream society and established religion is so outraged by these radical concepts, and this alien religion—that an angry mob with torches and pitchforks burns down the Temple and martyrs the Prophet.

But see, here is the thing: we have already changed the world so much that even now—63 years later and decades before the fictional story is even set—that extreme backlash reaction is inconceivable. The real-life Church of All Worlds and the worldwide Neo-Pagan movement it founded and fostered is already over half a century old, and it is far too late to stamp it out. Modern Paganism has long been recognized as the fastest-growing religion in the English-speaking world (and growing exponentially in many other countries as well). Paganism is now widely accepted as practically mainstream, and persecution of our people is almost nonexistent. Annual public "Pagan Pride" events are now held in many regions of the country, and metaphysical stores may be found in every large city. The war is over, and we won! Three generations have already grown up and are raising their own children and grandchildren in a world transformed by the new Pagan renaissance.

We have embraced, fostered and participated in the shaping of the Feminist movement, the Deep Ecology ecospirituality movement, the Civil Rights movement, sexual liberation, legalization of herbs and psychedelics as sacraments, LGBTQ+ rights, radical environmentalism, etc. And we have named, encouraged, and fostered the rise of two entire movements which have grown directly out of these realizations into full communities: the Neo-Pagan movement, and the polyamory movement. We have planted our roots deep into the fertile Earth, while, like a tree, our branches reach towards the beckoning stars.

We have indeed made the world safe for people like us! Now let us boldly go where no one has gone before—unto the Awakening of Gaea...

And this is the Ultimate Conspiracy—for when you know enough to grok what it's all about, it's too late; you're already one of us!

OZ's Personal History of CAW

By Oberon, Primate *(August 27, 1994; updated August 18, 2024)*

1st Decade: the '60s

In the Fall of 1961 I began my freshman year as a Pre-Med student at Westminster College in Fulton, Missouri. There I met Lance Christie, the first person I had ever encountered who seemed to be the same species as I. Each of us had felt that we were something very different from our parents and the people around us as we were growing up, and had been on a quest to find our own People.

Lance had already begun a small proto-group out of his high school chess club in Tulsa, Oklahoma, which had coalesced around Ayn Rand's novels-in particular, her vision of the "Atlantis" community in *Atlas Shrugged.* Lance's friends, as I, had all been avid science fiction readers (we cut our teeth on Heinlein juveniles), and had been particularly taken by the recurrent theme of the emergence of a new stage in human evolution *("Homo Novus").* We sorta thought of ourselves as the potential new Cro-Magnons in a world of Neanderthals.

The similar thinking that Lance and I had brought with us to college brought us together in many late-night discussion sessions, planning how we might contact others like us, form a community, start a movement, etc. Lance wanted to create a foundation or institute: "Christie House"—"a total-environment educational institution which would theoretically produce Ayn Rand heroes, alias Maslonian self actualizers." Inspired by *Atlas Shrugged,* I envisioned an alternative community hidden in some remote wilderness fastness...

I joined (briefly) the Phi Kappa Psi fraternity, and Lance and several others started an alternative fraternity called Mu Omicron Alpha (MOA), which gathered together a lot of what were at that time called "spooks."

And then, in October of 1961, *Stranger in a Strange land* (SISL) by Robert A. Heinlein arrived in Lance's mailbox as the Science Fiction Book Club selection of the month. He finally got around to reading it in late March of '62 "and was seized with an ecstatic sense of recognition." Lance turned it over to me on April 4, saying that this one book dealt with much of what we had been thinking and talking about, and had articulated many of our own thoughts.

I read it over the next couple of days, and was similarly enthusiastic. We talked long about the vision therein, and on April 7, 1962, the two of us shared water, pledging to begin living a new dream, and bringing others into it.

In the novel, Valentine Michael Smith was a human born on Mars as the sole survivor of a crashed first expedition, and raised by Martians. Upon being brought back to Earth twenty years later, he established the "Church of All Worlds," built around "nests," a fusion of congregation, group marriage, and intentional community. A basic concept was "grokking," i.e., the ability to be fully empathic (literally, *"drinking").*

Heinlein's SISL introduced us to the ideas of Immanent Divinity ("Thou Art God"), Pantheism ("all that groks is God"), Sacraments (water sharing), Priestesses, social nakedness, intimate extended families as a basis for community; and, of course, open, loving relationships without jealousy; and joyous expression of sexuality as divine union. By defining "love" as "that condition wherein another person's happiness is essential to your own," SISL changed forever the parameters of our relationships with each other, especially in the sexual arena. And all this in the context of a legal religious organization—a "church"—which could have all the rights and privileges granted to the mighty Church of Rome!

During the Summer of '62, we all separated, Lance to Tulsa, Penny to Springfield, Ohio, Martha to Elgin, Illinois, and I to the Colorado Rockies for my second year of working at Grand Lake Lodge in Rocky Mountain Nat'l Park. That was my Summer for finding myself. I spent many hours sunbathing naked out in the woods, meditating, reading Any Rand, and writing letters. This was the period of Atl's gestation. Our underlying philosophies were formulated at this time, and the thinking that would culminated in the first edition of the *Atl/an Logbook* was crystallizing in the high mountain air. Toward the end of that pregnant Summer I managed to accumulate enough days off to hitchhike from the high country of Grand Lake down to Tulsa a few times to meet and share water with Dagny and see Lance again. Lance, Penny,

Martha and I all drove down to Tulsa to share water with Dagny, Hank and others of Lance's old high school chess club, the spawning ground of the original vision. This was the first of what would come to be many cross-country pilgrimages over the following decades, as small groups of us travelled in carloads from one end of the land to another to attend festivals and science-fiction conventions, make new friends and lovers, and share water.

We began thinking in terms of an organization to bring Heinlein's (and our) vision into being. Lance and I were both in the Psychology Dept. at Westminster, and we devised a plan: all incoming students were routinely given the Edwards Personal Preference Schedule (EPPS), which rated their attitudes on fifteen scales based on Abraham Maslow's work on self actualizing personalities. Lance and I got hold of our own test results, noted the matching patterns in several key areas, and then designed a student project, implemented in the Fall of '62, of correlating the EPPS results of all the other students looking for the same distinctive pattern of matches (particularly an "M" in the center five scales). Those we found we then contacted turned them on to SISL, and recruited them int our water-brotherhood, which we called *Atl,* an Aztec word meaning both "water" and "ancient homeland of our ancestors." A small Caribbean fish-tiki became our token, as I carved dozens of wooden replicas for our water-brothers.

This approach was amazingly successful, and by the time Lance and I graduated in 1965, we had over 100 Atlan water-brothers (including most of the MOA crowd) and were publishing a regular newsletter, *The Atlan Torch.* We also had a growing anthology of our writing , musings and favorite quotes, called *The Atlan Logbook. The Atlan Torch* was the first "underground" paper to be published at Westminster, and it developed quite a following, especially among the faculty, as we focused much attention on issues of free speech and academic freedom.

Our great mentor during this period was Gale Fuller, head of the Psych Dept. at Westminster. He had a big house and grounds on the edge of town, and we spent many hours talking around the fire. It was his influence that persuaded me to shift my major from Pre-Med to Psych, Soc and Anthro.

Martha became pregnant over Xmas break of 1962, so we got married a few months later, on Feb. 16, and had our son, Bryan, on Sep. 15 f '93. We thus became the first students in the history of Westminster to be married and have independent housing. Our apartment became an off-campus clothing-optional haven for our growing Nest of water-siblings, and we never lacked for volunteer babysitters! Bryan may have been the first 2nd-generation child born and raised in the Pagan community. Martha and I undertook to create an Atlan environment in our Fulton home. We maintained an open house at all times, encouraging people to drop by at their leisure. On weekend evenings there was usually someone with a guitar, and conversation was interlaced with folk singing. Our pad acquired the reputation among friends as a place where they could be themselves, and among our enemies as a den of iniquity. These were good times!

Outside of the town of Fulton were some long-abandoned strip-mines which had supplied clay for the local brickmaking industry. These had become overgrown with small trees and grasses, with beautiful green and turquoise pools nestling among rolling dunes of calcite crystals. These were lovely, paradisal places which no-one else seemed to know about, so in warm weather we commandeered them for our weekend campouts, skinny-dipping and sunning during the days, and singing (those were the days of folk- and protest songs, and "hootenannies") and telling stories around the campfire at night as we guzzled Lance's infamous Sangria. We were introduced to marijuana in this idyllic setting, beginning our long affinity for "sex'n'drugs'n'rock'n'roll." Social nakedness and outdoor lovemaking was very liberating, and we carried these ways back indoors during the cold Missouri winters, posting a "Did You Remember To Dress?" sign on the inside of our door. *Bewitched* and *I Dream of Genie* were new shows on TV, and we appreciated the little touch of magic in the media.

During my college years, I took every course offered in comparative religions, history, philosophy, psychology, anthropology, and the natural sciences. The Senior Colloquium assignment was to design a new religion, and my thesis, "Freedom Through Existentialism," drew upon our Atlan perspective in trying to actually live out our visionary ideas in an experiential experiment, laying the foundation for the actual Church we would come to create.

Lance and Penny were married in Tulsa on Aug. 7, 1964, with Martha and I driving down to be matron of honor and best man. After the wedding, they moved to Kansas City, where Lance got a job with the health department. About this time we obtained our first car, a 1960 Volkswagon camper. We made our first use of it in a trip to Hidden Valley nudist camp in Illinois; our first contact with organized nudism. We enjoyed our experiences at the camp immensely, and I for one felt as if a shadow had been lifted from the world. That Christmas, Martha, Bryan and I drove to Florida for a Yule vacation, where we visited various nudist camps.

After we left Westminster in 1965, Martha and I worked the summer back at Grand Lake Lodge in Colorado, where Bryan learned to talk (his first word, after "Mommy" and "Daddy," was "horseshit!"). In the Fall, I went on to graduate school at Washington University in St Louis where I had a scholarship in Clinical Psychology. Lance went on to the University of Oklahoma in Norman. We founded Nests in these places, and continued publishing separate editions of *The Atlan Torch.* Martha was studying in Kansas City to be a Montessori teacher, and I would drive all the way from St Louis on weekends to be with her and Bryan; we hung out a lot at Sycamore Hollow nudist camp near Lawrence, Kansas, which we later learned was once frequented by Robert Heinlein!

In '66-'67 we rented a big old house in downtown St Louis, which we shared for awhile with a Boston debutante named Pam Lawry and a Black radical named Bill Taylor. We identified strongly with *the Addams Family* in the new TV show, and painted much of the interior black, with red and gold trim.

Sybil Leek, who had just published her *Diary of a Witch,* came through in '66 on tour of the US, and we met briefly; it was my first encounter with anyone of the Craft. After a disappointing year of rat running in grad school, I got a job with the Human Development Corp. (HOC), enlisting in the "War on Poverty." Our St. Louis Nest joined a Beatnik coffeehouse cooperative, "The Agora," through which we met Jim Igoe and others.

A column in *The Atlan Torch,* called "Atlan Annals," eventually became its own round-robin members-only "apazine," in which we discussed our unfolding plans and visions. At this time (1966-'67) two different directions emerged: most of the Atlans wanted to keep our water-brotherhood a secret fraternity, operating underground. Others of us felt that our vision needed to be taken to the greater society and made more influential in shaping the kind of world we wanted; and also to be more accessible to other potential Atlans as-yet-undiscovered out there.

Eventually, due somewhat to the influence of Kurt Vonnegut's novel *Cat's Cradle,* it was decided to split into two separate groups: The Atlan Foundation, headed by Lance, would remain underground and work in secret to influence various social systems (see the last chapter of Rimmer's *The Harrad Experiment).* The Church of All Worlds would incorporate legally and go public, with me as its Primate. This decision was implemented in the summer of 1967.

CAW began its public life at a fund-raising garage sale at a St Louis Beatnik coffeehouse over that Labor Day weekend. I was then invited to be a regular speaker there on Thursday evenings. Having just come across the word *pagan* in an historical context in an article called "Functional Religion" by Kerry Thornley (an early Keristan and one of the founders of the Discordian Society), I introduced myself as "Your Friendly Neighborhood Pagan," thus beginning the first usage of that term to apply to this new religion I was promoting, later extending it to encompass the entire emerging movement of Nature-based and revivalist pre-Christian religions, including not only Witchcraft as European shamanism, but also Egyptian, Greek, Norse, Druidic, Hindu, and various Classical and indigenous tribal traditions, such as Polynesian, Native American, African, etc.

Within a few months I had developed a significant following, including John Patrick ("Tiny") McClimans, the first person to actually join the new CAW. (John was ordained as our third Priest at Oimelc of 1970, and died of diabetes at Samhain of 1996). Money for legal fees was donated by Ravi Kristin, Boo-Hoo of the local chapter of the Neo-American Church, and we filed for State and Federal incorporation. Following the prescription in SISL, I had enrolled in a correspondence course offered by a small Christian seminary, Life Science College in Rolling Meadows, Illinois. My extensive undergraduate courses in religious studies provided most of the credits needed, and I received my Doctor of Divinity at the end of the Fall semester; I was then ordained by the CAW at Yule of '67.

In the Spring of '68, we took over another coffeehouse that had been run by a consortium of Christian churches. They had called it "The Exit," but we renamed it "Instead," setting up our first Temple upstairs (the coffeehouse was in the basement of a huge five-story Victorian mansion on Gaslight Square, the St. Louis equivalent of the Haight, or Greenwich Village; the whole place renting for $75 a month!). We opened on March 1, 1968; our State of Missouri Incorporation came through on March 4, and the first issue of *Green Egg* was published on March 21. A draft dodger who was hiding out under the name of "Jefferson Davis" became our coffee-house manager, and a young folksinger named Frank Batton was our main attraction. Ed Whitehead, a crazed Hippie artist and publisher, moved his press in upstairs and put out an underground paper (later producing our first mainstream magazine, *The Pagan!*). (Ed died in 1993.) Atlan Virgil Elliot, a Beatnik artist/poet, joined the Boneshakers motorcycle club, soon becoming their President, and providing us with a dubious "honor guard." The bikers introduce us to "Pagan Pink Ripple," which we dutifully drank for years... During this time I did some presentations at the local college campuses. where we picked up Tom Williams; he was ordained as our second Priest at Beltane, 1969.

With the *Green Egg* as a vehicle, we began making outreach to other groups we considered to be Pagan, including Feraferia, and their brilliant and artistic founder, Fred Adams. Feraferia was heavily influenced by Robert Graves, and we assimilated a good deal of their material, including their whole festival cycle of the Sacred Round. With Fred, we founded the Council of Themis, the first Neo-Pagan ecumenical alliance, bringing in the Egyptian Church of the Eternal Source and our first Wiccan group, the Coven of the Cat. After a few promising years, gathering many members, the Council disintegrated around the takeover of Poke Runyon of the O∴T∴A∴ magickal lodge, who began ejecting groups who were into sex'n'drugs. Some of

the surviving groups went on to found, in 1972, the Council of Earth Religions.

Working now as a substitute primary teacher, I enrolled in Harris Teachers' College to get my Teaching Certificate in '68. During that Summer, we discovered a wonderful place to hold our CAW gatherings in the form of a sand and gravel quarry at Fenton, Missouri, which had been cut out of the Missouri River flood plain. For the next several years this isolated site provided us a fine private beach for skinny dipping, campfires and rituals; some quite spectacular.

The city of St. Louis kept denying us our occupancy permit on various technicalities, and Gaslight Square deteriorated over the summer due to an escalation of hard drugs and violence, so we had to abandon our Temple six month after we'd opened it, meeting over the next year in our homes to watch *Star Trek,* eat popcorn and Cheez-Its, be naked, and have many long talks far into the night.

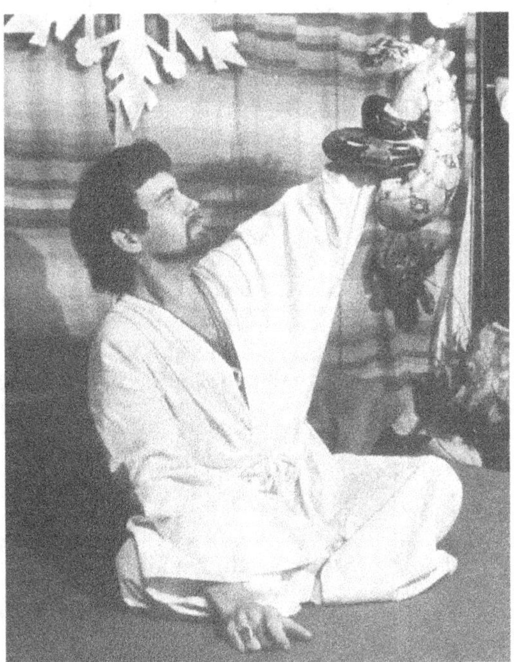

Tim Zell with his boa constrictor, Histah, 1968.

During this period I had a wonderful affair with an older woman name Patrice, whom I met as a journalist doing a story on Witches for Halloween of '68. She introduced me to the Unitarian Church, where Webster Kitchell, the Minister, and I became friends, and I ended up teaching evolution for their Sunday School the following Spring Webster and I went canoeing together, and published some of his sermons in *Green Egg* and *The Pagan.* Eventually he grew a beard and declared himself a Pagan, thus presaging the Pagan Unitarian movement that has resulted in CUUPS (Covenant of Unitarian Universalis Pagans) becoming a significant faction of both Paganism and the Unitarian Church.

On Labor Day weekend of 1969, the World Science Fiction Convention was held in St Louis, and naturally, the Church of All World had to be there in force. That was where we met Bill Morris (now "Orion"), who was a 17-yr-old Canadian from Winnipeg, Manitoba. He became a central figure in the CAW ever since.

2nd Decade: the '70s

At our Yule party in 1969, we had over 100 people crowding my living room, and we passed the hat for donations towards renting a new temple space. We collected enough, and set about looking for a suitable place, which we found a few months later, opening in March of 1970, just in time to celebrate the first Earth Day on April 20, as the only local church to participate. During preparations for this event, I met Julie, who, at 18, became my second "wife." Also that April, I had my first LSD experience upon the occasion of a total eclipse of the Sun. Our Temple was right next door to a Black Pentecostal church called "Mother Martin's Church of God in Christ," and one of the most amusing episodes of the time was when Tom and I were invited to do an Easter morning sermon there...

The summer of 1970 was filled with sex and acid, with many activities centering around our Temple and our secret beach in Fenton. That August, Martha, Bryan, Bill and I drove to Florida for vacation, meeting and visiting new and old Pagan friends. During that trip, at the insistence of Jim Igoe, I finally read Robert Graves' *The White Goddess,* which had a significant impact on my worldview. Subsequently, over Labor Day I had a cosmic acid vision of the Goddess, which I articulated in a series of revelatory thealogical essays published in GE 1971-73 (the "TheaGenesis" papers). This was the first published version of what later came to be known as the Gaea Thesis—a biological validation of the ancient intuition

that our planetary biospheere is a single living organism, Mother Earth. Thus Gaea, Pan and other Nature spirits became our Divine Pantheon.

These writings had a profound effect on the thealogical perspectives of the emerging Neo-Pagan community of the time, and were widely read, circulated and reprinted. By thus merging ecology with religion, the CAW became an early forerunner of the Deep Ecology movement. Through our focus on Mother Nature as Goddess, and our recognition and ordination of women as priestesses, CAW can also hold claim to be the first Eco-Feminist Church. Our only creed stated: "The Church of All Worlds is dedicated to the celebration of life, the maximal actualization of human potential and the realization of ultimate individual freedom and personal responsibility in harmonious eco-psychic relationship with the total Biosphere of Holy Mother Earth."

But once again the city was determined to shut us down, and we were denied an occupancy permit for our new storefront temple. The local election campaign that Fall included a program to "clean up" the nasty counterculture, and along with various other Hippie establishments, such as the local Free Radio (with Elizabeth Gipps), we found ourselves being setup and busted. Throughout the case, Mother Martin from the church next door was one of our staunchest supporters. While all charges were eventually dropped, the attendant negative publicity, especially in the wake of the recent Manson murders, sent us underground again, and we closed the Temple for good.

That Fall Julie went off to college, and Tom Williams and I enrolled in Witchcraft training under Deborah Letter (later Bourban), who had just opened The Cauldron, the first occult store and Botanica in St. Louis. These studies culminated in Craft Initiation in the Spring of '71, and we began infusing more Wiccan material into our CAW liturgy.

In the Winter, Bill and I drove up to Julie's college to spend some time with her. In April, Martha moved out of the house and Julie moved in. I donated the house to the Church and took a vow of poverty.

During the Summer of '71 we were engaged in attempting to purchase land for a rural CAW community, which we intended to call

"Lothlorien." Several families who were planning to go in on the purchase had sold their homes and ended up living for a few months with Julie and me while the negotiations dragged on.. By the time the landowner finally admitted that he was reneging on his deal with us because he'd gotten a better offer from a real estate developer, the couples had broken up under the pressure of all trying to live in our basement. Carole Maddox, with her kids Tad and Sarah, and Judy O'Rourke with her children Laurie, Sandy and Chip, all remained living in my home as we struggled to build a group family. As the man of the house and sole breadwinner, I had three women and six kids all requiring my attention, love and support. Other than my own 8-year-old son, Bryan, these were the first Pagan kids we'd encountered, and for the first time in his life, Bryan now had Pagan playmates. While I enjoyed the benefits of a large communal family, we were not really equipped for it in our two-bedroom house, and Carole and Judy, with their kids, moved out in the Fall, though we remained friends ever after (Judy died in 1993). However, Julie and my relationship, having just started to live together, was severely strained by this experience, and never fully recovered.

The 1971 World Science Fiction Convention was held in Boston, and Julie and I made the pilgrimage to attend. On that trip we connected with Robert Rimmer, author of *The Harrad Experiment,* and stayed a few days at Seth Many's infamous "Lewd Commune" in Cambridge. It was there that I finally initiated correspondence with Robert Heinlein, and his warm and lengthy letters back have been published in both *Green Egg* (#82, 85, 89) and his posthumous *Grumbles From the Grave.* Of great relief was his assurance that: "I have never expressed 'antagonism' or hostility to 'nests' or 'water brotherhoods.' This is sheer fabrication. I would like to throw such a lie into the teeth of anyone saying so, if I knew who he were. On the contrary, a number of 'nests' have indeed gotten into contact with me. I have treated them with politeness. I have standing invitations from several to visit them. I think I am on good terms with every such organization which has taken the trouble to get into touch with me." (RAH to TZ 1/20n2) He also stated that "I have enjoyed

reading the *Green Egg* and have been stimulated by it."

Susan Roberts had just published *Witches U.S.A.,* and we met with her in New York, where she introduced us to many of the Witches in her book, including Ray and Rosemary Buckland, who had introduced Gardnerian Witchcraft to the US. We also met Theos and Phoenix, Leo Louis Martello, Gwen Thompson, Ed Buczinsky and Herman Slater.

During that trip, Julie and I stopped off in Philadelphia to visit with Mike and Penny Novack and some of the Pagan Way people. Several of them had kids, and we were surprised to learn that they were not raising their children in a Pagan way, but sending them to Christian Sunday school! "The Pagan Way," it turned out, was mainly a front for Wicca, and up to that time the Craft was seen by most of its practitioners as less of a religion than a kind of secret magickal society, with no place for children in its rituals and practices.

Although CAW had been the first Neo-Pagan/Earth Religion to obtain full Federal recognition as a 501(c)(3) on June 18, 1970, we had initially been refused recognition by the Missouri Department of Revenue on the basis of our "lack of primary concern about the hereafter, God, the destiny of souls, heaven, hell, sin and its punishment, and other supernatural matters." With the help of the ACLU, the ruling was overturned as unconstitutional in 1971, resulting in much favorable publicity for the Church, and people flocking to us to conduct Pagan marriages. *Green Egg* continued to increase in scale and influence, as the "inside journal" of the growing worldwide Neo-Pagan movement.

In 1972 three Pagan families with kids joined up, finally developing a real 2nd generation context for our "Pagan family values." These were Carolyn Clark, Don and Alene Wildgrube, and Tom and Freda Kullman. The kids all fell in quite well together, and remained best friends for many years.

Over Labor Day of 1972, the World Science Fiction Convention was held in Los Angeles, and Julie and I traveled there with my boa constrictor, Histah, where we won the Grand Prize in the costume contest (as "Cernunnos and Ceridwen") and connected with the West Coast Pagan community, including Gwydion Pend-

Tim & Julie as Cernunnos & Cerridwen at LAcon 1972

derwen, Alison Harlow (one of the judges in the contest), Fred Adams of Feraferia, Harold Moss and Donald Harrison of the Church of the Eternal Source, and Isaac Bonewits. Alison and Gwydion brought us up to Ukiah, where they were in process of buying into Greenfield Ranch, a 5,600-acre cattle ranch which was being developed as a Hippie homesteading community. We fell in love with the place, and vowed to return someday to live there. Julie and I also joined Nemeton, a Pagan network newly formed by Gwydion and Alison, with a high-quality newsstand magazine of the same name

Late '72 brought us our first confrontation with the Fundamentalist Christian anti-occult crusaders in the form of Rev. Hershel Smith and his "Witchmobile," full of displays and items of occult paraphernalia. Smith described himself as a "former warlock" who, at the age of 13, sold his soul to the devil, cutting open a live puppy and drinking its blood. Stationing his "Witchmobile" outside of St Louis' New Life Evangelistic Center, Smith issued a public challenge to debate anyone on the evils of Satanism, Witchcraft and the occult. Eight members of CAW and five Witches showed up at his show on Dec. I, where I stood and accepted his challenge, to a response of being violently hustled from the room. A press conference was held the next day with CAW Clergy plus Gavin & Yvonne Frost of the Church & School of Wicca. NBC and CBS covered the event. Smith never showed up, and the Pagans carried the day. (This historic event was reported in GE 52.)

In the Spring of 1973, Julie and I broke up. I was quite shattered, but found solace in my Nest and High Priestess, Carolyn (ordained at Beltane--#4), who, with her Appalachian Druidic Craft background, continued the Wiccan training I had begun under Deborah Letter. Roberta ("Bobbie") Kennedy from Ohio was ordained at Litha (#5), and Don Wildgrube at Lughnasadh (#6). That Summer I hitchhiked out to Wyoming for the 4th of July Rainbow Family Gathering, on the way to which I was arrested for hitching and spend a weekend in the Colorado State Prison. While in Wyoming, I visited with Bonnie Sherlock in Lander, and receiver an initiation into her Tradition, a blend of Wicca and Lakota.

The continuing publication of my "Thea-Genesis" series resulted in an invitation to be the keynote speaker at the 4th Annual Gnostic

Carolyn Clark & Tim Zell, Beltane 1973.

Aquarian Festival in Minneapolis, during Fall Equinox of 1973, where I was interviewed for *Playboy* and met my soulmate, Morning Glory. It was the Pagan Romance of the Year, and we were handfasted on Easter Sunday, April 14, 1974, in a spectacular public Pagan ceremony which was written up in all the local papers and filmed by a special crew from a Japanese TV company. Isaac Bonewits and Carolyn officiated (both managing to catch their long hair on fire from the altar candles!). Margot Adler was Maid of Honor, and sang Gwydion's "Beltane Wedding Dance."

At Litha I passed the mantle of High Priest over to Don Wildgrube, having held it for the traditional seven years. Morning Glory was subsequently ordained as a Priestess (#7) at Lughnasadh.

Tim & MG as Peter Stag & Virginia, Discon 1974.

The 1974 World Science Fiction Convention ("Discon") was held in Washington, DC, and MG and I drove out to attend. We won the prize for "Most Primal" in the costume contest, as "Peter Stag and the High Priestess of the Goddess Columbia," from Philip Jose Farmer's *Flesh*. We also returned to Minneapolis at Mabon for the 5th Gnostic Aquarian Festival, where we met and shared water with Robert Anton Wilson. He became a regular contributor to *Green Egg* over the next few years, prior to the publication of his *Illuminatus* trilogy, with Robert Shea.

Our continual search for land in the country on which to build a community involved us in various ventures. We held several festivals at a lovely place south of St. Louis where there was a pond and cave. Don Wildgrube got us in contact with Herta Drnec, who owned a place of large open fields and a small creek which she called "Pangaea." Our Summer Solstice there in 1975 brought Harold Moss of the Egyptian Church of the Eternal Source all the way from Burbank, California.

Our St. Louis Nest soon grew too big to be contained in one place, so we formed two: one out in Overland, which was hosted and presided over by Don Wildgrube; and another in the City, hosted by Tom Williams. The former became more of an "outer circle" training group, while the latter, more inner-circle, we called the "Dog Star Nest" (because it was the "Sirius" group...). There was a lot of overlap, as we avoided scheduling competing dates, and we all got together for Festivals. While Don taught excellent classes in Tarot, astrology, and applied magic," others of us discovered magic mushrooms...

Morning Glory had come from Eugene, Oregon, and she gave me two years in St. Louis to pull up stakes and move to the West Coast. On my 33rd birthday, Nov. 30, 1975, I quit my job as Supervisor of Social Services for the Human Development Corp., rented out the house, bought an old school bus, and over the next few months we rebuilt the engine and the interior into a motorhome ("The Scarlet Succubus"), heading West in May of '76.

After many adventures on the road, we made it to Greenfield Ranch in time for Summer Solstice at Alison Harlow's newly-acquired 220-acre parcel of Coeden Brith ("Speckled Forest"). Then we spent a year in Eugene, parking initially in Anna Kom's driveway, where we taught classes on "Celtic Shamanism" at Lane Community College and founded the student Coven of Ithil Duath. The materials we developed for this course became the foundation upon which the HOME Tradition was eventually established.

In August I did a two-week fast and vision quest in the wilderness across the river from the

MacReady Hot Springs, which constituted my 2nd degree initiation into Shamanic Witchcraft. It was at the University of Oregon in Eugene that our continuing researches into the roots of myths and legends revealed to us the long-lost secret of the Unicorn.

When we excitedly disclosed our discovery to Alison, she invited us to settle as caretakers on Coeden Brith, adjacent to the 55-acre parcel that Gwydion had just purchased and named *Annwfn,* the Welsh Underworld. There we were given the mission to raise the Unicorns, and to this end, the three of us formed the Holy Order of Mother Earth (HOME) as a magical monastic order of stewardship and ritual. Greatly inspired by both the Ranch celebration (where Marylyn Motherbear and her kids offered a wonderful live performance of Roald Dahl's *James and the Giant Peach),* and the Pagan gathering at Coeden Brith, we moved in at Summer Solstice, 1977, posting our old "Did You Remember to Dress?" sign at the gate. The tradition of holding a Litha festival on the land continued over the following years, with the largest celebration exceeding 200 people. Gwydion always created the rituals, which centered around the Battle of the Two Brothers (Stag-King vs. Bull King; Oak King vs. Holly King...).

Gwydion Pendderwen planting redwood seedlings.

When Morning Glory and I left St Louis, CAW had Nests in Missouri, California, Illinois, Kansas, Wisconsin, Iowa, Minnesota, Pennsylvania, Tennessee, New York and Ohio. We were then publishing three periodicals, *Green Egg, Mythos and The Pagan!* We had left the administration of the CAW and the publica-

tion of the *Green Egg* in the hands of the remaining Clergy. Then Tom Williams and Orion, "following in their Primate's knuckleprints," pulled up stakes to join MG and I in California. After only a few more issues of GE, the financially-strapped Central HQ decided to sell off our printing press, and the magazine ceased publication. Subsequently all Nests except Milwaukee dissolved due to internal conflicts. Don Wildgrube and some of the members of the Overland Nest reorganized as the Earth Church of Amargi (an ancient Sumerian word meaning both "freedom" and "return to the Mother").

With the assistance of Gwydion and Willowoak, we transferred our main CAW headquarters to California, receiving State in corporation on Sept. 14, 1978. The sale of our house in SL Louis had been intended to provide funds for establishing a CAW community in California, but some of the people back there were reluctant to part with the money, and the delay in it being transferred to our new HQ effectively crippled our own CAW programs for the next few years.

Meanwhile, Morning Glory and I were living out in the woods, homesteading in a Pagan community as we'd always dreamed. Charlie Leach and Michael Hurley soon followed us from St Louis to California, and we met more Pagans and other people in the larger Ranch community whom we were able to bring into the Church. These included Gwydion, of course, who merged his publishing network, Nemeton, with CAW and donated his land to the Church. But the most significant person we brought in at this time was Anodea Judith, whom we perceived upon first meeting to be a potential CAW Priestess. It was while living at Coeden Brith that Morning Glory and I carried out our project of resurrecting the Living Unicorns back into the world. We also raised baby deer and wild pigs we found in the Spring, and lived much like wild animals ourselves, going naked over half the year.

Starting in 1977, Gwydion began organizing an annual New Year's tree planting festival for which he created a special branch of CAW Forever Forests. Over the following years, hundreds of people came out to plant thousands of cedar, pine, Douglas fir and redwood on logged-over land on Greenfield Ranch and other places This active combining of the spiritual with the ecological brought us into contact with Eart First! (co-founded by Atlan Lance Christie), wherein CAW became an active presence, participating heavily in the Redwood Summer of 1990

Starting in 1977, Gwydion began organizing an annual New Year's tree planting festival for which he created a special branch of CAW Forever Forests. Over the following years, hundreds of people came out to plant thousands of cedar, pine, Douglas fir and redwood on logged-over land on Greenfield Ranch and other places This active combining of the spiritual with the ecological brought us into contact with Eart First! (co-founded by Atlan Lance Christie), wherein CAW became an active presence, participating heavily in the Redwood Summer of 1990.

In February of 1978, we drove up to Seattle with Alison in the Scarlet Succubus for a founding meeting of the new Covenant of the Goddess. While we were there, Morning Glory had to fly down to Los Angeles for a family emergency, and I drove back alone. I decided to check out the Bigfoot Information Center run by Peter Byrne in the Oregon Dalis, where I came upon the little-known existence of a full-scale replica of Stonehenge over on the Washington side of the Columbia River. At the Maryknoll Museum, I learned that the replica had been built in the 1920s by railroad tycoon Sam Hill, who intended it as a war memorial to WWI dead. He had chosen that location because it was the only place in N. America where two eclipse paths would cross in this century. The first had been in 1921, when the altar stone was laid. The next was due on Feb. 26, 1979!

In July I hitchhiked up to Eugene for the Oregon Country Faire and the subsequent Oregon Rainbow Family Gathering. While high in a tree at the Faire, I had a vision of the coming eclipse, and circulated widely a cryptic note and image: "The prophecies will come/When Shadow mates with Sun."

A number of key Priests and Priestesses of the Pagan community came together the following February at the remote Stonehenge location (100 miles east of Portland) to create a spectacular ritual for 3-4,000 people. This was a truly awesome experience, with all-night drumming and dancing around the campfire in the center of the ring-as our giant shadows cast by the fire danced around the circle of stones, the references to Stonehenge as "the Giants' dance" became clear! As the energy reached a crescendo, we screamed and lifted our hands to the clouded sky—which was suddenly clear and filled with brilliant stars. The sense of timeless community we all felt in the morning, as we stood within the shadow of the Moon, simply cannot be described. This event was covered widely in the media, as it was the only place along the eclipse path (other than an Indian reservation to the East) where the clouds were cleared so people could actually see the eclipse itself. Walter Cronkite said on the evening news that "While the Pagans and Druids claimed not to be seeking any converts, we think they may have won some from the Weather Bureau!"

Stonehenge eclipse, Feb. 26, 1979.

It was shortly after the eclipse that I had a mystical experience with a wild otter which resulted in my being given the name "Otter," which I bore until the Fall of 1994. Orion Stormcrow, formerly Bill Morris, was ordained (#8) at Litha, 1979; he later became Director of Nemeton and Rites & Festivals, General Administrator, Publisher of *Green Egg,* and President of the Church.

3rd Decade: the '80s

In the Spring of 1980 our first Unicorns were born, and the next few years for Morning Glory and me were occupied almost entirely with that venture, as we dealt with massive publicity and exhaustive travels. We had to leave the land for the Summer through Fall to live in the home of our agents, David and Janet Hodgehead, in Los Gatos. We first appeared in public at the Renaissance Faire in Novato, where we were given a stall way at the back to take photos of folks with a live Unicorn. I recall two guys hanging over the fence arguing about the animal grazing in the paddock: "That can't be a real unicorn!" snorted one. "It is too," said the other. "I saw it on TV!"

At the Octacon SF convention in Santa Rosa in Oct. '80, dressed as "Schmendrake the Magician, Molly Grue and the Unicorn" (from *The Last Unicorn* by Peter S. Beagle) we won first prize in the costume contest and introduced Lancelet the Unicom to Theodore Sturgeon, who cried and called him "my son" (one of our favorite Unicorn stories was Sturgeon 's "The Silken Swift"). I met a woman named Clea there, and she came to live with us for awhile the next Spring, when we adopted two baby deer. She later became known as Harmony, and is a fixture at the Renaissance Faire.

OZ & Lancelot at Canada's Wonderland, 1982.

In June of '81, Gwydion organized a great public Pagan Litha Festival in Berkeley which was sponsored by "Church of All Worlds," "Holy Order of Mother Earth," and "Nemeton." It was quite successful, including Gwydion 's special "Faery Shaman" ritual. But the blatantly Pagan posters all over the Bay Area got the three sponsoring groups listed in all future Fundie literature as "Satanic" organizations! Morning Glory and I spent most of that Summer on Chautauqua, traveling throughout the Pacific Northwest with the Flying Karamazov Bros. and a number of other great performers from the Oregon Country Faire. My son, Bryan, and MG's daughter, Rainbow, accompanied us in these adventures.

March 26-28, '82, saw the first major Goddess conference in the form of "Goddess Rising," held in Sacramento, California. It was organized by Ann Forfreedom, and many leading figures in the US Pagan community were featured as speakers, including Margot Adler, Jim and Selena Fox of Circle, Erica Jong, Luisah Tiesch, Isaac Bonewits, Ann Forfreedom, Charlie Murphy, Cerridwen Fallingstar, Gwydion, Alison, Morning Glory and I, and others too numerous to recall. Though the event lost money, it was a great success in bringing together so many key people to meet and touch minds and hearts.

In the Summer of '82, MG and I didn't even see each other for four months, as we were on separate circuits to present our Unicorns at every Renaissance Faire in the United States and Canada. At the Texas Ren. Festival I met Bella Dona Carter, and at the Maryland Ren. Faire, I met Jeanne; both ladies were to become significant in my life, and we managed to travel to get together once a year or so over the years. Later, Dona took me to Europe and Peru, and Jeanne took me to Alaska.

On Nov. 9, 1982, Gwydion was killed in a car wreck. This was the first death in our Family, and we were plunged into deep grief, along with much of the Pagan community who had known Gwydion, or been touched by his music (he having been the first Pagan bard to produce recordings of his songs). It was a major watershed for all of us, and years and lives were caught up in dealing with the new responsibilities of sacred land stewardship. Ayesha, Anodea, Farida, Anna Korn and Oz Anderson were appointed the first generation of Annwfn Stewards.

In May of 1983, inspired by our experiences with Renaissance Festivals all over the country, Morning Glory and I conceived and founded the Ukiah Hometown Festival, which became an annual event ever since. For years we led the parade down Main Street, in full Ren Faire regalia, with a live Unicorn.

In the Fall of' 83, I took a ceramics class at the local community college, where I met and fell in love with Diane Darling. Our relationship soon became a triad, and she moved onto Coeden Brith the following Spring, with her son, Zachariah, who was then eight years old.

By the mid-1980s, aside from the continuing Milwaukee Nest, CAW survived only in California, focused around Annwfn and adjacent Pagan-held parcels of Greenfield Ranch. In this rural retreat in the Misty Mountains of

Mendonesia, our Pagan homesteading community had grown more coherent and focused over the years, as we merged our various magical traditions into the Holy Order of Mother Earth (HOME), celebrated the phases of the Moon and the changing of the seasons together, had our babies born and growing up on the land, sang our songs and told our stories around the campfire, built our houses, developed the springs, planted gardens and orchards, and really lived the semi-mythical lives of ancient Pagan tribal peoples. Our Beltane celebrations became the major event of the year, surpassing Litha, with Walpurgisnacht (May Eve) becoming our most elaborate ritual. The institution of May Royalty since 1988 greatly shaped our entire community and seasonal cycle, incorporating Kids' May Games as well to select a May Prince and Princess.

In the Summer of 1984, having finally made some money by the leasing of Living Unicorns to the Ringling Bros./Barnum & Bailey Circus, Orion, Morning Glory, Bryan, Rainbow and I took off to New Orleans for the Annular Eclipse of the Sun, beginning an ongoing series of Magical Mystery Tours to be sponsored by the Church's myth-research branch, the Ecosophical Research Association (ERA), founded m 1977 by Morning Glory.

In February of '85, the ERA mounted a diving and video expedition to New Guinea to hunt for the "Ri," reported to be the real-life analog of the legendary Mermaids. Eight members of the Church went along, solved the mystery (they turned out, alas, to be Dugongs), and made our report to the Cryptozoological Society. We also connected with fellow Pagans in Australia, and visited the estate of Norman Lindsey, the great Pagan revivalist artist of the 1920s-'30s, subject of the gorgeous 1994 movie, *Sirens.*

The Mermaid expedition was bankrolled by the Circus Unicorn lease and other investors but it did not pay off financially, and left us pretty broke. When we returned, Alison asked Morning Glory and me to leave Coeden Brith. We relocated in October to the Old Same Place with a private beach on the Russian River, where we were able to hold skinny-dipping parties and Summer festivals for upwards of 100 people. Diane moved in next door.

Upon leaving the land, I worked for a few months as a counselor at a school for problem kids before I was fired for using Tarot. I then went to work for a desktop publishing business where I first encountered Macintosh computers In the Spring of '86, in partnership with the folk from the computer business, MG and I opened our dream store. "Between the Worlds," with the theme of Science, Fantasy, Magic and Nature. We brought Diane in as a buyer and bookkeeper but there was not enough capital to pay adequate salaries, and we had to quit after a year. I went into free-lance desktop publishing, and MG took a lab job at the hospital.

MG, OZ & Diane. Painting by Robert Herreschoff.

In the late 1980s, following our emergence from eight years of living in the wilderness, the Church began reorganizing under the six-year Presidency of Anodea Judith (ordained at Beltane, 1985--#9). The membership program was radically upgraded to include a Progressive Involvement Program (PIP), intensive training courses and a new members newsletter, *The Scarlet Flame.* Anodea founded Lifeways as a teaching branch of CAW, offering classes, workshops, "Magic 101" (incorporating class materials MG and I had developed in Eugene and rituals we all had created under HOME), and training towards ordination. The 1987 publication of Anodea's *Wheels of Life* (which I illustrated) brought us new respectability. Activities and membership increased dramatically during this period as CAW awakened from its bucolic slumber.

In March of '87, Dona Carter and I went on an ERA-sponsored pilgrimage to ancient sacred sites of Spain, France, Italy, Greece and Crete. It was an amazing journey, and excerpts from my journal provided much material for GE. That year, CAW commemorated the 20th anniversary of "The Summer of Love" by sponsoring a huge public "Be-In" at the local park. A day of tie-dye and music culminated in a beautiful passing the torch" ritual for the Next Generation that left many in tears.

In April of 1988, the California Institute of Integral Studies (CIIS) in San Francisco, under the direction of pioneer psychedelics researcher Ralph Metzner, hosted a conference on "Gaia Consciousness: the Goddess and the Living Earth" Anodea, Diane, Morning Glory and were invited to be presenters and panelists, along with dozens of very significant figures in the growing academic Gaian community, such as Merlin Stone, Elinor Gadon, Brian Swimm, George Sessions, Matthew Fox, etc. Many important contacts were made, and several key people joined the CAW as a result, including Ralph Metzner and Elinor Gadon.

The first issue of *Green Egg (The Next Generation!)* appeared at Beltane, 1988, the 20th anniversary of its original publication. With Diane as Editrix and me as Publisher and designer, GE quickly resumed its former position of prominence among Pagan periodicals. Sadly, Robert Heinlein died on May 8, before we could send him a copy.

On March 19, 1989, Morning Glory and I commemorated our five-year triad relationship with Diane ma beautiful three-way handfasting ceremony at Annwfn, attended by all our tribe. Anodea and Orion officiated, and Sandahbeth of Amber Tide sang David Crosby's "Triad.' Shortly after, MG and I conducted handfasting rites for Diane and Gary Ferns, MG's ex-husband, whom we had introduced to each other. We became a family of four adults and three kids.

Since we had *Green Egg,* people kept asking us "What about ham?" So we initiated a kid's supplement, with Diane's son Zach as editor, and called it *HAM (How About Magic?).* The first issue was Mabon, 1989, and other kid editors took their turns over the years. Our CAW "Kid Pack" became a very important dimension of our community, with kids' events a regular part of our celebrations. An increasing number of our young adults have grown up in this tribe, some now with children of their own!

4th Decade: the '90s

The 20th Anniversary of Earth Day was celebrated worldwide on April 20-22, 1990, and CAW Nests all over the country were active participants. Locally, I designed the official logo (the Gaea Earth-face) and our Ecotopia Nest represented the Earth Religions in a major Interfaith Service. The following weekend we participated in the Whole Life Expo in San Francisco, interfacing for the first time with the New Age community. A very important contact made at that event was with Deborah Anapol of Intinet—an ardent proponent of multiple relationships.

Our interfaith work continued with participation in an ongoing Interfaith Council sponsored by Gordon Melton, and sending Anodea and Melissa Penn as delegates to the 1993 Parliament of the World's Religions in Chicago, where CAW became a signatory on the "Declaration of a Global Ethic."

Over Memorial Day weekend of 1990, the Heartland Pagan Festival in Kansas City hosted a Church of All Worlds Grand Reunion, where CAW was honored for its contributions to the emerging Pagan community, and having stuck together through all those years. Along with many of the current gang (accompanied by Oberon, the miniature Unicom), many Waterkin from the old days showed up, including Lance Christie (with his 2nd wife, LaRue), Don Wildgrube and Carolyn Clark; and many tales were told (and videotaped).

Our belly-dancing nightingale, Deborah Hamouris of Gaia's Voice, was ordained as a Priestess (#10) on 9/9/'90. During the Samhain season of that year, the ERA sponsored a Magical Mystery Tour to Machu Picchu in Peru. Led by Anodea, 13 of us (including Dona Carter) made the pilgrimage, where we connected with native Quechua shamans and did powerful combined rituals to magically unite the Pagan peoples of the Northern and Southern hemispheres.

CAW Grand Reunion at Heartland Pagan Festival, 1990. Left front, **OZ.** Kneeling behind banner: **Orion Stormcrow, Tom Kullman, Mark Kullman,** *Wayne Ochs, Ed Short II.* Directly behind them: *Don Wildgrube, Carolyn Clark,* **Tom Williams.** Back row, L-R: **Anodea Judith,** *Morning Glory, Fred Buck,* **Tzipora Katz, Annie Heartsong,** *Steve Frischer, Jim Ware (Morgyn), Spencer Knapp,* **Howard Nelson, D.J. Hamouris,** *LaRue & Lance Christie,* **Cary Robyn** (photographer). In very back with a white hat, **Jim Chamberlain.** Right front, *Diane Darling, Oberon the Faerie Unicorn. (Italics=deceased)*

In Sept. of 1990, CAW began conducting an elaborate annual reconstruction of the Eleusinian Mysteries at Pinnacles National Monument near Gilroy, California. Around 20 new pilgrims were Initiated each year, and we looked forward to extending this rite to other suitable sites across the United States and into Australia, where the seasons are directly opposite, and Persephone will go into the Underworld in one hemisphere at the same time as she emerges in the other.

At the 1991 Midsummer Gathering of the Tribes in Georgia, Julie showed up and we renewed our long-severed friendship. At that festival, I proposed the establishment of the Universal Federation of Pagans to be the first all-inclusive worldwide Pagan ecumenical alliance. The UFP was incorporated Dec. 18, 1993. At Starwood that year, Morning Glory and I first presented our "Bouquet of Lovers" workshop, which was surprisingly well-attended, and became much in demand for following years. This was based on Morning Glory's article, "Bouquet of Lovers," published the previous year in *Green Egg* #89, wherein we first coined the terms *polyamory* and *polyamorous.*

In the Summer of '91, Richard Ely, our "Gaealogist" husband to Anodea. led a group of us on an ERA Magical Mystery Tour to Crater Lake and the Lava Caves. While we were away, the entire Soviet Union collapsed overnight!

Over Labor Day, Intinet and PEP (Polyfidelitous Educational Pursuits) co-sponsored a PEP-Con in Berkeley for which CAW was invited to do the opening and closing rituals, as well as workshops. This was the first contact between the poly-sexual community and Pagans. Our table was right across the hall from that of Kerista, the 30-year-old utopian organization that had coined the term and concept *polyfidelity.* A few months later, Kerista disbanded, and *polyamory* became the universal term to designate multiple relationships.

That year, with 52 pages and a four-color glossy cover, *Green Egg* won the Silver Award from the Wiccan/Pagan Press Alliance (WPPA) for "Most Professionally Formatted Pagan Publication."

1992 was the 30th anniversary of the Church, and a Grand Convocation was held in August, with an attendance of about 200, once again including Lance and LaRue Christie. It was covered by a photographer from *National Geographic,* though the magazine never published his article. The location was the beautiful 93-acre V-M Ranch in Laytonville, where Orion and Annie were then living. We fell totally in love with the place, with its open ritual meadows, wooded camping areas, giant boulders, year-round stream, abundant spring water, and the lake right in the center of the property. At our main ritual, we worked magic that this paradisal place could come into our hands as a future home and sacred lands for the CAW.

Main ritual circle at the CAW Grand Convocation, August 1992. Photo by Phil Schermeister.

"Van" Van Atta, owner of the V-M Ranch, was the inventor of the Van deGraaf generator and had been, among other things, chief scientist at Lockheed, Sunnyvale, for a few years. Upon his retirement in 1973, he had moved to Laytonville with his wife, Winnie, built their dream house (with a solar water heater!), and became the radical environmental columnist for the local newspaper.

On Nov. 20, 1992, Church of All World became the first legally-incorporated non-Christian church in Australia, with High Priestess Fiona Judge (ordained May 23, 1994--#1) and Australian Regional Director Anthorr Nomchong. They began putting on major CAW-sponsored events, particularly an annual Pagan Summer Gathering.

In 1992 GE won the WPPA Gold Award for "Readers' Choice" as well as the Dragonfest Publishers' Awards for "Most Attractive Format" and "Best Graphics." HAM won the Dragonfest Award for "Best Fiction."

In the '90s, CAW Priesthood were increasingly invited as presenters to various Pagan festivals around the country, traveling a CAW emissaries to the larger Pagan community. In the wake of these visitations, new Nests began springing up like mushrooms.

In 1993 and '94, we conducted a recreation of the ancient Greek Panathenaia at the Parthenon replica in Nashville, Tennessee, where a 42 ft. statue of the Goddess Athena is the largest indoor statue in the Western world. In October of '93, we moved the *Green Egg* offices out of Diane's and my homes, and rented a real office building in downtown Ukiah, which became the Administrative Office of the Church as well. GE won the WPPA Bronze Award in '93, and Aeona Silversong was ordained at Mabon (#11)

At Beltane of '94, Morning Glory and formally ended our 5-year handfast with Diane, and in July, Diane left *Green Egg* to be succeeded as Editor by Maerian "Sun" Morris, our two-year May Queen and new bride of Orion (wed Nov. 12 at the V-M Ranch; Morning Glory and I officiating).

Pam and Jesse Skaar donated their 175-acre farm in Kentucky, which they named "Heartspring," to the Church Their dreams included a Pagan cemetery, as well as hosting festivals— such as the "Grow Closer" Festival sponsored by our Midwest Regional Nest Council, and initiated that August at Lothlorien in Indiana.

At the '94 Eleusinian Mysteries, I took on the role of Hades; the first time in my life I had ever aspected the Dark Lord. The experience had a profound effect on me, and a week later I was given and accepted a new name: Oberon. The same weekend I was doing the Mysteries, Morning Glory participated in the National Sex Symposium in San Francisco, addressing issues of polyamory and Paganism.

Avilynn Pwyll was ordained at Samhain (#13), and Richard Ely at Yule (#14). In 1994 GE again won the WPPA Gold Award and several others. We also began forging alliances with other Pagan groups we felt a kinship with. The first of these were Avalon Isle-Order of the Royal Oak in Atlanta, the Church of Iron Oak in Florida, and the Aquarian Tabernacle Church in Seattle.

At the Craft Wise convention in April of '95, where I was a presenter, I met Liza Gabriel, who became one of the great loves of my life.

She came out to Califia for a short visit in the Summer, and a two-month visit the following Winter, where we began laying the foundations for a new group marriage. The fourth partner in this multiple relationship was Wolf, a wonderful lover of Morning Glory's, who moved from Houston to San Francisco in Nov. of '95 to be closer to us. (Wolf, MG and I made quite a splash when we appeared as a triad on the Marilyn Kagan talk show in Sept.) And the fifth element was Wynter Rose, who showed up at Beltane '96. At the 1995 PEP-Con in August, held at Harbin Hot Springs, Morning Glory and I were invited to be the keynote speakers. A significant percentage of the attendees now were Pagans, quite a few members of the CAW.

The Ravenhearts at the V-M Ranch— Wynter, Wolf, Liza, OZ, Morning Glory. 1997.

Green Egg again won the WPPA Gold Award for 1995, and in 1996, went to a bi-monthly publication schedule. With Beltane that year, we began festivals at Heartspring in Kentucky, where we held our Annual Meeting at Lughnasadh.

In May of '96, GE editor Maerian, newly ordained at Beltane (#15), made an ERA pilgrimage to the Oracle of Delphi in Greece, while the Clergy Council met in retreat at Annwfn and held vigil, linking with her through a synchronized time she was immersed in the Castellian Spring. At that retreat, Anodea passed the mantle of High Priestess to Morning Glory. Upon her return, Maerian brought a Vision of the re-activation of the Oracles.

While I was away at Starwood in July, Morning Glory and Wolf represented our growing family at the Polycon at Harbin.

On Sept. 29, Morning Glory, Wolf and I were joined in a triad handfasting officiated by Anodea Judith and Richard Ely. Liza and Wynter participated as "Ladies-in-waiting." The following weekend, Liza and I drove out to Grass Valley, CA for a reunion of the old Council of Themis, hosted by Fred Adams & Svetlana Butyrin of Feraferia, and attended also by Harold Moss & Donald Harrison of the Church of the Eternal Source, Poke Runyon of the O:.T:.A:., Nelson White of the Knights Templar, and others. The proceedings were recorded for posterity.

In 1994, "Van" Van Atta died at nearly 89, and Winnie followed in '96. As Van had thought well of CAW when we held our Grand Convocation here, we entered negotiations with his heirs towards purchasing the V-M Ranch. A few CAW folks who wanted to create some sort of community on the Ranch began meeting to discuss the possibilities. Regrettably, these meetings eventually broke down due to conflicts over who should be involved, and official CAW negotiations were suspended.

Other significant conflicts also arose in the Fall of '96, the most serious concerning one of our Bards, Adam Walks-Between-Worlds, who stood accused of numerous improprieties around sexual manipulation, leading to a big hearing and extensive heated debate concerning the issues raised on all sides. Due to the severity of the concerns, Adam resigned his position as Bard and was banished from the Church. During these troubled times, Night An-Fey was ordained at Samhain (#16), and the mantle of GE Publisher was passed from me to Orion.

Meanwhile, the offices of CAW Central and the *Green Egg,* along with various CAW members, moved onto the V-M Ranch. These included Aeona, Melian and Apple of the BoD and GE staff, and Sunny & Gordon, our King and Queen of the May. When Liza finally made her transition from Mass. in December, our entire 5-person family pulled up stakes to move into Van and Winnie's 4-bedroom house. Our housewarming was a wonderful Yule festival, attended by around 50 people.

On Feb. 20, Adam WBW was found shot to death in the home he was visiting in Orange County, CA. No suspect was ever found.

Sadly, Pam and Jesse of Heartspring broke up, and the land was sold at auction in April of '97, dashing that dream of a CAW Sacred Center in Kentucky just as we are beginning another in Califia.

At a special open "visioning session" of the Board which was attended by over 20 people in person with links to many others through the Internet, the 35th anniversary of Lance and my first water sharing (April 7, 1962) was honored by declaring this date as "Founders' Day"—a time to share water in healing and reconciliation.

Farida Fox, our charming Faery Crone, was ordained at Annwfn's Beltane (#17), and with Litha we began a schedule of Summer Festivals at the V-M Ranch. In June—upon the vacating by Aeona, Melian and Apple—Orion, Maerian, and their three wonderful kids moved onto the V-M Ranch, back into the house Orion had previously inhabited with Annie.

At Ancient Ways, held in early June at Harbin Hot Springs, our entire 5-person family presented a new version of "Bouquet of Lovers" that was attended by over 70 people. Shortly afterwards, we adopted the family name of "Ravenheart."

On June 27-29, Starwhite hosted a gathering of Scions, Clergy, and other interested Waterkin from around the country for a weekend visioning over decentralization and restructuring of the CAW. It was a powerful experience, and people left with a renewed sense of hope and purpose.

Lughnasadh at the V-M Ranch was also the occasion of the CAW Annual Meeting. In celebration of CAW's 35th anniversary, Orion dubbed this festival "CAWnvocation II." A significant overhauling of the Bylaws was accomplished, and Orion was re-elected President. In September, Morning Glory led an ERA Mystery Tour to Greece and Crete.

But when our lease on the V-M Ranch expired, we decided that it just wouldn't work for us. We vacated the Ranch in Jan. of 1999 and our Ravenheart Family moved into a new home in Petaluma, CA, which we called "Shady Grove."

The New Millennium

The "Second Phoenix" phase of CAW lasted until 2002, when a hostile takeover by our Ohio-based Board of Directors led to a complete collapse and attempted dissolution of the Church. I was commissioned that summer to write a book for New Page Books and had no time or energy to engage with the hostile faction of my Church. I simply walked away and devoted my attention to writing the *Grimoire for the Apprentice Wizard* and founding the Grey School of Wizardry: www.GreySchool.net.

In March of 2005, Jack Cain, one of the caretakers at Annwfn, showed up at our house and asked me: "How would you like to have your Church back?" In updating the insurance for our upcoming Beltane, he had discovered that despite the perfidious Ohio BoD supposedly discorporating the Church the previous year, they had failed to notify the IRS, and had overlooked the fact that our California incorporation was still extant. All we needed to do was file a change of address for our primary office from Toledo, OH, to Cotati, CA, and we were back in business!

There was much to do as we set about rebuilding our beloved Church from the ground up. The people in Ohio told us that all the CAW records had been stored in boxes in a garage, and were destroyed by water due to a leaky roof. That pretty much cleared the deck for us to recreate the next incarnation of CAW any way we wanted, without any undesirable baggage from the past.

We adopted a metaphor for the history of CAW as a Phoenix, periodically immolating

OZ's statue of the Millennial Gaia, 1998.

itself only to rise again from the ashes. This would be the third resurrection, the previous phases being in St Louis 1967-1976, and Mendocino County, NorCalifia 1985-2004.

We called a special meeting of all surviving CAW Waterkin at Beltane, and elected a new Board of Directors, with me as President and Morning Glory as Vice President. And we began a process of examination of every aspect of CAW spanning more than 40 years, to determine what had worked, and what hadn't. There were many important lessons embedded in those four decades, and it was important to assimilate them and apply them to the new structure we would be creating out of the wreckage.

I finally understood that I didn't have to put up or argue with antagonists in the Church, and, as Primate, I could just kick 'em out. We concluded that the process of Circle advancement leading automatically to Clergy ordination at the 7th Circle—as we had done in the Mendocino era—was a mistake; and decided to return to the concept we'd had in Missouri of Circle advancement as a process of self-actualization. We decided to retain the labels of "Seekers" and "Scions" for the first two Rings, but change the third (Circles 7-9) to "Beacons", to better reflect our new Vision of such folks as exemplars and Elders.

Henceforth, we would develop separate criteria, qualifications and application processes for Clergy, which would take two forms: licensed Ministers and ordained Priests/Priestesses.

And long-time Scion Cat DeVille proposed an entirely new model for our organizational Bylaws, which the Ohio BoD had abolished and replaced with a so-called "Constitution." Cat proposed a brilliant structure of "Canons," following the traditional model and terminology for Church law and governance. (After several years of work, the new Canons were adopted at the General Curia on June 27, 2010.)

Morning Glory and I spent much of 2005 writing, editing, and formatting our CAW liturgy, developed through the Holy Order of Mother Earth, into a book form: *Creating Circles & Ceremonies: Rituals for All Seasons & Reasons* (New Page, 2006). We included everything we'd originally compiled in *HOME Cooking* and added the additional two books we'd planned.

The Ohio BoD had ceased publication of *Green Egg* after the Nov.-Dec. 2000 Millennial issue (No. 136). In 2007, our dear friends and lovers Ariel Monserrat and Tom Donohue proposed resurrecting GE as an online e-zine, with the motto: "Legends Never Die!" A beautiful full-color downloadable PDF, as well as a print edition, they published it 'til 2016). Then Sylveey/Dawn Selu continued 2016-2018; Alder Moonoak (2018-2021); Elisabet Carlson & Ducie Corrales (2022). And now Brahn th' Blessed/Samm Dickens & Katrina Rasbold (2023). https://greeneggmagazine.com/

Feb. 13-16, 2009, CAW was back at Pantheacon, pulling out all the stops. We had just received the first prototype of a 30" tall Garden Goddess of my Millennial Gaea statue, and we set Her up in front of our Mythic Images booth. Everyone loved Her, and it was a real delight to see small children come up and hug Her—even give Her a kiss. We hoped to have these life-size statues available for purchase later in the summer. Unfortunately, as of this date (August of 2024) this project is still in process. However, with production now being handled by Pacific Trading Company, and distribution by Jay DeForest, She is now available in four sizes: 4", 8", 14" and 24": www.themillennialGaea.com/

Our biggest offering at Pantheacon in 2009 was a spectacular "Phoenix Rising" ritual to dramatize the resurrection of the Church of All Worlds, the healing of MG and me personally, and the new sense of hope engendered by Obama's election, in these darkest of times. We spent months writing and rehearsing the script, casting all the parts, and making props, masks and costumes, including a spectacular feathered Phoenix headdress/mask that I would wear over fiery-feathered winged robes, and replicating full-size the elaborate wig of leaves and critters of the Millennial Gaea for Morning Glory to wear. I also had to create a little electrical "hearth" which could be turned up to look like coals igniting into flames. Four quarter altars and other room decorations also had to be designed, as well as masks and costumes for the five Elemental dancers.

At Pantheacon, on Valentine's Day, the room was packed, and the ritual was a tremendous success. It began in near-darkness, with fog machines filling the center of the circle with mist. Participants became passengers on a "ship of fools", guided by a Navigator (Eric), and arriving at a forgotten island, where the last

Priestess (Wynter) tended the hearth in the temple of Gaea. But the sacred fires had gone out, and all that remained was a large mound of ashes. Helios (Cougar), the Sun-God, crossed from East to West, bringing a bit of illumination, as Gaea (MG) entered, reciting Algernon Swinburne's evocative poem, "Hertha". The Priestess told her sad tale, of how all her hopes, dreams, and work had turned to ashes, and invited the "passengers" to identify with their own lives, tossing their ashes onto the heap, and fanning the coals. As they caught fire, a Phoenix (me) emerged from under the grey ashen blanket and rose to full height, wings outstretched. And this is what the Phoenix said:

"I arise. I arise from the ashes, reborn yet again. I am the Phoenix, ever-dying, ever-resurrecting. I am the hope in every heart, never dying, however wounded. I am the dream in every head, never forgotten, however diminished its grandeur in coming true. I am the light in every eye, still burning, however dimmed by remaining open through the darkest times. I am you.

"I am born of the dance of the Earth and the Sun—as are all of you. You are my people, and I am your avatar. We are one.

"We are Pagans and magickal folk— bound to the endless cycles of the Spiral Dance, from the vast wheeling galaxies to the double helix within your every cell. We know that there are cycles of destruction and creation; times of despair and times of hope; darkness and returning light; death and rebirth—all reflected in the Mystery of the Phoenix. We know that what goes around comes around, and Darkness must always yield to Light.

"Black holes turn inside out to become brilliant quasars, filling the universe with energy. The bitterest winter rolls around to balmy spring, when Life springs forth anew. Out of every Dark Age is born a glorious Renaissance, in which all good things flower and flourish. Death eternally comes 'round to rebirth. And the deepest, darkest, longest night inexorably yields to the blazing sun of a New Dawn.

"We have lived through rising tides of prosperity and the still waters of peace. And we have lived amidst gathering clouds and raging storms. Our spirit remains strong, and cannot be broken. We will not turn back; nor will we falter.

"There may come a day, billions of years hence, when Light fails, Entropy triumphs, and Darkness falls forever over all the worlds. But this is not that day! For this day, dedicated for millennia to Love, heralds a New Dawn, and a new Rebirth. On this day, we choose hope over fear, unity of purpose over conflict and discord. We choose rebirth!

"In the glory of the rising Phoenix, Hope shall be rekindled in every heart; forgotten Dreams shall be reawakened in every mind; and the light of Love shall burn in every eye. This is the way of things, and it shall not be denied! Thus shall it be in our personal lives, in our Religion, in our Nation, and on our Planet. And thus the long tragedy of human history brings us inevitably toward the Awakening of Gaea!

"They thought us dead, along with our hopes and dreams for a better world. But they were wrong. We live! We Are Alive!"

OZ as Phoenix. Guerneville Festival of Fools, April 2009.

Tragically, Morning Glory, my cherished lifemate of 40 years and CAW's beloved High Priestess died of multiple myeloma (blood and bone cancer) on May 13, 2014, leaving a vast hole in my life and heart, and in the heart of our community. She died at home, in our Temple, surrounded by family, friends, lovers, and more than 370 Goddess images She had collected from around the world. We all had a sense that They were welcoming Her into the Pantheon. Her body was laid into the Earth at Annwfn, with an apple tree planted over her heart; to rest in the bosom of Mother Gaea until she may return again in new flesh. Her grave overlooks the campfire circle where we have held our rites of Beltane (and Walpurgisnacht) for the past 30 years.

Arranging all the legalities for MG's green burial secured Annwfn as an officially-recognized cemetery for full body burials—something MG herself had tried to do for decades without success. This is a final legacy to the Pagan community from one of our eldest and most revered Priestesses. And over the years to come, I expect that many other Pagans will want to have their green burials at Annwfn.

After burying Morning Glory, I remained at our home (RavenHaven) for another year, while searching with friends for a suitable new home. In October of 2015, I moved in with Anne and James Lloyd in Santa Cruz, CA, where we opened a center in town we called the Academy of Arcana. (https://academyofarcana.com/) It featured a store, a library, classroom, museum, meeting space and offices, which Mama Maureen and I shared. Sadly, it was not economically viable, and drained all my personal resources over the next two years, forcing us to close at the end of Nov. 2017, and put everything I owned into storage.

The following Midsummer, 2018, in MG's little red Prius, I embarked on my legendary two-year "Walkabout of the Wandering Wizard," driving back and forth and up and down all over the US, with a few side trips to the Yucatan, Guatemala and Ecuador with my longtime consort, Dona Carter.

I spent four months in Salem, MA with Gypsy Ravish, attending the 2018 Parliament of the World's Religions in Toronto. After another four months in Nashville with Kadira Belynne, I was invited to the Venusian Church Longhouse in WA, where I spent the next 2½ years, departing at Samhain of 2022 for a couple of months in MI before settling in Asheville, NC, where I became engaged to a wonderful Priestess, Lady Rhiannon of Serpentstone. We were married on May 17, 2024. She has a devoted community, and I have been enthusiastically adopted into it.

Meanwhile, I continue to write books (20 so far) and appear at Pagan events around the country—now with my wife Rhiannon.

The non-fictional Church of All Worlds has evolved far beyond Heinlein's original fable, to which we may be considered the sequel. The Nest is still the basic unit, and there are still nine concentric Circles of member involvement, named after the planets and grouped into

Rhiannon & Oberon's handfasting, May 17, 2024.

three Rings. Each Circle's activity includes study, writings, magical training, and wilderness experience, as well as active participation in the life of the Church.

In the Old Days of CAW (i.e. 1967-2002), progress through the RINGS led to automatic ordination into the Priesthood at 7th Circle. We aren't doing that in this current 3rd Phase. While we still expect much of the criteria of attaining 7th Circle to apply to potential Priests and Priestesses, this is no longer a direct correlation. Some of this training may come from elsewhere—such as the programs of other Traditions and Schools. And that will count.

And most important—attaining 7th Circle in CAW is now associated more with the original concept of self-actualization, and CAW members of the 3rd Ring (i.e. Circles 7-9) are now known as "Beacons" rather than "Clergy." They may or may not also be ordained, but that is no longer a given just because they've attained the 3rd Ring. Consider the role and title of "Beacons" to be non-clerical, reflecting rather that such folks have come a long way in their personal evolution towards self-actualization, and will hopefully be a shining example to others. Beacons are elders, mentors, exemplars, inspirational visionaries, leaders (as in "on the leading edge"), authorities (as in "authoritative", NOT "authoritarian"), sages, mages, etc.

But CAW Priests and Priestesses are those who have a specific calling towards religious service to the CAW community and beyond. They are expected to have a firm grasp of CAW liturgy (as presented in our book, *Creating Circles & Ceremonies*), and be able to design and conduct rites and rituals as called upon: handfastings, baby blessings, rites of passage, initiations, Nest meetings, Sabbat rites, Mysteries, etc.

They must be able to provide pastoral counseling, and have a firm grasp of clergy confidentiality. In essence, CAW Priests and Priestesses should be able (like 19th-century Christian missionaries) to go to some far-off place and establish a full CAW religious presence and create a local CAW community in accord with the premises and principles of the CAW Tradition. Clergy applications ask for experience, credentials, references, essays on vocational calling and why one wants to serve in this capacity; as well as supportive petitioning and testimonials from the congregation that wants them to be so recognized.

Training for CAW Priests and Priestesses should reflect and be at least somewhat equivalent to the kind of training offered in seminaries for the Clergy of other faiths. We wish to utilize other available programs, such as those offered by Earth Traditions Ministry, Solantis Institute, Cherry Hill Seminary, Star King Divinity School, the Grey School of Wizardry, Witch School, etc. This will enable our Clergy and Clergy candidates to pick up additional training and experience they may not already have.

Separate from the issue of CAW Priesthood, however, we now also offer simple Ministerial licensing. The criteria for this are far less extensive than those for CAW Priests and Priestesses, as Ministers are not expected to provide a full range of Clergy services to the CAW community. A Ministerial License from CAW entitles the bearer to perform legal weddings and other Rites of Passage, offer pastoral counseling, visit people in prisons or hospitals, serve as Chaplains in prisons and military, etc.—wherever a legal Ministerial License would be useful.

In the business arena, the Church is governed by the Board of Directors, which determines policy and business matters, and the Council of Elders and Clergy Council, which address spiritual concerns. There is an annual General Curia to which all Waterkin are invited to discuss matter of interest and import, and Clergy ordinations are conducted. Anodea's

"Golden Age" Presidency (1985-1991) was succeeded by that of Tom Williams (1991-94). When Aeona Silversong became President in 1994, CAW became possibly the first international church to elect an all-women Executive Council. Orion Stormcrow was elected President in 1996, followed by Starwhite in 1998, and LaSara Firefox in 1999. Jim Looman in Ohio held the Presidential reins from 2001-2004, terminating the 2nd phase. I was elected President in 2005, and I still hold that position.

The remaining leg of our triadic leadership consists of the Sacred Royalty in the form of our annual May Queen and King (with their Ma Princess and Prince), and our Underworld Kin Hades and Queen Persephone. These roles pass to different people each year and are selected rather than elected. Our Queens and Kings have no temporal authority but lead by example and serve the community as avatars, holding court at various festivals. We treat them as we ourselves would wish to be treated, for "as these vessel fare, so fares the Tribe."

Worship in the Church involves weekly of monthly meetings which are usually held in the homes of Nest members on a rotational basis Nest meetings and rituals are traditionally he! skyclad, but this is not required. A chalice of water is always shared around the Circle either as the opening or closing of the ceremony.

We have created a new Tribalism, where we relate to each other as members of a tribe with interconnecting clans and families. And our Tribe, in turn, is one of the Nations of Earth religions, bound together by our love and reverence for our Mother, the Living Earth. We welcome all who wish to join with us honorably. The most common statement we hear from ne members is "I feel like I've come home to my people at last!"

Welcome home! Enter the Nest!

My CAW Experience

by Julie Epona O'Ryan (May 17, 1993)

IF I HAD TO THINK OF THREE WORDS to describe the CAW I would choose: Loving, Transformative. Courageous. These words, concepts, are the hallmark of my experience within CAW. I have been on a spiritual quest for the past two decades, looking for the religious experience that would embody these concepts. I have searched for: a personal. conscious relationship with the Divine; an experience of personal healing by the Divine; a group of like-minded people who would accept me as a member without condemnation. I did not find what I was searching for within Catholicism, Pentecostalism, Sidha Yoga, Bahaism, Mormonism, or the Twelve Step process (by itself); I found what I searched for within the Church of All Worlds.

Loving

I found a loving community, a tribe of lovers. Many of the religious paths I have traveled professed love, but few could define it; was 'love thy neighbor as yourself' any more understand- able than 'Perfect love and perfect trust'? To understand love as that position where another person's happiness was essential for your happiness, defined the concept clearly. Coupled with the belief that love shared is love multiplied, a powerful bonding is formed. I have been able to 'feel' the bondings within the center of CAW, the energy field that holds the tribe together, Love.

From my first experience of CAW, at the Grand Convocation of August 1992, it seemed to me that this tribe is held together by a network of lovers. The web of energy linking Otter, Morning Glory, Diane, Anodea, Orion, Richard, Tom, and Annie was so physically tangible as to be almost visible. I felt this web reaching through the entire tribe, including everyone that reached toward it. And there was a subtle difference here that set this apart from some of my previous experiences: this web did not reach out and grab me. It did reach out to meet my extended hand, but I had to make the initial move toward it.

Having made that move toward love, I was able to see just how complex this web is.

Here were people who cared about each other, who were able to support and, when necessary, confront each other. This ability to confront, to face conflict, was what convinced me to become a part of this tribe. Here I saw differences of opinion—strong, emotional differences—faced with maturity and respect. Here was open, verbal, honest confrontation; not passive-aggressive, back-stabbing, whispering in comers. Here was a willingness to live with differing points of view; not a directive for homogeneous thought. Here were adults willing to listen to each other, and express their own views, without allowing the conversation to degenerate into name-calling and other childish games. (That this tribe is blessed with several highly skilled mediators and negotiators was also obvious.) This highly complex, mature, adult love for each other was empowered through the open, guilt-free, telepathic sexual intimacy that is shared within the web.

I feel that the longevity of CAW, the energy that holds this church together cannot be separated from the sexuality of the web. Here is the group who insisted on taking Heinlein seriously, willing to make the telepathic-sexual connections needed to hold a tribe together. Here I experienced what I had previously learned as theory: that Magic is Not Metaphor; that Perfect Love and Perfect Trust is not symbolic; that sexual union is the ultimate worship of immanent Divinity. Here were the people who had kept the dreams of Heinlein, Leary. and Rimmer from fading into history; sharing and multiplying their love as the center of gravity that holds the CAW community together.

Transformative

I have undergone a miraculous transformation from having participated in a series of rituals conducted by the Church of All Worlds. First, I want to share how this transformation came to be. Second, I will tell you what has happened to me and for me. And let me assure you that I do not use the word 'miraculous' lightly. What has transpired has been a miracle, a direct intervention of the gods in the events of human experience.

My personal miracle has taken place through a series of rituals, and experiences, and over a period of many months. To say that I came to CAW desperately in need of healing is a gross understatement. Since finding and connecting with CAW during the Grand Convocation, I have participated in the Eleusinian, Ostara, Teddy Bear's Picnic, Walpurgisnacht, and the May Day celebrations. I have also been blessed with the spiritual guidance and training of one specific Priest along this path. I have faced many fears and won freedom, left my depression in the under- world and been reborn joyous, sacrificed my addiction to Hades and had the compulsion lifted, came as a guest and learned to play; my self-esteem was healed as I became Dragon's treasure, and my lust has been transfigured from sin to sacrament. More succinctly, my life has been completely changed, and for this I will be eternally grateful.

The rituals changed me because I believed they could; my belief was empowered by the subliminal message of the Priests and Priestesses. 'This is real; this is happening now; this is being done for you.' The Eleusinian initiatory ritual has not been recreated because it was important for the Greeks; the months of research, design, and rehearsal that went into the creation of this ritual were not done purely out of a love of history and pageant. The Eleusinia has been recreated because it is important for spiritual growth, now, today, in this tribe. And this is true of the other rituals that have been created/recreated by CAW. I have felt that each ritual I have participated in has been created with the understanding of its transformative potential, and a willingness to activate this potential.

I believe that the number of trained therapists, educators, negotiators within the CAW clergy is an important factor in the church's ability to create ritual that transforms the 'real' world. As a society, we became separated from the reality of the gods and goddesses centuries ago; through depth psychology, an understanding of how the mind works, we have been able to heal this separation. With a clergy educated in how to enable others to make a connection with the archetypes. rituals can be enacted that trans- form the participants. The amazing thing is not that these rituals can be created: the astonishing thing is that the CAW clergy are willing to make the commitment to the tribe to support their transformation.

How the CAW rituals become transformative becomes more complex than merely believing in the potential. The contract between the healer and the healed is one of shared karma, that spiritual energy of action and consequence that holds our life experience together. The healer contracts to hold the energy of the gods for the duration of the ritual, allowing the Divine to act through them, to become them, and accepts the transference that is the consequence of this role. The participant, the one to be healed, contracts to perceive the other as divine and to accept the reality of emotional imprinting that is the rational consequence of this action. The relationship be- tween the two people sharing this experience is changed forever: the spiritual exchange remains as a dimension of their shared reality. The willingness to enter into this contract is where I have experienced many other religious practices fall short, for the contract binds the two individuals together. I have met many priests, ministers, 12-step sponsors, who are unwilling to make this commitment and who therefore fall short of allowing true healing to take place through them; the CAW clergy do not hide from the commitment. The love that binds the web together potentiates the healing. 'How' is understood.

Courageous

I am in awe of the courage practiced by the Clergy of CAW. I have stood in Circle, from night until dawn, as the Priests and Priestess have held the Gods and Goddesses present within their beings and have allowed these entities to act according to their own agendas.

I have been in Circle many times as the gods were invoked, channeled, drawn down. I have seen many priests and priestess hold the divine presence for a moment or many minutes, as this deity acted and spoke, mostly within the parameters of the known mythos accompanying this god or goddess. I have acted as Priestess in this way myself. But what is practiced by the CAW clergy is an order of magnitude more complex, intense, different, from the practice I had been familiar with.

I have been witness to the evolution of the Gods. I have seen Zeus humbled, transformed, and watched as his consciousness was raised. I have seen Demeter, Persephone, and Hades progress in their evolution. This process, of allowing the Gods to be transformed by the reality of the twentieth century, to allow their mythos to evolve, is a pioneering of spiritual wilderness. Once the myth is permitted to expand beyond its known boundaries, no one, perhaps not even the gods themselves, knows what will transpire. And this act, of stepping out into uncharted spiritual lands, takes great courage.

I have found that if I have come to the ritual believing that what is done is done in truth and is not metaphor, if I have come bonded to the other participants, if I have come prepared for transformation, if I have come in courage to step beyond my known boundaries—then there is no way of knowing who I will be when I return from the ritual. This act requires perfect love and perfect trust of an intensity I had never imagined possible. I have been given the love, support, and courage to undertake this challenge by the clergy of CAW.

In conclusion, I must admit that I am in love with the Church of All Worlds; I have been transformed by it; I have been empowered by its courage. And for all of this I am filled with gratitude. And while I have many journeys and much to learn ahead of me. I feel that I've climbed the mountain, I've found the Grail; and, my, what a strange and wondrous trip it's been!

The CAW Vision Into Tomorrow

by Oberon Zell, Primate *(August 24, 1993)*

AS I WRITE THESE WORDS, CAW's registered membership has just passed the 500-mark, and is climbing exponentially. Like all Pagan groups, we of course do not proselytize, but we do try to make ourselves available, and occasionally we even extend invitations to select people we'd really like to have on board. Few have declined.

But this phenomenal growth rate is already presenting major challenges, and these will intensify, for we have many more seekers arriving on our doorstep than we have room to accommodate. Already we have far outgrown our original 55-acre sacred land of Annwfn for local festivals, and are having to look to larger facilities. This means land-based CAW communities, with temples, great halls, circles and henges. Schools, libraries, museums and omnisteries will surely follow, offering residency programs, summer camps and retreats. Perhaps entire villages, as of Olde...

Beyond a mere lack of physical room, we have at present far too few Priests and Priestesses proportionate to our expanding membership. By the end of 1993, we will have only seven ordained Clergy and one licensed Minister, and all of these still located in northern Califia! We will achieve another quantum leap similar to our Australian incorporation when we start ordaining Priests and Priestesses in other states and countries. As yet, many of our far-flung Nests and solitary members have had little or no experience with our unique and extremely effective CAW ritual and magical techniques, and are probably relying on various Wiccan models for their rites. We are now assembling a book of CAW liturgy. Thus will our rites and Mysteries spread throughout the world. I look forward, for instance, to seeing a Southern Hemisphere complement of our Eleusinian Mysteries happening in the proper season—Autumn—but at the opposite end of the calendar year from the corresponding Northern equivalent. Thus there will always be a Goddess in the Underworld, somewhere.

In the 1987 edition of her *Drawing Down the Moon,* Margot Adler noted that the most important development in the Pagan community in the '80s was the proliferation of public Pagan festivals. CAW has been putting on such events since the mid- '70s, and these will continue to increase, both in size and frequency. We are delighted to see CAW Australia hosting the Pagan Solstice Gathering and the All Worlds Festival and Feast while we here in the States put on Beltane, CAW-con, Panathenaia and Eleusinia.

So far, the entire Pagan community, CAW included, has remained largely invisible to the mainstream culture, in spite of over 500 Pagan periodicals being published, and more books on the Goddess and Her People than anyone could possibly keep track of. Countless interviews in every known medium over the past quarter-century have still failed to bring our mere existence into public awareness.

But this state of obscurity cannot last forever. Eventually, and I believe soon, we will achieve critical mass in the public consciousness. We will be "discovered." And when people suddenly realize that we are everywhere, and have been all along, like the mycelium spreading underground, there is bound to be a substantial reaction. And we'd better be prepared to handle it, because some of it will certainly be a vehement backlash from terrified fundamentalists of various monotheistic persuasions, who will see their own children joining us, to dance naked and ecstatic under the full moon. For their time, as foretold in their own prophecies, is coming to an end, while ours is just beginning...

Many legal battles will have to be fought to establish our rights (and our rites!). I predict that, ultimately, we will win them all, both in the courts and in the public media.

For our thirty years of experience have also shown us that, when we can coherently present ourselves and what we stand for, most people react very positively. After all, we advocate (and live!) compassion, brother- (and sister-) hood, integrity, love, Nature, and "traditional (i.e. tribal) family values." Our prime Deity is Mother Earth/Mother Nature—surely someOne with whom all can identify! And Paganism is really very familiar stuff to many people—after all, didn't most of us grow up on the Greek myths, Arthurian legends, Robin Hood, Tolkein, fairy tales, folklore and holiday customs? It's all in how you present it.

CAW is intended to be a catalyst for the coalescence of planetary consciousness. Our mythealogy is based on the Gaea Thesis—that all Earthly life, us included, comprises a single great organism, the living body of Mother Earth, known as *Gaea* to the ancient Greeks. Our Goddess is the very Soul of Nature! And our vision of the future evolution of this lifestream includes what Dane Rudyar has called the "planetarization of consciousness," and Teilhard de Chardin terms the "Omega Point." This implies the linking up of all sentient beings into a "global brain" wherein a vast collective consciousness emerges, just as we ourselves individually attain such consciousness sometime

during our first year of life. Thus will Gaea come fully into wakefulness, where now She but slumbers (and dreams...).

With this ultimate Vision, CAW has goals far greater than merely establishing nice, neat, little encapsulated "nests," meeting monthly or so and unconnected with the rest of our world. For many Pagan groups and Wiccan covens, that is adequate, but we Waterkin have a much larger vision: to re-unite the scattered children of Gaea, and bring the whole Family back together again!

Thousands of years ago, there was a messy divorce between our Earthly Mother and the alien Sky God who had displaced our true Father and raped our Mother into a forced marriage. Some of the children sided with the Stepfather and went with Him. Others remained with the Mother, to be bullied and persecuted for centuries by our former brothers (and some of our sisters). It is time for this separation to end. The word *religion* means "re-linking."

We have been divided and conquered. Our world has been split between Heaven and Earth, matter and spirit, men and women, humanity and Nature, body and soul, the darkness and the light. Western civilization is intrinsically alienating and alienated from the rest of the lifestream. The true function of religion is to heal that alienation, those splits, and achieve reunification. It is ironic that, in fact, much of the divisiveness has actually been caused by "churchianity" acting in the name of religion! But Paganism isn't merely another religion among many; Paganism *is* religion-in the very truest sense of the word. Our task is to bring together, and to heal.

Hatred divides us; love unites us. Thus it serves us to forge bonds of love and kinship with each other, even outside our own faiths. We treasure and hold sacred our ever-widening network of magical lovers. Though we must of necessity maintain a certain wary distrust of those whose beliefs require them to subjugate all dissidents, still we seek whenever possible to find common ground upon which to build our new temples of the spirit. More than merely "tolerating" diversity—we cherish it, celebrate it, and revel in it!

For after all, are we not all children of the same Mother? Thou art God; Thou art Goddess!

CAW/ATL Origins, Influences and History

By Richard Lance Christie *(1995)*

(Waterkin who have read the accounts of our early years as related in Margot Adler's Drawing Down the Moon, *will recall that the original Water-Brotherhood founded in 1962 by Lance Christie and Tim Zell was called "Atl." In 1967, when the decision was made to go public with the Church of All Worlds, Atl remained the secular branch, operating largely underground over many years, with Lance being the sole liaison between the two groups. Recently, incorporating as the "Association for the Tree of Life," Atl has become more public, and we thought that this current report, prepared by Lance, might be of interest to CAW Waterkin. Those who wish more information may contact ATL via e-mail: ATLandl@aol.com. https://mahb.stanford.edu/groups/association-for-the-tree-of-life/)*

OBERON, THEN TIM ZELL, AND I MET in the anteroom of fraternity houses during pledge week in early September 1961. Westminister College was then strongly Greek, with about 90+ percent of the all-male students belonging to and living in fraternity houses—which saved the college from having to worry about dorms. I don't recall the exact incident which introduced us, but it probably occurred because one or the other of us made a wisecrack observation about the absurdity of the social customs of the tribes to which we were participant observers, and the other immediately realized that here was someone who shared the same "reality tunnel" (as Robert Anton Wilson later termed it). We dived into talking about concepts that we had encountered in science fiction and Ayn Rand concerning the arbitrary and often absurd character of conventional social norms and taboos. Later Oberon wrote that I was the first person he had ever met that seemed to be a member of the same "species" as he. One thing which Oberon and I found we had in common was the feeling that we were a species of "green monkeys" living on a Monkey Island populated almost entirely by a species of "brown monkeys." (The brown monkeys' species name supplied by Georgia attorney Ned Mudd, who I encountered as an Earth First! co-conspirator in the late 1970's, is *Homo erectus asphaltus.*) We decided the name of our species was "Atlans," for purposes of labeling discussion, and as I see it we basically adopted the water sharing ceremony from *Stranger in a Strange Land* as a symbol of the fact that the "Atlans" had an "alien" point of view—we were "strangers in a strange land" inhabited by *homo erectus asphaltus* with strange, nonsensical, and often self- and other-destructive customs as we perceived them, and in the ceremony we were recognizing and encouraging the celebrants to celebrate their "green monkey"-ness and to undertake searching for understanding—to "grok" reality rather than accepting the conventional definition of it, which didn't wash with the celebrant anyway, which is why they were affiliating with each other in the first place.

Both Oberon and I grew up as "green monkeys"—wondering whether we had been accidentally dropped into a clutch of the young of a different, more primitive primate species. I remember my first day at kindergarten: my mother had walked the route from the school to our home, about a mile, with me previously. She dropped me off and I sat in the room watching all the teary *sturm* and *drang,* the aggression and acting out, genuinely puzzled and rather aghast at the incomprehensible, unconstructive and often destructive, behavior going on around me. I taught myself to read when I was three, and was reading at the 6th grade level when I entered elementary school—my schoolteacher grandmother's *McGuffy Readers* from 1890. Growing up, again and again I encountered stories of how the people who were today considered seminal giants, geniuses, major contributors to the evolution of civilization, had been met with hostility, persecution, and seemingly deliberate (or else profoundly stupid) misrepresentations by the authorities, elites, and publics of their time. Looking about me, I figured out about the age of 14 that western technological civilization was proceeding on an unsustainable course. I had not encountered the concepts of ecology, organic agriculture, renewable energy, or the Gaia hypothesis at that time, but when I did, they fit right into "receptor sites" in my intuitive understanding. I did encounter Ayn Rand in high school, and although I thought she went overboard with her positivism, the idea her writings nurtured in my consciousness was that power elites are heavily invested in maintaining the status quo by keeping the general public ignorant and afraid. This understanding was greatly amplified for me when I turned 21 and established a relationship with my father, a Columbia University professor who studied the authoritarian personality, the Machiavellian personality, and issues of political power psychology his entire career.

From our early teens, both Oberon and I read science fiction. Through science fiction, we were exposed to several concepts which became part of our world view. One concept is that authority's first agenda is defending and maintaining its power, and that authority will react irrationally against any person or force that threatens authority's sense of security in power. Another was that all sorts of alternative cultural arrangements were possible, and many of these alternatives made more sense to us than those which our culture had chosen. Science fiction was, and is, a major vehicle for those who wish to be social critics to try out "what if" scenarios to both explore the end result of current cultural, technological, and political trends, and to explore possible solutions to contemporary or likely future problems.

During high school and college, Oberon and I were exposed to Hugh Hefner's "Playboy Philosophy" series, which in turn referenced us to such works as G. Rattray Taylor's "Sex in History" and works on the psychological fear of women and the feminine. Like many high-IQ types growing up in the 1940's and 1950's, Oberon and I scored high on the feminine end of the masculine-feminine scales of various popular psychological tests circa 1960. These scales were based on stereotypical interest and activity preference choices, and one scored masculine if one liked competitive sports, shooting small furry animals, and monster truck

rallies and hated books, nature, and the arts. The concept that we were introduced to through these works on the history and function of sexual stereotyping and sexual power relationships was that the "feminine" aspect of reality had been demonized, subordinated, and the exploitation and persecution of the feminine principle was directly linked to the exploitation of nature, with which the feminine was identified.

Enter the Stranger

Then *Stranger in a Strange Land* came as my Science Fiction Book Club selection of the month. Heinlein went much further than other science fiction authors we had read with the themes spelled out above. He took on basic cultural assumptions about sexual relationships, death and life, and religion and, for us, demonstrated that the obverse of our cultural norms made as much if not more sense in respect to these issues. For us, Heinlein's water-sharing ceremony symbolized the understanding that "thou art God" (the godhead is immanent in nature, not external from material reality. As I say, the difference between a paranoid and a Pagan is that the paranoid says, "I'm Jesus and you're not" while the Pagan says, "I'm Jesus, but so are you."); "I am but an egg" (the notion we have about reality is a construct of schematas derived from sloppy and incomplete observation of partial data, constantly subject to major and minor revisions if we keep our eyes peeled and deal honestly with what we observe); and "grokking" as the concept of understanding one aspires to—for me, "grokking" consists of achieving a profound empathy which is the obverse of the detached scientific observer (which we know to be mythical from quantum mechanics, which clearly demonstrates the observer is part of, and alters through participation, the system "observed").

In short, our first water sharing was a symbolic affirmation of these understandings.

A.S. Neill, *The Realist,* and other books: A.S. Neill advocated a child-rearing technique which was directed at developing the capacity in the child for autonomy, problem-solving, etc.—a person who was socialized to be neither ignorant nor fearful. As we saw it, Neill's template was one formula towards raising self-actualized human beings. As to *The Realist,* I have no idea where that came from; probably from

Oberon. It had no influence on me that I can remember. A body of literature which did have a profound influence on me is all the humanistic and Gestalt psychological works; the latter in particular deal with undoing the cultural conditioning which separates one from being an authentic human being, as opposed to a well-conditioned, superstition-ridden, obedient little rower on the bench of the technotrireme.

Christie House, MOA and Animal House

First, let me say that I made it very clear at the time that "Christie House" was a stand-in for a far better name I hoped would nominate itself. The idea I was attempting to describe might be described today as a deconditioning refuge, a place designed to recondition one from externalizing one's authority, being afraid of one's sexuality, etc., towards having the capacity and skills needed to take responsibility for one's own programming based on one's discovery of one's authentic proclivities. Later on, Jack Hurley, who used to be resident staff at the Esalen Institute in Big Sur, described to me how people would come to resident workshops there and make major breakthroughs in how they related to themselves and others, then would confront returning to the demands and relationships of their homes and work in which their new skills were not instrumental and the environment, given the sensitivities they had developed, painful. Jack concluded by remarking that Esalen needed a "good employment agency and a good whorehouse" attached for its Gestalt-based interventions to make lasting changes in people's lives. I think "Christie House" represented my intuition that one needed a longer-term environment than a week workshop at Esalen to develop enduring ways at dealing with the world with integrity expressing an authentic self.

The satirical fraternity I and some others constructed at Westminister College from among unpledged oddballs was "Mu Omicron Alpha," MOA—a flightless, extinct bird. We did not have a residence hall or meeting place. Instead, what the participants did was to take on the fraternities at Westminister in such competitions as community service projects and the float parade. MOA, which had an active "membership" of about eight at best, kept ending up

winning these contests against established fraternities with circa 60 resident members. And yes, we were deliberately flipping the bird at the Greek system, which is where an "Animal House" association comes from.

The rationalization for "sex, drugs, and rock n' roll" acting out in the context of self-actualization lies in the observation that the strong streak of Puritanism or Calvinism in our culture conditions one to be suspicious of and deny the pleasure principle, which is symbolically equated to the feminine principle. At this point in my life, I think means of relieving inappropriate conditioned inhibitions and learning to embrace pleasure with joy that are easier on the liver and less disorienting than free-form partying are preferable; as best I can recall, I always did. However, we didn't have such means at our disposal, and we were exploring "If it feels good, do it" along with "you are responsible for your own consequences."

ATL/CAW split

The fundamentals of the ATL/CAW split lie in the different proclivities which Oberon and I had and have. SISL suggested to Oberon that an effective way to promulgate an alternative set of values and behavioral norms was through a church, which Heinlein observed occupies a "null area in the law" (as Jubal Harshaw put it). Oberon places far more emphasis on sexuality issues in our culture than I ever have, and saw the church as a place which could nurture healthy sexuality (in the mental hygiene sense).

By nature, Oberon is an artist, visionary, and warrior leader type: somewhat of a "Captain Kirk" archetype. His warrior side moves him to challenge authority and open up people's views through a form of public guerilla theater which appeared and has been part of the CAW expression under his influence. I come from a long line of Scottish engineers, and am more of a "Mr. Spock/Scotty" archetype. I and a large contingent of Atlans who are more the technonerd type did not feel called to participate in Oberon's public theater/church approach, but instead were and are interested in working out the technical and socioeconomic details of how to run human civilization in an ecologically sound way. My original thought at the time of differentiation of the water brotherhood into

CAW and ATL was that CAW would develop a Gaian religious value structure, support for and public awareness of it, while ATL quietly developed the Gaian technology of ecological right livelihood, and that the two would be brought back together at some point in the future. As Lyryal may have informed you, I am in discussion with CAW about doing exactly that, through feeding the ATL-aggregated eco-economic technology into the Earth Steward Path structure in CAW.

As to the differentiation, the technonerd contingent of Atlans were geographically centered around Norman, OK, to which I moved, while Oberon was in St. Louis and developed CAW there. Oberon started with the Heinleinian elements of the water-sharing symbology, congregations as "Nests" with an open field as to the sexual and emotional relationships among the participants, and a church structure to give the experiment protection and identity before the law; but it was not initially a Pagan theology that defined it.

It is important to understand that Oberon's development of CAW as a neo-Pagan church followed from his TheaGenesis vision. My theistic contribution to the fundaments of CAW lay in my observation that the classic Pagan teleology had the One (Godhead) splitting into a male-female polarity. The loom of duality on which the Pagan material world is stretched is composed of a polarized sexual energy. The desire of the separated portions of the godhead to reunify into the One acts through and is sacralized in sexual attraction, and a transient transcendent experience of unity is achievable in sexual intercourse. In this Pagan world view, there is no good-evil polarity, and the female and male energy manifestations are different but equal aspects of the holy whole.

Starting with Manicheanism and on through Christianity, the revealed patrist religions posit the split from the one being into a good-evil duality. In my view, this is a setup for both theological and cultural schizophrenia, because one must fight and eschew evil rather than reconciling with it to return to oneness. The problem with the concept of evil is that it is irreductibly relative to your own idea of what is good and bad for you, what is good and bad for you may be different from what it is for another, and there are plenty of examples of where one's

idea of what is good or bad for one proves to be mistaken. The revealed patrist religions induce nuttiness in another sense because they clearly have several gods running around (if it is a supernatural being with supernatural powers that belong to gods in many other religions, it is a god) yet claim to be monotheistic, and even worse, that the one god is omnipotent. If Allah or Jehovah is omnipotent, then the evil god in the pantheon has to be operating with the permission of the *queso grande* god. Bertrand Russell, among others, has written brilliantly on this dilemma, so I won't pursue it here. I do want to add that the ancient fear of a malevolent Nature is sacralized in the revealed patrist religions as a fear and denigration of the female, and such religions deify the male intellectual principle (e.g., the Logos) which is portrayed as having divine providence to control the irrational feminine.

I disagree with the idea that the ATL contingent had any intention of being "secret and underground." We didn't, and we aren't. We just didn't feel called to participate in the public guerilla theater of CAW and the intense social commitment involved in the "nest" congregation. As to being "agnostic," the Atlans are, as a group, invested in the religious worldview Aldous Huxley describes in his "perennial philosophy." I do not regard that as agnostic, although it is certainly not a conventional institutional religious stance in our culture. ATL and its members have not sought attention because we find that fame or notoriety places demands and constraints on one's time and attention which we would rather devote to enterprise we find more rewarding and productive.

I think it is correct that ATL and CAW stopped exchanging members about 1972. CAW actively proselytized and grew in membership, while ATL did not grow in "membership" very much. In terms of longevity and stability, ATL has added a few people over the years and has not lost anyone except to death, while the turnover in active members and clergy of CAW has been large. The Atlans decided to turn ATL into a non-profit corporation twice, the first time in New Mexico; we then dissolved that corporation and incorporated the Association for the Tree of Life (an ancient symbol which satisfied the acronym) in Utah in 1987. ATL is currently a 501(c)(3) tax-exempt non-profit corporation "seeking ecological economic solutions" (as it says on the letterhead) which is pursuing various projects in organic agriculture, renewable energy, environmental restoration and biodiversity, local food and energy security, wilderness and watershed preservation.

ATL and CAW's relationship never ceased, at least in respect to their ongoing leaders. Oberon has used me as a sounding board over the years, so I have had a hand in a lot of the organizational and theological infrastructure of CAW. I've turned up at various CAW events over the years, received *Green Egg* and the *Scarlet Flame,* etc. Sprinkled through these publications are occasional articles I wrote. As far as I know, relationships by all parties were always amicable. The difference was not in fundamental religious viewpoint—the Atlans are all Gaian perennial philosophy, God-innate-in-nature types—but in practice. From an Atlan point of view, the CAW folks appeared to us to be gratified by dressing up and acting out being Pagans, doing rituals, and working on sexual issues. We didn't knock any of that—whatever rubs your Buddha—but we are basically lone wolf types who get our transcendent "ah ha" jollies out of solving problems and comparing notes with each other, and find dealing with committed monogamous sexual relationships quite enough of an emotional and spiritual challenge to our particular capacities.

Oberon Zell & Richard Lance Christie, June 2005.
Arches National Monument, Moab, Utah.

Association for the Tree of Life

ATL is currently a collaborating organization in the Spine of the Continent ecological restoration initiative, which seeks to restore and conserve a network of core habitats and wildlife corridors from the Brooks Range in Alaska down through the Rocky Mountain cordillera through the Sierra Madre range in Mexico. ATL is developing the ecological systems plan for the part of the Colorado Plateau which wasn't included in the Grand Canyon ecoregion's plan.

As part of the ecological restoration initiative collaboration, ATL is developing a set of papers we call "the renewable deal" which describe the Best Available Management Practices (e.g., for domestic livestock which successfully avoid losses to predators such as wolves), and Best Available Technologies (e.g., for renewable, non-polluting energy sources and agricultural practices) which, if universally implemented, would produce the quads and calories of energy needed to support the U.S. economy and population while abating competition for natural capital, permitting us to restore the ecological integrity of our environment without collectively starving or freezing to death in the dark.

Since the human body is also an ecological system, and ATL activists are concerned with maintaining their health and vigor into old age so we can continue to enjoy "good deed doing," we have compiled sets of notes on health topics with emphasis on what can be done to prevent health problems and treat them when they occur by means of non-prescription natural methods and substances.

As to change over time, Oberon and I recently compared notes and agreed that we are both the same radicals with the same ideas that we started out with in the 1960's. I have not done as much towards developing an ecological operating manual for a Gaian human civilization as I had fantasized, but I have assembled the pieces such that I have the feedstock for writing that operating manual. I had the good sense to pick a long-lived line of durable Celts to be born to, and my diet and exercise regimen (organic farmer, you know) is pretty much optimal for maintenance of health and functionality into extreme old age (I currently have the blood pressure and blood chemistry of a fit 35-year-old). I very likely have 40 productive years left to me, and propose to make better use of them than I have the past 40.

OZ NOTE: Lance died of pancreatic cancer on Oct. 28, 2010. Born in 1944, he was 66 years old. He completed The Renewable Deal *for ATL*

Church of All Worlds Position Statement given at the Parliament of the World's Religions

by Anodea Judith, High Priestess *(September 4, 1993)*

THE CHURCH OF ALL WORLDS IS AN eclectic, polytheistic, Nature oriented religious community. We worship deity in many forms, both masculine and feminine, with special emphasis on the Goddess, seeking to restore the archetypal sacred feminine to Her rightful place among the divine. To this end we support and train women as Priestesses, as well as male Priests. We are pantheistic in that we see deity as immanent within every living being, within all Nature, and within the Holy Biosphere of Mother Earth, whom we regard as a living being of divine proportions, most commonly referred to as Gaia, after the Earth Mother Goddess of ancient Greece. As deity resides immanently within each one of us, we support the growth of individuals to achieve their maximum potential, serving the divine through the evolution of our own and others' consciousness. As our divine selves are strengthened through contact with others, we foster the growth of tribal community through shared spiritual experiences, commitment to service, and continuous self-examination. We are committed to evolving theaologies that are life-affirming, that offer alternatives to war and exploitation, oppression and ignorance, racism and sexism. We value and reclaim the ancient myths of our ancestors, and seek to enliven and evolve them through group rituals and worship of the seasonal cycles in the unfolding spiral of the year. We seek to restore the lost connections between Heaven and Earth, mind and body, male and female, light and darkness, culture and planet, humans and Gods.

Science and Technology.

We do not see religion as separate from science and deplore the separation of spirit from matter that has occurred in the minds of scientists over the last 400 years. We fervently support studies in biology, astronomy, cosmology, geology, paleontology, zoology, botany, physics, chemistry, anthropology, psychology and sociology. Each of these disciplines is an adventure in discovering more about the nature of immanent deity that is the fabric of our universal home. We are committed to helping the world awaken to an understanding of the larger planetary and universal systems of which humans are only a part. Knowledge is power against ignorance, and can lead to understanding. Reductionism and scientific materialism, however, do little to foster a spiritual understanding of the larger creation, or to connect the individual with the divine nature of reality. Science has much to offer us and gives us much to be thankful for, but it cannot provide the answer to the questions that arise in spiritual seeking.

Our religion seeks to regard all things in their totality, which includes being aware of both their light and their dark side; and this applies especially well to technology. Technology can assist humanity by helping to advance consciousness and relieve human suffering. The creation of computer nets, information fields, communication net-works, and faster means of travel are all useful tools in creating global communication that can help connect and awaken the neural net of our planetary Gaian intelligence. When technology is wielded by the hand of greed and domination, to the point of harming the biosphere, then it becomes a tool of *deicide,* and we feel it is a sacred duty to resist and expose the harm that this causes to humans, animals, and the ecosystem. We do not see technology as a replacement for spiritual values, but as a tool for communicating those values to more people. It must be used in balance and with consciousness of its effect to the seventh generation and beyond.

Diverse paths of worship.

As our name, **Church of *All* Worlds,** might imply, we do not require the severing of any other religious ties in order to join our church or become part of our spiritual community. We open our arms to many paths, which include but are not limited to Shamanism,

Witchcraft, Voudoun, Buddhism, Hinduism, Sufism, Gnosticism, and Christian Creation Spirituality. We combine these roots with other threads from transpersonal psychology, body-oriented disciplines, artistic expression, paths of service, and science fiction, which helps us to dream the future. Looking forward and helping to create and sustain a healthy and meaningful future is an important element of the Church of All Worlds. We are less concerned with Creation theology than we are with "Evolution Theology;" meaning we are more concerned with our current *purpose* on this Earth than how we got here.

Environment and population.

Since the most important deity within our theaology is the living being of Mother Earth, we are deeply concerned about humanity's threat to the health of the biosphere through population expansion, exploitation, and domination by humans of other species We support the right of each living child to a healthy family who can responsibly provide for them financially, emotionally and spiritually. We fight for stronger reproductive rights that can prevent abortion, but should abortion be needed, we strongly support a woman's right to choose her destiny according to the counsel she receives from the Goddess within. We feel that it is unethical to force a woman to bear an unwanted child into a world that has too many humans, and deplore the sexism of male-dominated society that would impose such a law on other human beings, and on the already overtaxed resources of our Beloved Mother Earth

We affirm the interconnected nature of all life and seek to create a world of interdependent harmony, assisting the evolution of Gaian consciousness and the awakening of humanity to their true potential.

To these ends we summarize our mission statement as follows:

> The *mission of the Church* of *All Worlds is to evolve a network of information, mythology, an experience to awaken the Divine within and provide a context and stimulus for reawakening Gaea and reuniting Her children through tribal community dedicated to responsible stewardship and the evolution of planetary consciousness*

Declaration of a Global Ethic

THE WORLD IS IN AGONY. THE AGONY is so pervasive and urgent that we are compelled to name its manifestations so that the depth of this pain may be made clear. Peace eludes us...the planet is being destroyed ... neighbors live in fear...women and men are estranged from each other...children die!

This is abhorrent!

We condemn the abuses of Earth's ecosystems.

We condemn the poverty that stifles life's potential; the hunger that weakens the human body; the economic disparities that threaten so many families with rum.

We condemn the social disarray of the nations; the disregard for justice which pushes citizens to the margin; the anarchy overtaking our communities; and the insane death of children from violence. In particular we condemn aggression and hatred in the name of religion.

But this agony need not be.

It need not be because the basis for an ethic already exists. This ethic offers the possibility of a better individual and global order, and leads individuals away from despair and societies away from chaos.

We are women and men who have embraced the precepts and practices of the world's religions:

We affirm that a common set of core values is found in the teachings of the religions, and that these form the basis of a global ethic.

We affirm that this truth is already known, but yet to be lived in heart and action.

We affirm that there is an irrevocable, unconditional norm for all areas of life, for families and communities, for races, nations and religions. There already exist ancient guidelines for human behavior which are found in the teachings of the religions of the world and which are the condition for a sustainable world order.

We Declare:

We are interdependent: Each of us depends on the well-being of the whole, and so we have respect for the commu-nity of living beings, for people, animals and plants, and for the preservation of Earth, the air, water and soil.

We take individual responsibility for all we do. All our decisions, actions and failures to act have consequences.

We must treat others as we wish others to treat us. We make a commitment to respect life and dignity, individuality and diversity, so that every person is treated humanely, without exception. We must have patience and acceptance. We must be able to forgive, learning from the past but never allowing ourselves to be enslaved by memories of hate. Opening our hearts to one another, we must sink our narrow differences for the cause of the world community, practicing a culture of solidarity and relatedness.

We consider humankind our family. We must strive to be kind and generous. We must not live for ourselves alone, but should also serve others, never forget- ting the children, the aged, the poor, the suffering, the disabled, the refugees and the lonely. No person should ever be considered or treated as a second-class citizen or be exploited in any way whatsoever. There should be equal partner- ship between men and women. We must not commit any kind of sexual immorality. We must put behind us all forms of domination or abuse.

We commit ourselves to a culture of non-violence, respect, justice and peace. We shall not oppress, injure, torture or kill other human beings, forsaking violence as a means of settling differences. We must strive for a just social and economic order, in which everyone has an equal chance to reach full potential as a human being. We must speak and act truthfully and with compassion, dealing fairly with all, and avoiding prejudice and hatred. We must not steal. We must move beyond the dominance of greed for power, prestige, money and consumption to make a just and peaceful world.

Earth cannot be changed for the better unless the consciousness of individuals is changed first. We pledge to increase our awareness by disciplining our minds, by meditation, by prayer, or by positive thinking. Without risk and readiness to sacrifice there can be no fundamental change in our situation Therefore we commit ourselves to this global ethic, to understanding one another, and to socially beneficial, peace fostering and Nature-friendly ways of life.

We invite all people, whether religious or not, to do the same.

Given at the 1993 Parliament of the World's Religion September 4, 1993 In Chicago, Illinois, USA. Proudly endorsed by the Church of All Worlds Board of Directors Oct. 10, 1993.

> *NOTE: The above is just a synopsis of the far longer document, a 9-page* Declaration of a Global Ethic. *It is an attempt to articulate principles common to the ancient guidelines for human behavior found in the teachings of the religions of the world, that are now and will be pertinent to this present day and future years. Consider its words from your own perspective, remembering the guidance imparted to you by the wise ones of your tradition, whatever that may be.*

Church of All Worlds Encyclical on Reproductive Rights

May, 1993

Preamble:

This is the first of only two Encyclicals ever put out by the Church of All Worlds. It was written in May of 1993, by five Priestesses: Anodea Judith, High Priestess and President; Diane Darling, Editrix of *Green Egg;* Anna Korn, Willowoak Istarwood, and Morning Glory Zell.

Among them, these women have lived all of the following salient experiences: abortion, live birth, midwifery, raising one's own child, raising another's child through adoption or step-parenting, giving up a child for adoption, miscarriage, successful birth control, and sterilization.

Encyclical:

The Church of All Worlds supports a variety of spiritual experiences, knowing that diversity brings richness and stability to organizations as it does to ecosystems. Therefore, the writing of an "official position paper" is a novel and difficult thing. Yet in light of the old axiom that a people who will not stand for something will fall for anything, we feel impelled to take a stand against the threat to deny women their right to control their own bodies and the timing of their offspring.

One of the few pieces of "dogma" (if you can call it that) that the CAW does hold is the sanctity of the Goddess. Fundamental to the Goddess as Great Mother, the first and oldest, is the wonder of reproduction. The miracle of a body producing Life, whether it is the body of the Earth, of an animal, a plant, or a human being, is feminine divinity manifest. The Goddess is sacred. So are all aspects of Her fertility.

Yet today's cultures do not regard mortal women's reproductive ability with anything approaching this sense of sanctity. Too many women have been molested as children, raped as adults, beaten as mothers, relegated to low paying jobs, denied birth control by religious and political institutions, and threatened with denial of the right to terminate pregnancy. Prenatal care is often hard for poor women to obtain, and birthing is dominated by a gender that has never experienced it. Mothers are frequently alone, poor, undereducated, too young or otherwise inadequate to the monumental task of raising a child. Social support for every aspect of human reproduction is lacking in major ways.

If a woman wishes to terminate her pregnancy because of ill-health, lack of emotional or financial capability, to prevent her, thus forcing a child to compound and endure these adverse conditions in life, is cruel in the extreme. The ill effects of forcing incarnation into a body that is drug addicted, or where the mother's life is threatened, are pronounced, but subtle harm is also done when the body and psyche are formed in an environment flooded with the biochemical and psychological effects of maternal fear, anger, depression, resentment, rage, despair, horror and hate.

In a world already bursting with too many bodies, forcing a woman to bear a child under adverse circumstances shows a violent disregard for the sanctity of life and disrespect for the Goddess, women and the environment. True "right-to-life" concerns the quality of existence, before and after birth, as well as the health of the overall web of life, already stressed by human overpopulation.

The presence of Life permeates all creatures, from the great whale to the tiny germ. It animates the sperm and ovum as much as the zygote. Life is created by the dance of the Lord and the Lady in the photosynthetic trysting of the plants, and flows along the food chain to the animals and beyond into the dark Earth again. The issue is not Life per se, but one of adequate life support. It is patently obvious that if church and government were seriously concerned with the right to life, the issues of gun control, nuclear weapons, the waging of war and environmental degradation would be addressed.

Throughout history, laws governing the rights of women's reproductive capacities show a consistent correlation with patriarchal cultures and periods of military expansion. In Ninevah and Rome it was a criminal offense for a woman to seek an abortion, but each newborn baby was placed at its father's feet that he might choose to raise it up, smash it with his foot, or order it exposed. Bearing and raising children against their wills keeps women in a dependent position and serves the continuance of patriarchal values, but the freedom to manifest intelligent timing and a well-prepared situation allows the woman to honor her responsibility as well as her health, career goals, and emotional needs.

We, who revere life and all that it entails, individually and collectively face and address these problems. It is our intention and will to see the events of reproduction universally respected as sacred and to enact the restoration of the sanctity of responsible reproductive choice.

The process begins long before abortion becomes an issue, with healthy, relevant and honest sex education for all persons, especially teenagers. Intensive research into safe and effective means of birth control for both sexes must be funded and tested in humane ways that do not exploit women, men or animals. Universal access to acceptable birth control methods, regardless of socioeconomic status or age, is essential, as are the information, support and means to avoid sexually transmitted diseases. It is the sacred duty of both men and women to prevent unwanted conception. The question of abortion can be largely circumvented by the religious use of birth control.

Sensible counseling and high-quality, inexpensive medical support for all aspects of pregnancy are essential. A pregnant woman deserves unbiased comprehensive information regarding options available to her. She has a right and a duty to be aware of the immediate and long-term effects of diet and drug use, of the importance of pre-natal care, of the availability of alternative birthing procedures, of choices in child health, of parenting education and child-care services, of accurate information on the adoption process, and of the medical and psychological impact of abortion.

She deserves compassionate professional support that respects her decisions and religious convictions, whatever they may be. To bring a child into the world is a commitment of utmost responsibility. To determine to terminate a pregnancy, whatever the underlying reason, is also excruciatingly difficult. A woman who has discovered herself to be pregnant deserves time and space without harassment to consider her course of action. She may wish to sort through her options with her lover, priestess, Goddess, family and friends.

Should she decide to carry through with her pregnancy and become a mother, a woman deserves her community's unstinting support in helping her arrange appropriate medical or midwife care, make financial plans, get relationship or other counseling if desired, and then raise the child in the best environment for both of them in a celebration of the life brought into the world and of the courage of the woman who chooses to do so in a responsible manner.

If she decides to continue her pregnancy and then give the baby up for adoption, a woman has the right to counseling to help her through the adoption process and to prepare her for the moment of parting. She has the right to see, touch and hold her baby at birth, if she wishes, and both the birth mother and the child have the right of contact with each other when later the child wishes to know his or her genetic ancestry.

If the decision is to terminate the pregnancy, abortion is best completed as early as possible, when the medical risk is low and before the fetus becomes an independently viable life form. Research into past lives, rebirthing and hypnotherapy indicates that a spirit comes and goes from its growing body starting in the second trimester, staying longer and longer towards the end of gestation. If the mother feels this, she may make peace with the spirit of the unborn through internal communication, ritual or meditation, and perhaps explain her reasons for not continuing her pregnancy. Loving support from her family and, where desirable, the humble presence of the other parent, transform the abortion procedure itself into a solemn and sacred act.

Women have the right to unimpeded early termination of pregnancy that is affordable and relatively pain-free. Although it is unfortunate when unwanted pregnancies occur, women should not be punished by those who oppose abortion, view sexuality as inherently sinful, and consider an unwanted child just punishment, an ethically reprehensible stance.

For a woman who is certain that, for the balance of her present lifetime, she does not wish to become a doorway for new life, her reasonable options for preventing pregnancy include surgical sterilization. Others, for whom the final removal of reproductive capability is not appropriate, rightfully claim access to safe and reliable birth control as a basic right.

In summary:

It is ecologically, psychologically, spiritually and politically indefensible to bring unwanted children into the world. We are pro-life, regarding the quality of life for all beings to be of utmost importance. The Church of All Worlds unconditionally supports the right of a woman to make her own decisions regarding her ability to responsibly raise a child. We declare and defend a woman's right to safe, effective birth control and to a timely abortion whenever she should deem it necessary. We work for the rights of women to maintain and expand their reproductive options.

Church of All Worlds (incorp. 1968; 501(c)(3) 1970) www.CAW.org

Petition:

Pagan Doctrine on Reproductive Rights

We, the undersigned Pagan religious organizations, unconditionally support the fundamental right of every woman to make her own decisions regarding her ability to bear and responsibly raise a child. Pagans are pro-life, regarding the quality of life for all beings to be of utmost importance. It is ecologically, psychologically, spiritually, and politically indefensible to bring unwanted children into the world. Therefore, we support the basic right of all women to maintain and expand their personal reproductive options. We declare and defend every woman's Goddess-given right to safe, effective birth control and to a safe and timely abortion should she deem it necessary. As religious organizations, we hereby declare any attempt to prohibit, deny, thwart or impede any woman's access to a safe and timely abortion to be a direct violation of the First Amendment to the US Constitution.

Earth Religion Anti-Abuse Resolution

By Morning Glory Zell *(May 22, 1988)*

(The Earth Religion Anti-Abuse Resolution was written by Morning Glory Zell on May 22, 1988 and subsequently adopted by virtually every Pagan and Wiccan Path and Tradition, starting with the Church of All Worlds. Re-affirmation may be a purposeful act for us today.)

We, the undersigned, as adherents of Pagan and Neo-Pagan Earth Religions, including Wicca, or Neo-Pagan Witchcraft, practice a variety of positive, life-affirming faiths that are dedicated to healing, both of ourselves and of the Earth. As such, we do not advocate or condone any acts that victimize others, including those proscribed by law. As one of our most widely-accepted precepts is the Wiccan Rede's injunction to "harm none," we absolutely condemn the practices of child abuse, sexual abuse, and any other form of abuse that does harm to the bodies, minds or spirits of individuals. We offer prayers, therapy, and support for the healing of the victims of such abuses. We recognize and revere the divinity of Nature in our Mother the Earth, and we conduct our rites of worship in a manner that is ethical, compassionate and constitutionally-protected. We neither acknowledge nor worship the Christian devil, "Satan," who is not in our Pagan pantheons. We will not tolerate slander or libel against our churches, clergy or congregations, and we are prepared to defend our civil rights with such legal action as we deem necessary and appropriate. ♥

War and Peace on Sacred Earth
Church of All Worlds Encyclical on War

by Richard Ely, Priest *(Summer 1991)*

THE FUNDAMENTAL TENET OF NEO-Pagan religions is that Earth in Her entirety is a Goddess incarnate. She is all of Nature and Her names are many. Here we will call Her Gaia or Mother Earth, and those who honor Her before all others we will call Gaians. Gaia's rocks, seas and atmosphere are the sacred texts of Her evolution, and she is embodied in the living biosphere. Because an essential quality of the biosphere is interdependent interconnectedness, to harm any part of the web of life is to harm the whole. Thus all life is sacred, from the smallest microbe to the most evolved human being. Gaians believe that life should be taken sparingly, only in real need, and then after honoring the spirit of the organism that is to die. Most Gaians feel that the more conscious a being is, the less justification there is for killing it. Many of us would extend the definition of murder to include cetaceans, apes, elephants, ancient trees and other forms.

The "Common Themes of Neo-Pagan Religious Orientation" agreed upon in 1970 by the members of the first Pagan ecumenical council, the Council of Themis (of which the Church of All Worlds was a founding member), included the statement that: "We as Pagans deplore and censure all wanton violence and destruction, all exploitation, all murder, and all habitual coercion, including habitually punitive attitudes and practices. To Gods and men these are abominations." This position remains basic to our religion.

The Church of All Worlds categorically supports the right of all members of Neo-Pagan religions who honor Mother Earth as a prime deity to nonviolently oppose war in any and all forms. War is deacide, for it is destructive of the Goddess embodied in living beings. War results from various human communities having forgotten their collective origin in the sacred Earth and managing to demonize each other. War is the basic tool by which the patriarchal takeover and suppression of the Goddess was originally achieved and subsequently maintained.

Wars fought with high technology weapons are among the greatest ecocidal catastrophes, due to both the physical destruction in the theatre of battle, and the environmental costs of creating the war machine. High technology weapons exacerbate warfare by allowing killing without any conscious connection with the victims. Human beings become blips on a screen, and their suffering is denied.

Conscription is involuntary servitude. A soldier in the army of the State is essentially a slave who has little or no say in what his or her weapon will be, who the enemy is, or in what manner the battles are fought. Armies can be uses as agents of State terror, and soldiers have been required under pain of death to attack their own communities. There is no guarantee that such will not happen again in the United States in times of social unrest.

Even World War II, that most 'just' of wars, contained its share of massacre of innocent non-combatants by the Allies. Along with the atomic bombings of Japan, a prime example is the fire raid on Dresden in February 1945, which killed over 200,000 civilians and destroyed an historic city at the time when the German armies were collapsing. No significant military advantage ensued. If this is the action of the 'good' side, small wonder then that the Nazis were so evil. The difference between adversaries in World War II was more one of degree rather than kind, because both sides were willing to kill large numbers of civilians to achieve their 'higher' ends.

Gaians are clearly distinguished from Judeo-Christian pacifists who, at best, treat Gaia as a God-created object placed under the stewardship of humanity, and base their opposition to was on such Biblical passages as the Ten Commandments and the Sermon on the Mount. In contrast to Gaians, many monotheists see Mother Earth as a source of raw materials and convenient dump, an inanimate object to be subdued and risen above, or a source of demonic temptation.

Gaian pacifists who are also Wiccans would in part base their opposition to war on the *Wiccan*

Rede, the central moral tenet of 20th century Witchcraft: "An it harm none, do as you will."

Gaians also have the right to choose the path of the Sacred Warrior, to embody an ancient archetype who serves to protect the oppressed, the weak, the innocent, and holy places. Sacred Warriors revere life, even the life of their adversaries, preferring nonviolence to fighting. Martin Luther King and Gandhi were Sacred warriors. They did not demonize their opponents, but sought to transform them by awakening the sacred within them.

We are all fragments of Gaia; to kill each other is to kill Her. Even our enemies are sacred.

Gaean 12 Steps

By Anodea Judith

THE 12 STEPS OF ALCOHOLICS ANONymous have been used by millions of people for addressing a variety of habitual sins. The phenomena of addiction—being unable to do without something, until it severely alters your life--has been expanded from abuse of alcohol and other drugs, to food, sex and behaviors such as loving too much or having too little sense. We are, as Anne Wilson Schaef so aptly states, an addictive society.

Al Gore, in his phenomenal book *Earth in the Balance: Ecology and the Human Spirit,* states plainly that *as a civilization, we are wholly addicted to consuming Earth.* Piecemeal environmental solutions, such as recycling or carpooling, while useful, cannot begin to address the full scope of the problem. Like the wife hiding her husband's bottle, our denial and failure to confront the situation enables it to continue. Having already written a Pagan 12-Step alternative to the Christian context of the original 12 steps (GE 92, Ostara 1991), I here apply them on a planetary level:

1. Admitted that we were powerless over the culture's addictive consumption and destruction of the planet, and our environmental crises had become unmanageable.

2. Came to believe that the power of Gaea, the living Earth, could run the biosphere correctly and heal the destruction over time.

3. Made a decision to turn our will and the legislation of our lives over to the will of Gaea, as we understand Her needs through science and religion.

4. Made a searching and fearless moral inventory of the extent of the damage we have done to the planet.

5. Globally admitted the exact nature of our wrongs.

6. Were entirely ready to let the needs of Gaia override these short sighted policies and behaviors.

7. Humbly returned to simpler ways allowing our connection with Gaia to erode our destructive habits.

8. Made a list of all systems we had harmed, and realized the need to make amends to them all.

9. Created direct policies, legislation, and practices to address such harm wherever possible, without endangering lives.

10. Continued to monitor the way we live upon the Earth, and when wrong, promptly exposed it.

11. Sought through appropriate activity and spiritual practice, our conscious connection with Gaia, seeking knowledge of the planet and the power to live collectively in harmony with Her.

12. Having experienced a global awakening as the result of these steps, celebrated and sought other systems to apply them to.

UNIVERSAL FEDERATION OF PAGANS
Pagan Precepts
(1990)

THE MEMBERS AND MEMBER BODIES OF THE UNIVERSAL FEDERATION OF PAGANS practice a variety of positive, life affirming, Nature-based faiths which draw their inspiration from the indigenous traditions of many cultures, certain spiritual and artistic movements, and from sources as diverse as the human experience. We are dedicated to the enlightened celebration of Divinity which we find inherent in and manifesting throughout Nature, and to the wise and joyful stewardship of Her gifts. To this end, we see in general, to understand and emulate the diverse, complex, harmonious and mutually dependent forces and relationships of Nature and to discover our personal roles within them. Inasmuch, the following are the general foundations of Pagan spirituality, ethics, and practice:

Sacred Right of All Life Forms

As multiform Pagan people, we acknowledge that no philosophy, theory, religion or system of thought is absolute and infallible. Thus we find no justification for emphasizing one individual theory or way of life over another, except insofar as they affect others. Therefore, the Federation and its members enthusiastically support the sacred right of all life forms, Pagan or otherwise, to live their own lives, insofar as its concerns only themselves, as they see fit and without un- wanted obstruction or compulsion, and in particular, to eat and drink, to dress, to live, to associate, to make love, to worship, to gather, to travel, to think, to speak, to write and to otherwise express themselves as they see fit.

We see these as the self-evident, in- alienable birthrights of every life-form and the Federation will work to protect these rights, live in a manner commensurate with them, and be prepared to defend them using every means we deem viable.

Pagan Polytheism

Many Pagans feel that "the glory of creation is found in its infinite diversity and in the myriad ways in which our differences combine to create beauty and meaning." To this end, Pagans generally worship a multiplicity of Divine forms, usually beginning with the Goddess and the God. This is what is meant by Pagan polytheism.

Pagan Healing and Medicine

In general, Pagans seek all that is contributory to health and well-being from Nature and consider food, environment, attitude, and one's interactions to be inextricably linked to one's health. Pagans practice a variety of traditional and non-traditional healing methods with the understanding that health, like happiness, needs to be fitted to the individual.

Pagan Celebrations

As Nature is cyclical, Pagans tend to worship in cycles based on solar, lunar or other calendars. In general, Pagans celebrate the phases of the moon and the quarters and cross-quarters of the solar calendar. We also track the cycles that appear in ourselves, our friends and our environment, and so we celebrate Rites to mark stages in our lives such as being born, puberty, adulthood, marriage, giving birth, menopause, and death. There are other celebrations as well and many small rituals are used each day to mark the changing of cycles.

Pagan Experientialism

Pagans generally prize actions, information and relationships over possessions. Most of us seek life's wisdom through attention to a wide variety of experiences, including those experiences that are inner, or which transcend shared external references. Pagans normally give equal value to inner and outer types of experiences and respect the knowledge and meaning derived thereby.

Pagan Hospitality

Pagans tend to place a high value on the practice of friendship and community and are eager to fulfill the sacred duties of hospitality. To a Pagan, hospitality generally transcends mere accommodation, but extends to a sense of empathy, welcome, and reverence that many non-Pagans seldom achieve with- in their own families. Paean traditions often suggest that a visitor n ay be a God/dess traveling in disguise and there is often much friendly competition among Pagans to ex- tend the deepest welcome.

Unity of Magick and Religion

Pagans generally recognize that a spiritual force of great power imbues all Nature. It is this field that makes magick and life itself possible. Often, Pagans undergo rituals and practices to develop their understanding of this force such that they become wise and prudent navigators of its ways. Many of us see religion, magick, and wisdom-in-living as united in the world view of Paganism.

Complimentary Opposites

Pagans generally observe that the creative and magickal power of Nature tends to manifest in complimentary opposites such as male-female, light-dark, life-death, ebb- flow. Pagans tend to value both aspects of a pair equally knowing each to be necessary to the existence the other. And since divinity is as likely to manifest in female as in male form, we regard men and women as spiritually, and in all other ways, equal.

Sacred Eroticism

Most Pagans perceive Nature as endlessly and diversely erotic, sensual and spontaneous, and we value and find beauty in all consensual eroticism, sensuality and spontaneity as acts of pleasure, symbols an embodiments of sacred life, and as one of the sources of energies used in magickal an religious practice. In general, Pagans believe that life was meant to be filled with beauty, love, pleasure, learning and humor.

Concern for the Earth

Perhaps the most common and poignant Pagan deity is the Great Mother or Gaea; our living planet Earth. As we view the whole planet as our holy symbol we consider also Her health to be linked with our own health and Her sacredness to linked with our own sacredness. The Federation and its members are therefore careful to live in respectful harmony with our planet, Her life forms and Her systems. We also greatly resent and oppose any organization or individual which seeks to subvert the health or sacredness of the planet, Her lifeforms or systems, particularly when such acts are motivated by ignorance, fear and greed.

Pagan Hierarchies

Pagans reject hierarchies based upon dominance, and power based on the threat of force. Hierarchy in nature, like that of molecules, cells, and organs, is based upon systems within systems, a progression from forms that are simpler to those that are more evolved, more complex. Therefore we honor those who possess and share experience and knowledge greater than our own, and who undertake the responsibility of teaching others.

Pagan View of Old and New

Pagan religions are as old as humankind. The word "Pagan" is derived from the Lati *paganus,* "peasant," deriving, in tum, from the Latin *pagus,* "village." Pagan religions are Natural religions both in origin and in mode of expression.

And yet, as Nature demands evolution Paganism is a dynamic, constantly-changing practice that continually evolves through its interactions with other religious, cultural, philosophical and expressive forms. In particular, Pagans accept the positive, beneficial aspects of contemporary arts and technology, while maintaining an attitude of skeptical optimism towards their supposed harmlessness and ethical neutrality.

The Church of All Worlds Tradition

By Liza Gabriel, Oberon Zell, and Morning Glory Zell, 2002

I. The Future of the Church of All Worlds Tradition

As Founders, Elders, and long-term practitioners of the Church of All Worlds, we have come together to celebrate and proclaim what we see all around us, that the practices, traditions, and values of the CAW are now a Tradition of Neo-Paganism, like Wicca, and no longer wholly centered in any one organization or under any one authority. We honor the contributions of the people who choose to be affiliated with the legally incorporated organization called Church of All Worlds, as well as all of those people who follow this Tradition and choose other affiliations—or no affiliation at all.

We proclaim this in affirmation and support of all who identify with the principles and practices of the Church of All Worlds Tradition, regardless of their chosen organizational affiliation. We wish everyone who wants to have a Nest of this Tradition, or to practice in this Tradition, or to build a new Church or other organization in this Tradition, to be empowered to do so; just as Wiccans and other Traditions have room for many expressions. We want everyone of this Tradition to feel free to express this Tradition in his or her own way, answering only to the authority, institution or organization that each individual feels truly called to.

We do this for the sake of clarity and empowerment of all people practicing and cherishing the Tradition of the Church of All Worlds and in honor of all the loving and caring contributions to this Tradition by people who may no longer identify with any particular organization. The Neo-Pagan religious movement is growing fast. Deep within in it is the founding and seminal influence of the Church of All Worlds and the generations of Pagan leaders it has produced. Let us rejoice in our diversity and celebrate our common heritage!

As free Practitioners of the Church of All Worlds Tradition, we proclaim these values and practices as central to our tradition and in so doing acknowledge every group and individual's freedom to interpret these and shape them to their current context. We do not know what contexts future generations will encounter!

After reading the statements below, we invite you to join us in affirming the beauty and magick of the Church of All Worlds Tradition and to empower all of its practitioners.

II. Basic Principles of the Church of All Worlds Tradition

The Church of All Worlds Tradition is an eclectic tradition of Neo-Paganism. Its practices are intended as a means towards the best outcome for all. The CAW Tradition is ever-evolving with basic, inclusive practices as follows:

1 REVERENCE FOR THE EARTH

Practitioners of the CAW Tradition revere, honor, and protect the Earth. Most believe that our planet is a conscious living being—Gaia, or Mother Earth. Most revere Her as a manifestation of the Great Mother Goddess worshipped by human beings from the dawn of time.

2 IMMANENT DIVINITY

Practitioners of the CAW Tradition honor the God and/or Goddess as immanent in every human being, voiced in the common greeting, "Thou Art God," or "Thou Art Goddess." The deepest experience of the Divinity in other people and things comes through the process of *grokking*. Literally, *grokking* means "drinking." In practice it means expanding one's identity to include the whole being of another person or thing.

3 SHARING WATER

In harmony with the process of *grokking,* the water that is essential to all life is the primary Sacrament of the CAW Tradition. Water is Blessed and passed in a chalice, or otherwise shared. Often the last drops are offered to the Divine. Usually when a chalice is passed, the person passing blesses the person receiving the chalice by saying, "Never Thirst," "Thou Art God," "Drink Deep," "Don't spit in the cup," or other appropriate words. This ritual, more than any other, is the common practice of the CAW Tradition.

4 WATER KINSHIP

The intention of the Water Sharing ritual is to affirm bonds of kinship. Depending on the intimacy of the circle, four levels of this bond are common:
1. Affirming our connection to each other and to all life;
2. Affirming belonging to a tribe or tradition;
3. Affirming friendship;
4. A lifelong Commitment of deep communion, friendship, love, and compassion, which may or may not have an erotic component.

5 NESTS

Nests are the basic grouping of the Church of All Worlds Tradition and are composed of at least three people who have a consistent commitment to the Tradition. At least one member, the Nest Coordinator, should have at least one year experience and the blessing of other long-term practitioners of the Tradition. A Nest may begin with no experience and work towards the ideals of Nesthood. Some Nests are families. Others are social networks, or ritual working groups. They are usually small and intimate. Sometimes several Nests may form a Branch.

It is likely that the current legal organization called Church of All Worlds may choose not to recognize such Nests, Branches or the leadership status of these non-affiliated individuals or groups. Some unofficial Nests may choose to pursue affiliation with the legal organization at some point whereas others may choose to remain permanently unaffiliated.

6 FREEDOM OF EXPRESSION IN INTIMACY & FAMILY

The Church of All Worlds Tradition is associated with open attitudes towards intimacy and sexuality. How this is practiced differs widely from person to person and Nest to Nest. Practitioners of the CAW Tradition affirm and support the broadest diversity of intimate and familial expression consistent with a sustainable and ethical life. For example, CAW practitioners support same-sex bonding through marriage, handfasting or other means. While quite a number of practitioners of the CAW Tradition are monogamous, all support the full range of choice in relationship, including intimate relationships and familial bonds that contain more than two adults; in other words, polyamory.

7 A TRADITION THAT LOOKS EQUALLY TO FUTURE AND PAST

Four of the five practices above derive directly from *Stranger in a Strange Land*, the 1961 science fiction novel by Robert Heinlein in which the name "Church of All Worlds" first appeared. Some members of the CAW Tradition glow with pride over this fact, while others are embarrassed and do not wish to be identified with the book. There is no question that many aspects of the book are increasingly outdated.

What will never be outdated, however, is the Church of All World Tradition's embrace of the mythology of the future and of science and technology as sources of wisdom as valid as the sacred traditions of old. The CAW Tradition honors the ancient past and looks, with equal reverence, to the future.

8 FUN

Humor, enjoyment, play, fantasy, and all forms of pleasure are central to the ways that practitioners of the Church of All Worlds Tradition come together.

III. Practices of other Neo-Pagan Traditions shared in common by the CAW

1. **Polytheism.** Most but not all practitioners of the CAW Tradition believe that Divinity takes many forms and worship whatever form is meaningful to the individual. The Myths and Mysteries of many Deities provide deep sources of initiation and wisdom for practitioners of the Church of All World Tradition.

2. **The Wheel of the Year.** Like almost all Neo-Pagan traditions, the CAW Tradition celebrates the cycles of the seasons, especially the traditional quarters and cross quarters: Ostara, Beltane, Litha, Lughnasadh, Mabon, Samhain, Yule, and Oimelc.

3. **Magick.** Practitioners of the CAW Tradition sometimes use traditional and untraditional means to influence the course of events through the focus of personal will. They acknowledge, honor and use unseen forces beyond rational human understanding.

4. **The Rede**. Most CAW practitioners support *the Wiccan Rede* as a foundation: 'An it harm none, do as you will.' However, in the CAW Tradition, it is understood that all magic, whether it serves personal ends or not, is intended to move towards the best outcome for all. The Church of All Worlds Tradition looks beyond the perennial spiritual value of non-harming, and actively contributes to the evolution of the whole. What form this takes may vary widely.

5. **Casting a Circle.** Practitioners of the CAW Tradition frequently cast a circle by ritually drawing it with a blade, wand, or other power object. The circle then serves as a place of protection, holiness, and power in which religious and magical acts are accomplished. The ideal of every action and relationship inside the circle is *perfect love and perfect trust*.

6. **The Five Elements.** Practitioners of the CAW Tradition often use the traditional elements, Air, Fire, Water, Earth and Spirit and the corresponding directions East, South, West, North and Center as important parts of religious practice.

7. **Evoking the God and Goddess.** Practitioners of the CAW Tradition often choose individuals in their circles to serve as focal points and expressions of the Divine Male and Female. Divinity is also invited into the ritual circle on its own without being invited into a particular individual.

8. **Bardship.** The CAW Tradition is a rich source of song, chant, ritual, art, lore, scholarship, vision and so on. The practitioners of the Church of All Worlds Tradition who have made major contributions to the creative life of the Neo-Pagan Movement and the broader culture are too numerous to name. Innovation and creativity are valued and nourished.

9. **Influences of Other Traditions.** The CAW Tradition enjoys and embraces influences from all the world's religions and traditions in ways that complement its basic principles and practices.

IV. Conclusion

Our recognition of a broader CAW Tradition is a positive acknowledgement of what already exists within the diverse spiritual spectrum of the Pagan Movement. As such it should be viewed as an attempt to reach beyond the status quo and to heal past rifts by creating a larger, more inclusive pattern of identification. In the past there have been many polarizing issues that have divided CAW. Perhaps this unorthodox form of recognition can encourage peaceful coexistence and give birth to an informal resolution of these conflicts since actual agreements are not a possibility at this point.

The skilled and wise practitioners of the Church of All Worlds Tradition are too numerous to count. We know that many of them will join us in this affirmation of our tradition and heritage, and in addition will teach, write, and create their visions, answering to their own authority in the freedom and embrace of our evolving Tradition. We are counting on these people to contribute their rich and diverse wisdom to the world for the good of all. Our hope is for a cooperative and diverse honoring of our common values, heritage and practices.

We thus declare: *Make It So!*

CAW Precepts

O MATTER HOW WE FORMULATE our philosophy, the true test of our strength lies in our behavior—our ability to embody the principles we hold dear, and apply them in our daily lives to the building of relationships and community, the integrity of our actions, and the strength of character that inspires others to grow and transfoml the world around them. To these ends we advocate the following principles of behavior:

1. **Be Excellent to Each Other!** Thou Art God/dess. To truly honor the Divinity within each other is to treat each other with respect, kindness, courtesy, and conscious consideration. This involves honest and responsible communication, including the avoidance of gossip and rumor-mongering, and the willingness to reach for understanding rather than judgment. Learn how to communicate in a positive, life-affirming way. We prefer to avoid us/them and either/or thinking, and to instead take an inclusive systems approach that sees the Divinity in all living things. To this end we also deplore coercive behavior that does not respect the free will of others. We prefer to lead, not by guilt or coercion, but by inspiration and example; not only to be excellent to each other, but to strive for excellence in all our endeavours, no matter how seemingly insignificant. Tribal values we hold include Loyalty, Generosity, Fairness and Hospitality.

2. **Be Excellent to Yourself!** Again: Thou Art God/dess. Divinity resides within as well as without, so how you treat yourself is how you treat that Divinity. Self-abuse, whether through irresponsible use of substances, overwork, self-denial, self-deception, or simply running those tapes that undermine self-esteem, are all insults to the Divinity within. Treat yourself kindly, with compassion rather than judgment, and it will be easier to treat others that way. Take care of your body, home and possessions, as a piece of Gaia that has been entrusted to you. Be a conscious guardian to the Temple and the God/dess within.

3. **Honor Diversity!** In Nature a diverse ecosystem has more stability. There are many styles of living and ways of living, each of which has something to offer to the overall puzzle of life. Be open-minded and receptive to new ideas because this usually manifests in growth of the spirit and the mind. Learn about differences rather than judge them. Be willing to explore others' creative abilities to manifest a sense of well-being and confidence in their own Divinity. Sexism, racism, or rude remarks directed towards other's sexual preferences, body type or personal habits (insofar as they do not harm others) have no place in this community. **All life is sacred.**

4. **Take Personal Responsibility!** The necessary counterpart to individual freedom is the willingness to be person ally responsible for all of our actions, and for our effects upon the planet. Only through the practice of personal responsibility can we become responsible collectively and live a life of freedom and maturity. We are not a religion of gurus, Mommies or Daddies who can tell you what to do. As a religion that respects equality, we must take equal responsibility for making things happen, pre- venting harm, or cleaning up mistakes. To this end we also advocate one of the principles "taught in kindergarten;" **Clean up your mess!**

5. **Walk Your Talk!** Talk is cheap. It is fine and well to proclaim to be a feminist or environmentalist, to preach heady Pagan gospel, or to play holier than thou. It is only in practice that words become Truth, and change becomes manifest. But do not be afraid to fail, for in order to grow. our reach must exceed our grasp, and it is through failing that we learn.

Sexual Etiquette

Unity through Diversity is a founding tenet of the Church of All Worlds. Because of this, not everyone's idea of acceptable behavior is the same. So to avoid undue stress, confusion, and bad vibes, here are some reminders:

1. **Sexuality and the Sacred Freedom** thereof is one of our prime values, so respect it.

("All acts of love and plea- sure are My rit- uals.") Sexual activities that are engaged in by informed and mutually-consenting adults are *no one else's business,* and are not to be condemned or censured. By the same to- ken, it is *absolutely unacceptable* to attempt to pressure, cajole or coerce another into any sexual activity that they do not wish freely and wholeheartedly to participate in.

2. **Minor issues.** While the respect due sacred sexuality applies *in principle* to Pagans of all ages, the emotional as well as legal pitfalls involved make it imperative that adults avoid sexually- charged interaction with youths be- low the legal age of consent. There are spe- cific laws concerning age, and Clergy are mandated reporters.

3. **Be sure you interpret signals correctly.** A loving touch, hug or a mas- sage is not an in- vitation to coitus, so if your attempts at inti- macy or caring make someone uncomforta- ble, *stop!* And if someone touches you in an un- comfortable fashion, ***tell them!*** If that doesn't work, get a Priestess, Priest, or Festi- val staff member to help you. Please be sen- sitive as to how your affections are per- ceived/received.

4. **Practice safe sex!** Use condoms with all out- side your Condom Compact; and if you have a sexually transmitted disease), *tell your consort.*

Ritual Etiquette

THE CIRCLE is a manifestation of cyclic en- ergy in the form of a vortex. This holy time and sacred space is separate from the world and contiguous with all other Circles. The Circle is an animate universe between the worlds which we empower by our agreement. Therefore:

1. A ritual is not a spectator sport. If you don't wish to participate, please stay far enough away that your conversations, etc. won't in- terfere in the rite.

2. Leave your mundane self and earthly busi- ness outside the Circle, and enter with your magickal self. Enter the Circle in "Perfect Love and Perfect Trust," having worked through personal difficulties beforehand.

3. Meet everyone's magickal self as if for the first time, remembering that we have been partners since life began. Treat everybody and everything in the Circle with respect, tact, courtesy and love.

4. A ritual is a religious service, one in which considerable power may be raised; so please behave reverently and carefully in Circle.

5. Keep solemn silence except when Truth wishes to speak through you. Speak only Truth in Circle, and your magickal affirma- tions will have the force of that Truth.

6. A ritual need not be solemn, yet it should be serious in that humor should be used with purpose. Gratuitous remarks can disrupt the Circle's energy/focus, so please refrain from making them.

7. The best rituals are those that seem spontane- ous, yet they've often been planned care- fully. So look to those leading the rite for cues on when to join in with chanting, drumming, etc.

8. When moving about in the circle, always move in the direction of the casting (usually *deosil/clockwise).* Walk around the Circle if necessary, but don't walk across or against the flow.

9. Ritual objects are invested with power and should be treated **with** respect. A person's tools and musical instruments are private and should not be touched without permis- sion—especially anything wrapped, sheathed or boxed.

10. Once the Circle is cast, enter or exit only at great need. If you must enter or exit the Cir- cle, please cut yourself a door or have one of the ritual officers do so.

ONE OF THE PRIESTESS' AND/OR PRIEST'S JOBS is to channel the Goddess and/or God in the Circle. Help them:

- Watch them, listen to them, follow them.
- Empower them and the ritual by your partic- ipation. Feed your energy and visualizations through them into the Circle.
- Put objections aside and save criticism until later. If you cannot go along with something, leave the Circle.
- **WE ARE SISTERS AND BROTHERS IN CIRCLE,** but we work in different ways. Be sensitive to different needs and styles before and during a ritual. Respect the differences be- tween all magickal selves and include them, for they are all needed to complete the Circle.

Four Reasons Why Paganism and Polyamory Are Linked

By Elisabeth A. Sheff Ph.D., CASA, CSE The Polyamorists Next Door
In addition to multiplicity, Paganism and polyamory share other traits.

Psychology Today, June 5, 2017

What is Paganism?

Paganism is an umbrella term for a range of polytheistic Earth-based forms of worship. Popularized in the 1960s and 70s in part through the Church of All Worlds, Paganism in the United States is a "revival and reconstruction of ancient Classical and indigenous Nature-based religions adapted for the modern world." Part of this emphasis on nature means that Pagan beliefs generally place humans as one part of an interconnected web —not the top being with dominion over all others. Oberon Zell of the Church of All Worlds explains that "Pagans seek not to conquer Nature, but to harmonize and integrate with Her. Paganism should be regarded as 'Green Religion,' just as we have 'Green Politics' and 'Green Economics.'"

Why are polyamory and Paganism connected?

In a previous blog, Religious Attitudes Towards Polyamory, I explain how the majority of the respondents in my 20-year study of polyamory consider themselves atheist or agnostic. The second largest group reported that their religion was Paganism, followed by a substantial group of Unitarian Universalists and a smattering of Jews, Buddhists, and a few Christians. Investigating the link between polyamory and Paganism has led me to uncover four reasons for the significant overlap among Pagans and polyamorists in the United States.

1. Freedom to think outside the box

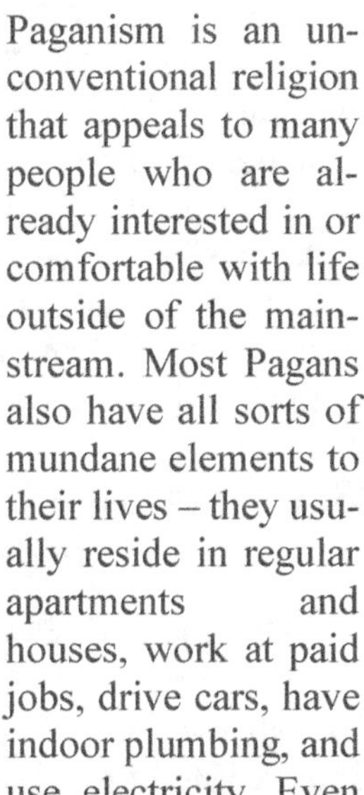

Paganism is an unconventional religion that appeals to many people who are already interested in or comfortable with life outside of the mainstream. Most Pagans also have all sorts of mundane elements to their lives – they usually reside in regular apartments and houses, work at paid jobs, drive cars, have indoor plumbing, and use electricity. Even so, they are often interested in the margins of social life and have been questioning social mores and norms for long enough to find and practice this unconventional religion. There are a few second- and third-generation Pagans living in the United States, but for the most part it is a religion composed of people who choose to find something outside of the usual bounds of religious thought. Polyamory also appeals to those who question social norms and seek out unconventional lifestyles. This shared fascination with the social margins means that Paganism appeals to polyamorous folks, and vice versa.

Furthermore, the practitioners of each occupy the same social sphere. Community norms among polyamorous folks define it as rude to judge Pagans as outlandish or freakish, and similar values among Pagan community members make it uncommon for anyone to (openly) degrade polyamorous folks for having multiple partners.

2. Multiplicity

With its reverence for multiple spiritual traditions that each have multiple deities, it is no surprise that Paganism recognizes a pantheon of goddesses and gods. Various deities are associated with different times of year, holy days, or specific types of assistance and thus meet a range of needs for worshipers. This presence of multiple divine beings and their ability to meet many different needs is parallel to polyamorous folks' desire to have multiple romantic partners meet a wide range of needs with diverse personality traits, interests, or specialized skills.

3. Alternative communities provide access to ideas and partners

Some polyamorous folks who had not previously heard of Paganism reported that they learned of its existence through contact with Pagans at poly community events or online poly discussion forums. Others reported that they were exploring alternative religious beliefs and stumbled upon the idea of polyamory through contact with Pagans. Regardless of whether they are Pagan or polyamorous first, being able to search in both communities for partners allows folks a larger pool of potential dates.

4. Same Founders

Possibly the single most important reason for the confluence between Paganism and polyamory is that they share the same founders in the United States. Among the founding pantheon of polyamorous community leaders, Oberon and Morning Glory Zell-Ravenheart are two of the most important figures. In his book *The Wizard and the Witch*, Oberon describes meeting Morning Glory in 1973 and beginning an adventure in alternative spirituality and relationships. Along with founding the Church of All Worlds, they created a template for multiple partner commitment ceremonies, crafted what has become a widespread image of a seated woman with the globe of the Earth as her pregnant belly, established a tribe of lovers and poly-affective kin, and published the *Green Egg*. Morning Glory is credited with coining the term *polyamory* in her essay *A Bouquet of Lovers* published in the *Green Egg* #89 in 1990. While Morning Glory passed away in 2014, Oberon is still alive and has established the Academy of Arcana, a center for polyamorous and Pagan community in Santa Cruz, California.

> **About the Author**
> **Elisabeth Sheff, Ph.D.**, is an expert on polyamory and sexual-minority families with children. She is the author of *Stories from the Polycule: Real Life in Polyamorous Families.*

Sacraments in the CAW

by Oberon Zell & Liza Gabriel
(from *CAW Membership Handbook,* 3rd Edition, 1997)

SACRAMENT IS SOMETHING REgarded as holy, or sacred. Ordinary acts or substances may be elevated to the status of Sacraments in a ritual context, thereby becoming gateways into a greater awareness of the beauty and power of the BIG PICTURE and our part in it. Article II, Paragraph 16 of the CAW Bylaws lists as one of our Purposes: "To make provisions to establish and ordain various Sacraments of the Church of All Worlds." Such sacraments may grouped into three categories: Actions, Rituals and Substances. *It is absolutely prohibited in the CAW that anyone ever be compelled or coerced into partaking of any Sacrament without their full knowledge and consent.*

Actions

Sacred Sexuality—

The appropriate expression of sexuality at each season of life is essential to a life fully lived. Sex is a source of power, creative as well as procreative. We have been taught that this power comes from polarity, a charged attraction of opposites, but that is only one of the many ways that sexual energy flows. People of similar qualities or of the same sex generate pleasure and power together. The giving and receiving of sexual pleasure is an endlessly varied art.

We are born out of this act of pleasure. This miracle has been a source of awe and a method of magic from the dawn of time. We all have in us somewhere the naive and childlike belief that if sex can create us, sex can create anything. Out of such simple beliefs some of the most powerful and effective magic in human experience is woven. Our bodies are the particular piece of the Great Mother especially entrusted to us. In the experience of that sacred trust, Sex becomes an act of worship, engaging and awakening the God and Goddess in our partners. "For behold; all acts of Love and Pleasure are My rituals." (Doreen Valiente, "The Charge of the Goddess") Thus we sanction all loving and responsible sexual relationships between informed and mutually consenting adults, whatever their gender, number or practice. We also advocate safer sex practices.

Ritual Nudity—

As in our founding novel, *Stranger in a Strange Land* (SISL), we encourage and practice (though we do **not** require!) "holy nakedness" in our Nests; and weather and privacy permitting, we conduct many of our outdoor rites "skyclad." Group skinny-dipping and hot-tubbing are long-standing traditions in the CAW. Naked bodies are honest, unpretentious, beautiful and sacred; we are "naked and unashamed!" We agree with "The Charge of the Goddess:" "And as a sign that you be truly free, you shall be naked in your rites." We support the establishment and maintenance of clothing-optional beaches, hot springs, and other sanctuaries for skyclad communion with Nature.

Environmental Action—

As our prime deity is the Goddess of the Living Earth, we regard Her maintenance and protection as our most sacred duty. We are in strong alignment with the rallying slogan of Earth First!: "No compromise in defense of the Mother Earth!" We support all forms of non-violent environmental activism, including highway and park clean-up campaigns, tree plantings, and demonstrations against despoilers of Nature.

Magick—

We define "Magick" as "the art of probability enhancement," or "coincidence control." The study, practice and mastery of such arts is a lifelong quest, involving the ability to formulate, embrace and shift the very paradigms that constitute our consensual "reality."

Rituals

Water Sharing—

The communion ritual of Water-Sharing is the quintessential rite of the Church of All Worlds. The rite is conducted simply by offering a chalice of water to another, while saying such ritual phrases as: "I offer you water; may you never thirst;" "May you always drink deeply;" "Thou art God (or Goddess);" "Water shared is life shared."

We have affirmed that **Water-Brotherhood** may only be pledged in person, and face-to-face. We have learned that this sacred act is not to be entered into lightly or without careful thought; it is a lifetime commitment to a bonded relationship, in which water-sibs promise to always "be there" for each other. This is the deepest and most intimate form of Water-Sharing, held in the "innermost circle."

As for **group Water-Sharings,** we do not consider these to be pledges of water-brotherhood on the same intense level of commitment as the personal sharings, but rather a communion of acknowledgment. We recognize two levels of group Water-Sharing: the large "outer circle" sharing affirming kinship in the great "Circle of Life," wherein "water shared is life shared" with "all that groks," which, of course, "is God/dess;" and the "intermediate circle" sharing among those attending any Nest, coven, or small group ritual, affirming the bonds of the group.

Seasonal Celebrations—

Central to all Pagan worship, including that in the CAW, is the annual cycle of seasonal "Sabbats" referred to as the "Wheel of the Year." Participating in these celebrations attunes us body, soul and tribe to the Great Round of Life's Mysteries: Birth, Growth, Death and Rebirth. The eight Sabbats are:

Ostara— Spring Equinox; Festival of Rebirth
Beltane— May Day; Festival of Sacred Marriage
Litha— Summer Solstice; the Longest Day
Lughnasadh— Festival of First Fruits
Mabon— Autumn Equinox; Festival of Harvest Home
Samhain— Hallowe'en; Feast of the Blessed Dead
Yule— Winter Solstice; Festival of Returning Light
Oimelc/Imbolg— Festival of Waxing Light

Rites of Passage—

These are rituals honoring and empowering life's transitions. Such passages include (but are not limited to) the following:

Birth— rite of *seining,* or baby blessing, in which infants are presented to the community, given names, God & Goddess-parents, and blessing gifts;
Menarche/Puberty (attaining fertility)— ceremonies commemorating girls' "first blood;" boys' coming of age;
Gender Reassignment— rite to commemorate a transition to a different gender from birth;
Adulthood— rites declaring independence and legal responsibility;
Taking Mates— rite of *handfasting* (marriage). May be for a year or for a lifetime;
Giving Birth— rites of delivery, motherhood and fatherhood;
Menopause (end of fertility)— rite of "croning" for women;
Elderhood— rite of "saging" for men;
Death— "last rites" include "passing," wakes, funerals and burials (or other disposition of the body, such as cremation and the scattering of ashes).

Initiatory Mysteries—

An Initiation is a magical metamorphosis; a ritualized transformation experience that introduces one to a new level of reality. Initiations, meaning "new beginnings," may mark life transitions, as in Rites of Passage, or they may signify entry into a mystical society. CAW-sanctioned Mystery Initiations include those of various Traditions of Wicca and Shamanism, and the once-in-a-lifetime Eleusinian Mysteries.

Nest Meetings & Esbats—

An "Esbat" is a full moon meeting of a Witches coven. Held in a ritual Circle, such gatherings focus on both worship and the working of magic—"probability enhancement"—for healing or other changes in the world. Nest Meetings of the CAW may be held as Esbats, New Moons, or more frequently as desired. The form is always a Circle, and Water is always shared in communion.

Personal Spiritual Practice—

CAW Waterkin are encouraged to establish and maintain a daily spiritual practice. This may include setting up a household altar, offering prayers and *puja* (rites), morning and/or evening meditations or exercises, meal blessings, and such other routine rituals as seem appropriate to the individual.

Divination— There are many techniques of divination, or "far-seeing," all of which are honored in the CAW. These include (but are not limited to) the following:

Scrying— trance-gazing into a crystal, mirror, bowl of water, fire, etc.;

Tarot and other card reading— random selection, display and interpretation of archetypal symbols on painted cards;

Rune-casting— interpreting thrown stones inscribed with Norse or other runes;

The I Ching— ancient Chinese book of proverbs keyed to hexagrams;

Astrology— correlation of Earthly events with celestial patterns;

Augery— interpretation of synchronous natural events, such as the flight of birds.

Elements

The four Elements, **Earth, Water, Air,** and **Fire,** are actually the four states of matter: solid, liquid, gas and plasma, going from lesser to greater energy. These comprise the Body, Blood, Breath and Energy of Gaia. All of material existence is composed of these Elements in varying combination, and so we honor them in our rituals. Many also add **Spirit** as a fifth Element. Within these broad categories may be grouped all the Sacred Substances:

Earth

Primal Ooze— A delightful way to experience the conjoined Elements of Earth and Water is via "Primal Ooze." The latest scientific thinking has it that wet clay formed the original template for the formation of DNA, four billion years ago. A pit filled with smooth wet clay provides a truly wonderful mud bath for slippery hordes of Waterkin! Clay is also, of course, a wonderful artistic medium, and, when we add Fire, becomes the most enduring of all artifacts.

Cheez-Its— The first heresy declared by the Roman Catholic Church was the *Artotyrite* heresy; a practice of the Montanist sect, who ate cheese on their communion bread. In the Church of All Worlds we affirm the right to diversity in sacraments by honoring the Artotyrites with *Sunshine Cheez-Its* (accompanied with an explanation of the symbolism, jokes: "What a friend we have in Cheez-Its;" "Cheez-Its saves," etc.).

Of course, **Bread, Fruit,** or other foods (such as the special selection of "underworld foods" eaten in silence at the Samhain "Dumb Supper") may be shared "snack-ramentally" as well. All such foods are considered to be the body of the God and/or Goddess. The most common phrases to accompany the passing of food are: "May you never hunger," or "May you always have sufficiency."

Chocolate— Chocolate is widely recognized in Pagan Circles as the Fifth Element. Celebrants are known as "Chocolytes" though those who over-indulge are known as "Chocaholics."

Chocolate beverages were considered a drink for the Gods during the time of the Aztec Empire. In Tantric practices a couple would place a square of dark chocolate between their lips and eat to the middle where they would meet in a long passionate kiss. This not only raises the Kundalini (among other things) but evolves the use of the taste buds in oral satiation.

Chocolate has a divine taste that is orgasmic as it melts in your mouth. The theobromine causes a euphoric state which satisfies the deepest of desires and most compelling of cravings.

In circle, when sharing this "snack-rament," the most common phrases are: "Thou art sweet," "Thou art creamy," and for the darker time of year, "Thou art bittersweet." When you have ingested this sacrament and reached true enlightenment, you achieve the realization that there "S'more than enough for everyone and some to share." *(—Aeona Silversong)*

Water

Water— This is the prime "official" sacrament of the Church of All Worlds; read all about it in *Stranger in a Strange Land!* Water is the essential foundation of all Terrestrial life, comprising 80% of our body mass. Water is the very blood of the Mother; the chemical constituency of the blood in our veins is the same as that of the ancient seawater of four billion years ago, which we assimilated into our bodies as we developed in the oceanic womb of The Mother.

We are all One—washed in the blood! Blood, sweat and tears are the waters of our lives. The physical properties of water, manifesting as solid, liquid and gas (Earth, Water and Air) at biologically compatible temperatures, and water's unique property of having a solid form that floats in the liquid, are what allows the possibility of life on Earth—and throughout the known universe.

All CAW rituals include a Sharing of Water, from a simple communion acknowledging of our water-kinship with all Life, to the lifelong commitment of Water-Brotherhood.

Of course, other liquids, such as **Wine** or **Fruit Juice,** may be shared sacramentally as well; they all partake of the "essence" of Water. As we offer wine, we may say, "Wine shared is love shared;" with juice we often joke, "May you always be juicy!"

Coffee— The "Javacrucian Mysteries" are enacted every morning in countless Pagan households and Pagan events: facing the rising Sun and holding the Mug of Brewe, the celebrant takes a first sip, then elevates the cup and intones, "Gods, I needed that!" And means it. Then begins the daily recapitulation of ontogeny...

Sects of the Javacrucian Tradition vary mainly around additives to the Basic Brewe:
> **The Left Out Path**
> **The Path of Delectable Darkness**
> **The Milky Way**
> **The Path of Sweetness and Light**

Associated cults include Teaosophists, Rastacolians, Mateyanists, and Chocolytes.

Air

Breath— Breath is a rhythm which accompanies every moment. Unlike our heartbeats, we can consciously control breath; holding it, speeding it up, slowing it down, making it shallow or deep, raspy or smooth. Yet when we are asleep or unconscious, our breath continues. Because breath can be controlled both by the conscious and unconscious minds, it is used as a bridge between the two. In many languages the word for spirit and the word for breath are the same: *ruach* in Hebrew and *esprit* in French. In other traditions the word for breath and life energy are the same: *prana* in Sanskrit and *pneuma* in Greek. Breath has been used since prehistory not only as a bridge between the conscious and unconscious, but as a bridge between body and spirit. Breath is the foundation of most sacred sex practices. It is used in ritual to raise and focus energy and to bring an experience of full aliveness, embodying the spirit and inspiring the body.

Music— Music plays a central role in almost every religious tradition. Diverse groups of people can grow very close very fast through an experience of music or singing. Music fills the air around us embracing everyone present and echoing in our souls. The Pagan community in general and the Church of All Worlds in particular are blessed with many inspired musicians and bards and these folk contribute to virtually every Pagan ritual and occasion, often inviting everyone to join in. The two most ancient and widespread sacred instruments are voice and drum. Both are intimately connected to the rhythms of the body—the voice to breath and the drum to heartbeat.

Fire

Campfires— The most ancient and distinctively human experience is that of sitting around a campfire, sharing songs and stories with your clan. A campfire automatically forms the focus of a primal circle, and scrying into the flames may reveal many things... Firewalking also has been learned and practiced by some of us as an initiatory and transformative experience.

Annwfn Moon Circle by OZ.

Candle-Burning— Burning candles of selected colors may be used in spellwork. Some of the most popular color associations are:

Red— Physical work, as in healing of people and animals; passion and sex;
Orange— Pride and courage; heroism and attraction;
Yellow— Mental work, meditation, etc.; intellect;
Green— Vegetation, as in gardening; fertility and prosperity;
Blue— Emotional work, love, etc.; peace and protection;
Violet— Power, wealth and good fortune;
Black— Blighting or binding;
White— Blessing, or anything you want!

Spirit

Psychedelics— Various plant-derived psychotropic chemicals have been used as sacraments in virtually every culture on the planet, including wine in Christian Churches and peyote in the Native American Church. These are "medicines" of great power, meant to be used only with reverence, and in a sacred manner. The magic of these sacraments lies in their ability to temporarily alter mundane consciousness and allow communion with the Gods. If such substances are to be used at all, it is the collective wisdom of the Ancient Elders that they should be used respectfully and reverently, with the full knowledge and consent of the partaker.

From time to time, the CAW Board of Directors has legally registered resolutions to establish and ordain as sacraments, to be used in a sacred and ritualistic manner, with full reverence, various psychotropic herbs and substances which were not currently proscribed or designated as controlled substances by the laws of any known municipality, county, state, province or country. Two of these are: MDMA ("Ecstasy"), registered 4/5/85; and *Salvia Divinorum* ("Diviner's Mint"), registered 1/19/95. Such registration does not constitute a recommendation that these substances be partaken of, but rather an acknowledgment of their sacred nature.

Dance— One of the most primal and prevalent scenes in Pagan life is a fire circle with drummers and dancers. Both freeform dancing and circle dancing are essential parts of our rituals and celebrations. Expressing the joy, sorrow and beauty of our lives through our bodies and through dance affirms our identity as part of the natural world and prevents our rites from becoming mere head trips.

Humor— Pagans in general, and CAW Waterkin in particular, seem to have an inordinate fondness for humor and jokes, both clever and dumb. Puns especially are virtually a trademark of our sense of humor, and the references from which these are drawn are an affirmation of our common group heritage. Among the most ubiquitous humor references in our tribe are:

Monty Python TV shows and movies;
Star Trek TV series (all!) and movies;
Firesign Theatre radio shows and albums;
The Addams Family TV series and movies;
The Hitchhiker's Guide to the Galaxy (by Douglas Adams) books, radio, TV, movie;
The Princess Bride book and movie;
Pirate movies, books, jokes, cartoons, etc.;
Science Fiction & Fantasy (esp. Robert Heinlein, Roger Zelazny, Robert Asprin, Terry Pratchett, Neil Gaimon);
Filk Songs, including endless verses to "Give Me That Old Time Religion!"

HOME Cooking cover by Nybor, 1997.

Whither Water Sharing
and What's With the Requirements, Already?

by Anodea Judith (for the CAW Priesthood Council)
(from *CAW Membership Handbook,* 3rd Edition, 1997)

THE RITUAL OF Water Sharing is the most fundamental ritual in the Church of All Worlds. Taken from the scene in *Stranger in a Strange Land* where Valentine Michael Smith innocently accepts a glass of Water from his nurse and becomes a bonded friend ("Water Brother") from that point on this ritual has far more significance than just the quenching of thirst. On Mars, water is the rarest and most precious substance, vital to life, so offering it to another is an act of intense love and commitment.

Water Sharing in CAW occurs on several levels and depths. The most common level is the public Water Sharing, where a chalice is passed around a large circle at a general event, and strangers and friends alike drink deep and pass blessings around the circle as they drink. This ritual signifies a bond of shared principles and tribal community, a momentary sip from the chalice that represents the Goddess, whom we all honor and adore. In drinking Water, we are drinking from the magical law of "perfect love and perfect trust." This means that even with strangers we don't know, we behave in a way that would not betray this law. We agree to be excellent to each other.

A deeper form of Water Sharing at this outer level is done among those attending any Nest, coven, or small group ritual; when sharing a spiritual experience with someone on a memorable hike; when joining other Pagan folks for a fine dinner and evening of conversation; when embarking on a project with another fellow traveler on the path. In such cases, this is a ritual of communion, affirming the bonds of the group.

A second level of Water Sharing is more intimate, and also has two depths. This level occurs between two people at a time (or combinations of two in small groups) and signifies the celebration of a deeper meeting of minds, hearts and souls. When meeting someone at a festival and making a deep personal connection; when honoring the partner of your new lover—these are occasions for this second level Water Sharing. In this sharing you are looking deep into your friend's eyes, and acknowledging that you have a sense of who they are, and that you want to honor that. This doesn't mean that you have to know everything about them, but that you know enough to recognize a kindred soul. You know enough to put your trust in them.

Your Water Sharing speaks to what you see in this person—acknowledges it, honors it. You tell them what you are offering them. The meaning of this Water Sharing is very important. It means that you are promising to never betray this person, to consider them an honored part of your life from this point forward. It means that you would help them in need if you could, that their suffering or their joy would add to your own. This is a heavy commitment, and it is not done lightly. Those who share Water on this level become *Water-Siblings (Water-Brothers, Water-Sisters). Waterkin.* Such bonds between adults and children of separate bloodlines may be known as *Water-Mothers, Water-Fathers, Water-*

Daughters or *Water-Sons.*

It is this second level of Water Sharing that we are asking of CAW Waterkin **who want to move deeper into the web of RINGS.** We expect our members to become Water-Siblings with each other. If you cannot get at least one person to trust you on this level, how can you be trusted with the sacred?

(The deepest level of Water Sharing may occur between bonded lovers, who are pledging their life-long love and commitment to each other. This is an acknowledgment of a deep soul-mate bond. It is a bond of intimacy, a dissolution of boundaries. Just what this bond may mean to specific individuals is a very personal matter and must be determined by those individuals; but suffice it to say the commitment is even stronger than the previous level of sharing. **This deepest sexual level is *not* a requirement for progression through the RINGS.**)

(In the early years of CAW, we practiced "catenative assemblage," in which we regarded the "Water-Brothers of our Water Brothers" to be our Water-Brothers as well. This proved unworkable as soon as people began sharing Water outside the First Nest, with folks who were not known to the others. Since the mid-'60s we have affirmed that Water-Siblinghood may only be pledged in person, and only among people who actually choose to conduct the ritual face-to-face with each other.)

Why is the second level sharing—that of Water-Brotherhood—a requirement for advancement in the web of RINGS? Why does it have to be done in person? Can Water be shared by mail or over the Internet?

CAW is now a large organization that functions on the principles of a small tribe. At its best, it functions like a group mind. At its worst, it can be a dysfunctional family. As we have grown in size, the nature of CAW has changed in many ways. Yet the spirit is the same. It is based on love, wisdom, camaraderie, and spiritual sibling-hood. Water Siblings or Waterkin.

First-level Water Sharings—those of group communion rituals—may certainly be done by mail, or even over the Internet. What is being affirmed here is kinship in the group Circle, or in the greater "Circle of Life." No pledge or commitment is being here implied beyond that simple yet pro- found acknowledgement of group kinship. But the personal bond is the core unit of Family, Tribe and Community. In order to preserve this sacred core, we must preserve the second-level ritual of Water Sharing in person. To preserve our integrity, we must have at least a web of people who know each other. We are too large for everyone to know everyone. But at least we can make sure that everyone who becomes part of the workings of CAW knows someone who will stand for them as a Water-Sibling. This criterion may not categorically screen out all those less-trustworthy types who may hide it well, but it certainly eliminates most of them. And those it doesn't rule out are bound by a law of magick. If they betray it, then they have to answer to the Gods for it. I believe this ritual needs to be done face to face, eye to eye, voice to voice. The chalice two people share Water from needs to be the same chalice, for it represents the fact that we are all drinking from the same chalice, drawn from the same well—the Earth, our home.

This requirement is a preservation of our integrity. If it slows the process down, then we must honor the principle: Waiting Is. Remember, it takes less time to do it right than it does to do it over.

Water-Sharing Ritual

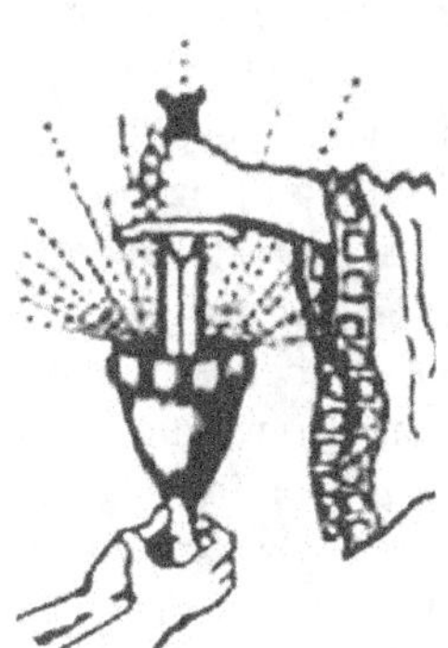

The Priestess and Priest consecrate the chalice of water. Then the Priestess holds the chalice aloft and says: "Behold the Water of Life! Whosoever shares this cup shall never thirst. For Water shared is Life shared!" She then takes a sip and passes it to the next person, saying; "May you never thirst," "May you always drink deeply," "Thou art God (or Goddess, as the case may be)." The chalice (or cups) is passed around the circle, with each person sipping and responding similarly. At the end, when all have shared, the remaining water is poured into a potted plant, or onto the ground, with a blessing such as "Mother Divine, we return what is thine."

Pool Water-Sharing Ritual

By Liza Gabriel & Oberon Zell

THIS SKYCLAD RITUAL IS DONE IN a swimming pool or shallow pond and involves sharing water both by passing a chalice and by being immersed together. The climax of the ritual is creating a whirlpool together while chanting. The ritual lasts less than an hour and can be done with anywhere from 10-20 people depending on the size of the pool. The ritual may be performed by a priest and priestess, or by one individual with assistants.

This is a ritual of bonding and connection with all life through water which flows through all life. Oberon and Liza created it for Craftwise in 1995, and it has since been done at a number of festivals as a very enjoyable way to introduce people to CAW and water sharing.

This ritual is held in a swimming pool or natural body of water. The air and water temperature should be comfortable for standing still in the water for a considerable period, say forty minutes. In a swimming pool this means 78°F or warmer. At one end (preferably in the West) an altar is built with a large chalice on it, plus an appropriate Goddess image, seashells, and smudging and water items. At night, candles are set at intervals along the edge of the water.

Participants are asked to get naked and line up outside the ritual space. A gatekeeper tells the people to enter one by one silently. If silence is not a realistic possibility, you could play canned music, have musicians playing or ask people to chant. People enter the water two by two. The priest and priestess stand at either side of the stairs into the pool. Either with their hands or with large shells, they pour water onto the people as they enter, also helping anyone who needs it to enter safely. They are motioned to circle clockwise around the pool, creating a circle along its edge.

When everyone has entered the water the Circle is cast by the priest or priestess. (Morning Glory cast the Circle with bubbles!) A chant is started that people will be familiar with, such as *"We are a circle within a circle."* Then The directions are called and the God and Goddess are evoked. It can be very beautiful for the God and Goddess to swim under water to the center and jump up out of the water together before they begin their evocation.

The priest and priestess give a short visualization rap about water and its magick, such as the "Blessing of Water." They explain that the intention and energy we put into this water will circulate through all life into eternity. Then the people are motioned into a clockwise spin, while shouting their intentions. The water in the pool quickly becomes a powerful vortex and care must be taken that no one is hurt. An appropriate water chant is chanted while the vortex is spinning, such as *"We all come from the Goddess."*

In a few minutes a completely chaotic scene will have emerged. At the climax everyone splashes wildly to release the magick. The priest, priestess and assistants must then stop the vortex and guide people back into the circle. Then the chalice is passed in a traditional water sharing (the chalice water may be poured into individual small medicine cups). As the chalice is passed, people are led in a chant: *"Drink deep, drink deep from the waters of life, water shared is life shared."* This chant can be done in a round.

The Elements, Goddess and God are thanked and the Circle opened, and people are invited to continue playing in the water or schmooze.

Bathing Beauty by Harold Gaze (1885-1962)

Rites of Passage

By Alder Moonoak & Oberon Zell

(from *CAW Membership Handbook,* 3rd Edition, 1997; updated 2024.)

RITUALS OF TRANSITION AND LIFE changes, called "Rites of Passage," mark significant periods in life, movement between life-stages, and personal transformations. These are rituals of honoring and empowerment. They are a public acknowledgment and recognition of growth. Just as the seasons pass in order, so do the stages of life. The inner and outer worlds mirror each other, so Rites of Passage provide a further link with the Earth and the Cosmos. Rites of Passage include coming of age, marriage or handfasting, pregnancy and birth, passage into Elderhood, handpartings, death and rebirth. The following general explanations come mostly from Alder Moonoak, a Priest of the Church of All Worlds:

Birth

When a child is born it is a remarkable event; when a child who is loved by many and nurtured by a whole community is born, it is a miracle. When we gather to name and honor a new baby, we honor life itself. Other terms for this rite are *seining,* or baby blessing. At this time those who will nurture the child are identified: Goddessmothers, Godfathers, parents, siblings and other loved ones who may have a part in the baby's life are recognized before all. We pass the new baby around the Circle, with magickal gifts and blessings for long life, health and happiness: "Live long and prosper..."

Coming of Age

This phrase originally meant "of age to marry," but in these days we no longer expect people to marry so young! Normally held between the ages of 11-13, the Coming of Age ceremony celebrates the onset of puberty in one's body and mind. From this point begins the exploration of our new and changing bodies. You must learn your own boundaries, likes and dislikes, and about your right to say yes or no when it comes to *your* body. Usually this rite is performed by adult members of the child's own sex, and may involve an initiatory ordeal and the giving of a magickal name.

Gender Reassignment

This can be as simple as having a menarche ceremony for a transwoman when she starts hormone therapy, or a ritual to celebrate a transman getting to experience puberty as a male. Some may want a ritual that ushers them from one gender to the other. The transition should be considered as an Initiation. Many possibilities!

Adulthood

This rite can occur anytime between the ages of 16-21, depending on the individual and local laws concerning "legal maturity." This ceremony heralds the beginning of the journey into adulthood, adding adult attitudes, abilities, responsibilities and maturity to our best youthful attributes. The rite usually involves a sacred/special place, a "Vision Quest," and a "rebirth" into the community of adult men and women. Some symbol is gifted to the new adult and s/he is honored before all—often with a new magickal name.

Handfasting (Marriage)

Choosing to live with a mate or partner is a commitment to that person, a joining of two independent beings because they are *more* together than they are apart. Handfastings are made "for as long as love shall last" because even though a couple may stay together for the rest of their lives, they also may not, and both choices are honorable. This rite sends them off on a joint adventure, with as much joy and passion as possible! Of course, same-sex and multiple partners may also be handfasted or wed. And if they should someday decide to part, a ceremony of **Handparting** will allow them to do so with honor and goodwill.

Parenthood

While Birth rites are centered on the baby, Parenthood is a ceremony for the new parents. It is a time for honoring the mother and father whose life journey has brought them to this place. We bless the new parents with a "baby shower" and a circle of love and support. This is a celebration, a party, a time for giving gifts, and of saying: "We're here if you need us—you don't have to raise this kid alone!"

Elderhood (Crones & Sages)

Elders, like children, are priceless treasures of our community. After the age of 50 or so, we may formally acknowledge and honor our Elderfolk for their wisdom, knowledge, skills, or whatever they have gained from their years on Earth. Often it's they who settle disputes, bless babies, and speak with greatest authority in councils. At this rite, another symbol may be gifted to them in recognition of their value.

Death/Rebirth

Near or at the time of death, we give comfort and compassion in a **Rite of Passing.** Beloveds gather to say goodbye, and to send the spirit out through the Circle. We ask that they be blessed with peace, a time of rest, and then a new journey, a new birth. After death, we remember them with a gathering called a **Wake.** This is a farewell party where we share treasured memories and stories. A **Funeral** may follow, in which a few chosen speakers may deliver a *eulogy* ("good words")—speaking of the impact of the departed person's life on theirs, and on the world. "What is remembered, lives."

A time of death is a sad time, but also one filled with hope and joy, for Death is part of Life, and just as the seasons turn, so we also will be reborn and continue. It is a time to let go and move on. Perhaps we may even have inherited a Guardian Angel in our lives: "May your spirit continue to guide us."

The Great Cycle, the Spiral leading ever forward, continues, one within the other: the moments of a day, the seasons of our lives, our lives themselves, generations, planets, stars, galaxies and the universe itself, all turn in the great Circle of Life. One of which we are proud to be a part, because fun, adventure and growth are the greatest treasures I can imagine!

The CAW Wheel of the Year

by Oberon Zell (from *CAW Membership Handbook*, 3rd Edition, 1997)

*Central to Pagan worship is the annual cycle of the seasonal celebrations, variously referred to as the **Sacred Round**, the **Cycle of Sabbats**, or the **Wheel of the Year**. The eight spokes of this Wheel are the Great Festivals, called* Sabbats *in Witchcraft. These occur at the Solstices, Equinoxes and Cross-Quarters midway between. As the year progresses, the rituals and myths associated with each Sabbat recapitulate the great Cycle of Life, from Birth to Death to Rebirth. Some version of most of these festivals are celebrated by nearly all indigenous peoples of the Temperate Zones, and most of them have even been assimilated into the Christian liturgical year, as Saints' days and Masses. A bonfire in the evening is the feature most common to all of these festivals.*

In the Church of All Worlds we have for many years been evolving a complex cycle of celebrations which have assimilated many elements of custom and folklore from our ancient Pagan heritage. We have drawn mainly from the customs of Western Europe and the British Isles, but as Greek mythology has always been a strong component of our collective Western lore, we also incorporate the Eleusinian ritual cycle into our seasonal observances. The main characters in our seasonal drama are Mother Earth (Gaea), Father Sun (Sol), and their children: the leafy Green Man (Florus) and Maid (Flora/Kore), and the hornéd Red Man (Faunus/Pan) and Maid (Fauna) (green=chlorophyll; red=hemoglobin.)

As the Wheel of the Year forms a circle, any starting point is arbitrary, and several of the Sabbats have been regarded as New Years in various traditions. For the purpose of this writing, we will begin, as if casting a Circle, with the East, and the Festival of Spring:

Ostara, also called *Spring's Height,* is the Sabbat of the *Vernal* (Spring) *Equinox*, occurring about March 21. It is named for Eostre ("Eastern Star," i.e. the planet Venus), Saxon goddess of dawn and fertility, who is cognate with Ishtar, Astarte, Ashera, Aphrodite, Inanna and Venus. The female *estrous cycle* of fertility and sexuality takes its name from Her. Eggs, bunnies and ducklings are, of course, all symbols of fertility, and are universally associated with this festival. This is the New Year on the Zodiacal calendar, and the name of each 2,000-year astrological age is based on the sign in which the Vernal Equinox falls in its continuing precession. Ostara is a festival celebrating fertility and birth, when Mother Earth bears two sets of Holy Twins: the Green Man and Maiden, and the Red Man and Maiden, representing the plants and animals. Hot cross buns *(paska)* are a traditional treat, representing the balanced Sun. In the Eleusinian Cycle, Persephone returns from Her six months in the underworld, reborn as Kore, the Flower Maiden.

At Annwfn, the children dye Ostara eggs (red is the traditional favorite color), and each egg has the name of a Goddess written on it.

These "oracular eggs" are then chosen blindly from a basket, and each person must learn the lessons of their chosen Goddess in the coming year. Ostara has been Christianized as *Easter,* another variant of the Goddess' name.

Beltane (Gaelic) or *May Day*

(traditionally the first of May, but astrologically falling several days later, at 15° Taurus), is the great celebration of sexuality: "Hooray, hooray, it's the First of May! Outdoor loving begins today!" The Sacred Marriage of the Red Man (Robin, Fauna) and Green Maid (Marion, Flora, Blodeuwedd, Maia) is celebrated in the Maypole Rite. (May marriages among mortals are considered ill-fated, however, as they are linked to the doom of the May King.) Leaping the balefire (made of nine sacred woods) is said to secure protection from evil, bring good luck, and increase one's fertility; and making love in the garden will cause it to flourish. Floral wreaths are worn and May Baskets left on doorsteps for loved ones. The Green Man dances with the Red Man, and men may dress as women. It is traditional to wear green, the color of the Faeries. Also called *Flora Day, Hare Day, Caedamh Dea Dia,* and *Summer's Beginning,* Beltane was Christianized as *Roodmas.*

The night before (May Eve) is called *Walpurgisnacht* (ostensibly named for St. Walpurgis, an English woman missionary to Germany who died there in 780ce; but *Walburg* is an old Teutonic name for the Earth Mother). This evening celebrates the begetting of Spring by Wodan and Freya, and the bonfire must be lit using spark from flint and steel. Walpurgisnacht is traditionally regarded as a night of madness, when the veil between the worlds is particularly thin; it is the opposite hinge of the year from Samhain, and the beginning of the Summer half of the year. Brocken Mountain in Germany is famed as the site of great Witches' orgies on this night. In classical times May Eve was the Festival of Hades, Lord of the Underworld

At Annwfn we hold an all-night ritual and Bardic on Walpurgisnacht, generally with a theme involving a journey into the mythic realm, or Faerie. We hold bawdy May Games to select the Queen and King of the May, who are crowned as Hornéd Man (Robin) and Flower Maid (Marion), and who become consorts and avatars for the men and women of our community during their reign (until Samhain for the King; a full year for the Queen). Children's May Games are also held to select a May Princess and Prince, and the new Royal Court will convene at festivals throughout the Summer season. Morris dancing and feasting are part of the Beltane celebration, and we have incorporated our own version of the Abbots Bromely Horn Dance.

The Maypole Ritual is, of course, the centerpiece of Beltane, and the women prepare the Maypole Crown, the Circle, the Yoni Gate, and the Hole, decorating them with ribbons and flowers; while the men go off to meet and bring in the Maypole, topped with a huge carved phallus ("John Thomas") inscribed with the years of all our Beltane celebrations. The pole is brought in through the Yoni Gate amid great merriment and sexual innuendos, crowned, placed in the Hole, and raised. The Maypole Rite is a Sacred Marriage of the new Queen and King, and he is bound to the Pole while she dances seductively around him. Everyone grabs an end of the many ribbons hanging from the Maypole Crown, and we dance the weaving dance to wrap the Pole and the King. As we dance and weave around them, the Queen may mount the bound King... After the weaving is done, she cuts him loose, and they are sent off to "swive" (make love) in the garden.

Litha,

also called *Midsummer* or *Summer Solstice,* occurs about June 21. Litha is the name of a Saxon Grain Goddess, cognate with Demeter or Ceres, and Her festival is one of joy, abundance and play. It was Christianized as St. John's Day. On this longest day of the year, picnicking, swimming and water play are customary, as are bonfires and fireworks in the evening. Cakes are shared with one piece containing a bean or other marker; the one who gets it is considered "dedicated" and required to jump the flames three times. Throughout Europe lovers clasp hands or toss flowers to each other across the bonfire, or leap through it together before disappearing into the woods and fields ("searching for the Midsummer grass") to make love under the stars. This celebration is specifically in honor of the Great Earth Mother Who nourishes us with Her bounty from Her everflowing cauldron, but we may also honor the Sun-Father at this time. Litha is a festival for families, marriage partners and children. It is the best time for marriages, and also a time for future visions and Faery favors.

At the Old Same Place we celebrate Litha with a big skinny-dipping beach party and pot-luck barbeque, with tubing down the river and a Primal Ooze pit. Fireworks light up the night, with drumming and dancing around the great bonfire. We may even have a performance from *A Midsummer Night's Dream.*

Lughnasadh (meaning "Games of Lugh"), traditionally August 1, but astrologically falling several days later (at 15° Leo), is named for Lugh, an Irish Solar God of ritual combat. It was traditional to hold faires at this time. Marking the beginning of "Earth's sorrowing Autumn," as Emer said to her husband Cuchulain, this Blessing of the First Fruits is also called *Bron Trogain,* or "Harvest's Beginning". As the *Feast of Bread,* it is commemorated by baking the first loaves of bread from the first grains to be harvested; the bread represents the body of the fallen God. Once a month-long festival held in Ireland at Teltown on the River Boyne (named for the Cow Goddess Boann, "She of the White Track," i.e. the Milky Way), Lughnasad (loo'-na-sahd) is traditionally celebrated with competitive games among men and boys. The winners are declared Champions and Heroes, and held responsible for the defense of the village. This is a festival dedicated to male energy, and Priests serve as the Green Man and Red Man, presiding over opposing teams. Male virility and sexuality is honored, including that between men. "Teltown marriages" lasting no more than a year and a day were once famous. The Irish Tailtean Games were originally held in honor of Tailtiu, mother of Lugh; but other competitive masculine games of strength and skill have traditionally been held at this time as well, including the Olympics, the Panatheniac Games, the Highlands Games, and modern football season. This festival has been Christianized as *Lammas,* or Loaf-mass.

Mabon, or *Autumn Equinox,* is named for the Welsh God of the Harvest, the Sacred Son of Modron ("The Great Mother"). He is the Green Man whose blood is intoxicating beverage: Dionysos (wine); Osiris (beer); and John Barleycorn (whiskey). The bay tree is sacred to Mabon, as its magical action is preservation, a time-honored Harvesttide occupation. Also known as *Harvest Home, Kirn Feast, Mell Day, Ingathering* and *Harvest's Height,* this festival commemorates the ritual sacrifice of the God and His descent into the Underworld, and the brewers' art that produces the sacrament of this season. In Latvia this harvest festival is called *Vela Laiks,* the "Time of the Dead." In Mendonesia, it is the festival of the Grape Harvest. Harvest Home is the traditional feast of Thanksgiving in England, but the Plymouth Pilgrims had a late harvest, so America's Thanksgiving is celebrated much later. The most universal tradition throughout Europe was the "Corn Dolly" made from the last sheaf of grain to be harvested. It was believed that the spirit of the grain resided in this doll and it must be treated accordingly, presiding over the Harvest Feast.

Autumn Equinox is also the time of the **Eleusinian Mysteries**, and the Holy Order of Mother Earth (HOME) enacts an annual recreation of this ancient Greek festival, in which Persephone, the Flower Maid, is abducted by Hades, Lord of the Underworld, to reign as His Queen for the next six months, until She returns at the Vernal Equinox. Those who are chosen to take the roles of Hades and Persephone for this rite become our Underworld Royalty for the Winter half of the year, holding court at Samhain, and offering counsel in matters dealing with personal Underworld issues.

Samhain (meaning "Summer's End") is the Celtic Feast of the Dead, when the veil between the worlds is thinnest, and departed spirits may return to commune with the living. Bonfires were lit and blazing straw from the fire was carried through the villages and over the fields. Traditionally celebrated on Oct. 31, Samhain (sow'-ahn) falls astrologically several days later, at 15° Scorpio. It is the opposite hinge of the year from Beltane, and is the Celtic New Year, marking the beginning of the Winter half of the year. Also called *Third Harvest* or *Winter's Beginning,* this festival has been thinly Christianized as *All Saints Day,* with the night before being called *All-Hallows, Hallowmas,* or *Hallowe'en;* long a favorite holiday for Pagans of all ages, and an occasion for masquerade, pumpkin-carving, and trick-or-treating. In

Mexico it is called *Dia de las Muertos,* the "Day of the Dead." In many lands, candles are lit in every room and food and drink put out for the souls. This is a time to honor our ancestors, remember our dead, and hail our descendants, and the most important element of Samhain Eve is the Rite of the Dumb Supper, a meal of "underworld" foods (mushrooms, nuts, black olives, pork, beans, chocolate, etc.) shared in total silence, wherein the spirits of the beloved dead are invited to join the feast and be remembered in honor and love.

At Annwfn, the King and Queen of the Underworld hold court, presiding over the Dumb Supper and the laying down of the May King's crown (an alternative to his ritual sacrifice!). One of our ritual dramas has the Red Maid seeking Her lost love, the Green Man, who descended into the Underworld at Mabon, and now reigns there as King. Scrying may be done at this time, with a crystal ball or concave black mirror. The Circle is considered to be held in the Underworld, and the energies move *widdershins* (counterclockwise).

Yule

Yule (meaning "Wheel" in Norse) is the Festival of *Winter Solstice,* around Dec. 21, and the longest night of the year. This is one of the most universally celebrated festivals, and in Northern countries, the most important, commemorating the birth of the infant Sun-God from the womb of Night. Yule is also known as the Festival of Lights, for all the candles burned this night. In ancient Rome it was called *Natalis Solis Invicti;* "The Birthday of the Unconquered Sun," and it took place during the longer festival of the *Saturnalia,* the greatest festival of the year, from which we get our New Year's image of old Father Time (Saturn) with his scythe. This was the first Pagan festival to be Christianized, in 354 CE, when the birthday of Jesus (originally in late September) was officially moved to the date of the Winter Solstice and called *Christmas.* The many customs associated with Yuletide (candles, decorated trees, Yule log, wreaths, pine bough decorations, gift-giving, wassail and caroling, costumed mummers' plays, mistletoe, "decking the halls with boughs of holly," etc.) are all Pagan, and provide a rich store of material for our contemporary celebrations. Yule is opposite to Litha, and while the emphasis now is on the Sun and Father Gods,

the Mother is still honored.

In Mendonesia, we try to acquire a Great Hall for Yule, preferably with a large fireplace. A ritual drama may enact the story of the first Yule, when the Sun went away and the children had to go and bring it back. Some of the characters in our Yule ritual may include the Wintery Queen, the Queen of Night, Father Winter, Father Time, Lucia (a maiden with a crown of candles), and, of course, the young Sun-God. We bring in the Yule Log amid singing and toasting; drink *athelbros* (traditional Scotts wasshail); exchange gifts; display the Wren; and share songs and stories around the fire, holding vigil until the dawn. We maintain that *somebody* has to stay up all night to make sure the Sun comes up in the morning...

Oimelc, Imbolc, Imbolg

Oimelc, Imbolc, Imbolg are variants of the name for the Cross-Quarter Sabbat traditionally celebrated on Feb. 2, but falling astrologically several days later, at 15° Aquarius. *Oimelc* (ee'-melk) means "ewe's milk" and *Imbolg* means "in the belly," referring to this as a festival of Pregnancy, Birth and Lactation. It is the celebration of the bursting of the locks of frost, and the bursting of waters as the sacred sets of Twins lower in the womb of the Earth Mother. The Celtic Festival of Waxing Light, it is also called *Brigantia,* and dedicated to Brigid, Irish Goddess of fire, the forge, inspiration, herbal healing, poetry and midwifery; customs of this festival include making a Brigit's Bed and Brigit Doll to sleep in it. Her festival marks the beginning of both the lambing and plowing season. Opposite the men's festival of Lughnasadh, Oimelc is celebrated with women's mysteries of birth and menstruation, and rites of passage into womanhood. It is a time of Dianic initiation, celebration of sisterhood, and woman-to-woman loving. Called *Lady Day* in some Craft traditions, Oimelc has been Christianized as *Candlemas* or *Candelaria,* and popularized as *Ground Hog's Day.*

At Annwfn, Brigit fires up the forge and leads us to each forge talismans in token of our pledges to complete some creative project during the year. The Goddesses reign, and two Priestesses may take the parts of the Red and Green Maids. At the Bardic around the campfire or in the Temple, we share poetry, songs and stories attributed to Her inspiration.

Seasonal Royalty in the CAW Tribe
The May Couple and the Underworld Regency

by Oberon Zell (from *CAW Membership Handbook,* 3rd Edition, 1997)

THERE ARE MANY different aspects to what we call "gods" and "goddesses." Some, such as Mother Nature and Father Time, are truly cosmic. Others, such as Mother Earth and Father Sun, are more finite, with material bodies to house their ethereal souls. Some, such as Pan, Eros, Yemaya, the Green Man, etc. are actually forces and powers of Nature. Still others, such as most of the familiar pantheons of Egypt, Greece, Ireland, Scandinavia, etc. are closely linked to the human community and embody aspects of human nature more than those of Nature Herself. There are deities that are totemic, such as Coyote, Eagle, Bear; these are the

collective souls of particular species. Then there are the humble Nymphs, Sprites, Fairies, Naiads, Dryads, Fauns and other spirits of place.

Each of these deities, at whatever level, may have *avatars*—living human representatives who carry Their energy and who manifest Their spirits *incarnate* ("in flesh") for however long they can hold it. In the Afro-Caribbean traditions, possession by the Loa or Orishas is carefully confined to the brief period of the all-night ritual. When we "call down the moon" and invoke the presence of the God or Goddess to attend our rites in the person of our Priest or Priestess, we always release Them at the end, when the Circle is opened. Being a vessel for divine energy is extremely hard on mortal flesh, especially, apparently, on males. Jim Morrison was a vessel for Dionysos, God of Intoxication, and Gwydion carried the energy of the Green

Man. Neither of them knew how to let go at the right time and they were both consumed to death by the Divine Fire.

The Church of All Worlds has evolved over the years a hierarchical structure similar to that of the British Empire: as they have Parliament to determine laws and political governance, we have our Board of Directors. As they have the Church of England to handle matters of religion and the Spirit, so we have our Priesthood Council. And as England has its Royalty, so do we have ours: the Queen and King of the May, and the King and Queen of the Underworld. The members of the Board are *elected* annually by vote of the membership. Priests and Priestesses are *ordained* for life after years of study and training. And the Sacred Royalty are *selected* each year by the Gods and the Tribe through participatory rituals.

Our Queen and King of the May are essentially avatars of the community, bringing together the epitome of the male and female energies and personalities of our tribe in a *heiros gamos*—sacred marriage—which is enacted on several levels in the Maypole ritual. Our Queen represents the Land itself as well as specifically being an avatar and stand-in for all the women in the tribe. Thus her reign continues throughout the year, progressing in stages through the full cycle of the immanent Goddess—Maiden, Mother and Crone. The King represents the People, bonded to the Land in love and service, and he is also an avatar and stand-in for all the men in the tribe. He is the Year-King, and his reign ends at Samhain, when he descends into the Underworld. But he may return to assume the Mantle of the Winter King and continue beside his Queen for the remaining months of the year.

Thus it is essential that the energies of *both* genders must be represented in our avatars. The two of them (with their Princes and Princesses) hold Court at the festivals of Litha, Lughnasadh and Mabon, whereat they may hear grievances and accept vows, dispense honors and awards to those they deem deserving, as well as grant favors, dub Knights, designate Bards and Champions, issue Letters of Marque, etc.

During the period of the May couple's reign, it is the privilege of the People to shower them with honors and hospitality. Every house They visit is blessed by Their presence, as is every lad or lass they love, every field they sow, and every meal they share. We treat them as we ourselves would wish to be treated, for "as fare these vessels, so fare we all."

In the late 1990s, reluctant to continue the practice of sacrificing (symbolically) our beloved King, and in deference to the love of his Lady, we introduced a new ritual of Transformation, of Death and Rebirth, whereby at Samhain we resurrect our May King as the Winter King (or "Rain King" in NorCalifia). He resumes the throne for the remainder of the year and he and his Queen continue to hold court together until the next Beltane.

Since we revived the ancient Mysteries of Eleusis in 1990, we have also come to embrace another royal couple: Hades and Persephone, the King and Queen of the Greek Underworld. Their co-regency begins with the Greater Eleusinian Mysteries at the Autumn Equinox, and continues through six cold months, until the Vernal Equinox, when Persephone returns to our world with the flowers of Spring, in the rite of the Lesser Eleusinia, or *Kore-thalia.* They hold Court at the festivals of Samhain and Ostara, and may do also at Yule and Oimelc (perhaps in conjunction with the Winter King and Queen), when, as with the May Royalty, they may hear grievances and accept vows, dispense honors and awards, grant favors, dub Knights, etc.

Another variation might follow the Welsh story of Pwyll and Arawn, in which the King of the Living and the King of the Dead change places for a season. This exchange might be enacted at Samhain, when the May King traditionally descends into the Underworld. (Starwhite has created a wonderful ritual for this.) Then the Lord of Annwfn would reign as Winter King beside the Queen of the May until the Spring, while the King of the Land resides with the Queen of the Underworld.

It is important to recognize that these offices carry no temporal authority. Our Sacred Royalty are not *above* us; they are *of* us. In a very real sense, they *are* us, just as the Earth is of us and we are of the Earth—that is the meaning of immanent divinity. Their royalty carries no right to issue orders, commands or decrees which must be obeyed. No one in our Tribe has that right—not Priest or Priestess, not members of the Board of Directors, not even our Founders.

There is mutual honor and duty inherent in these Royal offices, just as there is mutual honor and duty in the way the community relates to them. By honoring our Kings and Queens, we confer blessings upon ourselves and our homes. By blessing our homes and fields, they confer honor and good karma on themselves and the vessels who carry them. Various chosen couples who have carried the energies of King and Queen have added creatively to these evolving roles, and have received positive responses from the tribe.

When Heartspring was available to CAW members East of the Mississippi, we had two May Couples, the Eastern King and Queen and the Western King and Queen. We hope this practice resumes in the future as our Tribe grows.

May all who sit our Sacred Thrones bring great honor to the Gods and our Tribe!

Annwfn Maypole crown, 2012.

So You Want to Start a Nest?

by Morning Glory & Oberon Zell (from *CAW Member Handbook*, 3rd Ed. 1997) & Samm Dickens

The Church of All Worlds exists as a web of Nests and Proto-Nests; these groups are the basic congregation of CAW.

They are generally small and more intimate groups (as compared to a Branch which may be comprised of several Nests as well as unaffiliated members). CAW does not dictate the form or beliefs of a Nest; each Nest is essentially autonomous, setting their own rules, internal structure, goals, etc. They can be a closed coven or open grove, have a traditional focus or a more eclectic one, concentrate on Druidism, faery magick, ceremonial magick, or ecological activism, etc. While there are certain values and rituals such as water sharing that are common to CAW as a whole, there is no specific dogma that a Nest must follow.

Establishing a Proto-Nest. At least three active, registered CAW members meeting at least once a month are required to start a Proto-Nest. After a Proto-Nest has been in operation for a full year and has one Scion member (4th Circle or inward), it may be chartered as a full CAW Nest and be covered under our 501(c)3 non-profit status as a full congregation.

The first step in starting a Nest is to form a Proto-Nest. The requirements are (1) a **Name** for the Proto-Nest, (2) **contact information** for the Proto-Nest coordinator and (3) the **names and email addresses** of three paid members of CAW (inclusive of the coordinator) who wish to be part of the Proto-Nest. Also, (4) an application fee of $50.00 is required. This fee will be refunded if for any reason your application for a Proto-Nest is declined.

Granting of a Charter to a Proto-Nest is by application to and approval of the *Nest Coordinating Council*. A Proto-Nest will be on probation for one year and one day, at which point the Nest Coordinating Council will review the activities of the Proto-Nest and make the determination on the issuance of a Nest Charter. (The **Nest Coordinating Council** consists of

- the *CAW Nest Facilitator*, Samm Dickens
- the *Primate*, Oberon Zell {&/or any *Elder*}
- the *CAW Treasurer*, Mama Maureen and
- the *Membership Registrar*, Mama Maureen.

Diversity. The Church of All Worlds lives up to its name, evolving in diverse directions. What we offer here is a general program that works well in many different situations. The guidelines here are equally applicable to Branches or Nests.

Name your Nest. Come up with a clever name for your Nest. (*You may of course keep the name of your Proto-Nest if it has worn well.*) Consider doing a newsletter, blog or Facebook page that summarizes what happened at the last meeting and gives times, places and themes for the next few meetings.

Meetings. You might start out with getting together at new and/or full moons and expand from there. Meetings may be held in members' homes until your Nest grows too large—as long as you have reasonable privacy and freedom. We recommend rotating to avoid burnout and to give everyone a chance to host a Nesting. Hold some Circles outdoors, preferably in some remote place where no outsiders are likely to be about. A Pagan is truly a child of the natural world, and can commune better with the powerful Nature-forces when out in the open, even better in some place of wilderness. Work out your own programs for these meetings. As in *Stranger in a Strange Land,* we have found that nudity promotes openness and closeness though it is, of course, never required. ("*And as a sign that ye be truly free, ye shall be naked in your rites.*" *—Aradia, the Gospel of Witches*).

Refer to some of the books listed in the Bibliography (especially *Creating Circles & Ceremonies*) for specific rites. At each meeting, make it an order of business to decide when and where you will meet the next few times, and establish the themes of those meetings if you wish. Here are a few suggestions for themes, rituals and other activities for Nest meetings:

SOME IDEAS FOR NEST MEETINGS

Nest Activities	Rituals & Ceremonies	Other Activities
Movie/TV Nights	Seasonal Sabbats, Wheel of the Year	Dinners / Salons
Nest Nights Out (local pub?)	Breaking Bread, Sharing Water	Theme Parties
Classes/ Workshops	What a Friend We Have in Cheez-Its	Movie Parties
Work Parties	Skyclad Ritual (optional)	Concert Parties
Community Services	Firepit, Candle or Lantern Lights	Backyard Campouts
Lectures / Discussion Groups	Create an Altar (as you wish)	Camping Trips
Singing and Chanting	The Bond of Fire and Water	Excursions
Playing Music & Drumming	Spirit Work, Summonings	Presentations
Simple Rituals, Myth Enactments	Object Reading / Divination	Study Groups
Playing Sensitivity Games	Planning Future Nestings	Video Studies
Seasonal Games & Celebrations	Business, Tithing (Dues), Charities	Book Discussions
Beggar's Bowl	Craftwork, Artisanship	Special Guests
Healing Session, Reiki	Spellcrafting, Enchantments	Drum Circles
Storytelling, Poetry, Fairy Tales	Spirit Work, Releases, Closure	Bardic Circles

A model for an introductory meeting: People have been told what to expect, and have been asked to bring munchies or drinks. After everyone arrives, they are assembled into a circle. around a small altar. The Circle is cast *deosil* (clockwise), and the Elements and Deities are invoked.

On the alter are placed: Images of the God and Goddess, a potted plant, a mirror. To the West: a chambered nautilus or other spiral seashell; to the North: a crystal or fossil; to the East: a feather, a censor, or a bell; and to the South: a large red working candle. Also, a large chalice of water, and a bowl of Sunshine Cheez-Its. In the course of the evening, some of these altar objects may be passed around the circle, and people are encouraged to say a few appropriate words as they receive each.

Water sharing: After a few introductory remarks on the symbolic significance of water-sharing, the chalice is passed around clockwise with ritual phrases taken from *Stranger in a Strange Land,* such as "May you never thirst," "Water shared is Life shared." As the chalice passes from each person to the next, hands are joined. When it is returned to the host/ess, he/she then empties the final drops into the potted plant.

The chalice may then be refilled with wine, fruit juice, or more water, and passed around again, followed by Cheez-its. The most common phrases to accompany the passing of food are: "May you never hunger," or "May you always have sufficiency." Other snacks and drinks may also be shared at this time.

This simple ritual can be followed by many other forms of sharing. For an introductory gathering, pass the shell and as it comes to each person, they tell the tale of how they came to be here. At other times, the candle, crystal, feather, or other objects selected for their associations may be used, as people free-associate the thoughts that come to mind upon holding these objects.

The Sacred Bullshit Session: Eating together stimulates conversation and camaraderie. Business is discussed, plans are made for the next meeting, donations are collected, etc. Finally, the mirror is passed around, and each person looks into it, saying "Thou art God (or Goddess)" into their reflection. When it is time for the first people to leave, the circle is opened with a group hug. Ritual words of parting are said ("Merry meet and merry part, and merry meet again!"), and farewells are made.

Tailor your rituals to suit your own needs, bearing in mind that it is always the intent rather than the word which really counts. Put in your own ideas, and honor the Goddesses and Gods as you feel, deep within your heart, that they should be honored.

Naturally, one important aspect of your meetings will involve discussions of the philosophies of Paganism and the Church. CAW Central can provide you PDFs of CAW brochures you can print out. If you take on Nesting, people will expect you to know what it's all about! Add to your Pagan lore and make your own small enclave of Paganism a place of mystery and magic!

Themes. Plan special group activities, such as dinners, theme parties (our favorites are the Addams Family and Pirate Party), concerts, movie parties, campouts, excursions ("Magical Mystery Tours"), presentations, study groups, book discussions, videos, special guests, drum circles and bardics (in which everyone brings music, poetry, short stories, etc., and all take turns sharing in circle). So party on!

Grow by having members invite a sympathetic friend occasionally. The best way we've found to allow growth without interrupting the intimacy of the group, is to allow only one new person to be invited at a time. Then, after these new people have been to a couple of meetings they may wish to join CAW and your Nest. We encourage diversity and are absolutely non-discriminatory regarding race, gender, sexual orientation/practice, age, etc. At each meeting record names and contact info of all those who attend. When you have a couple dozen names, distribute the list to everyone, including CAW Central.

As your group expands, you may start widening your range of activities. You might set up workshops and seminars, promote and sponsor public events such as Pagan Pride days, run a recycling center, throw great feasts and festivals, publish a newsletter or magazine, promote and sponsor conservation and reforestation projects, start a wilderness sanctuary or retreat center, open a coffeehouse, put on benefits for appropriate causes, and countless other projects, limited only by the scope of your imagination, interests, talents and time.

If after reading this you're still interested in setting up a Nest in your area, go to https://caw.org/nests/ for a Nest Application form. We will list your Nest or Proto-Nest in *Green Egg* and our CAW Facebook pages. If you have problems or questions e-mail our Nest Facilitator, Samm Dickens, nesting@caw.org.

Prayer/Blessing of Water

By Kari Eckholt, adapted by Oberon Zell
(To all participants; holding up Chalice)

Contemplate now the waters running thru your veins, and the Earth, contemplate that the salinity of the blood plasma of our bodies, the salinity of the cerebral-spinal fluid bathing our nervous systems, and the salinity of our great mother oceans is nearly identical.

Listen to our message of love in the water, for we remember we are everywhere.

This chalice of pure water is the lifeblood of our Mother Earth and our very selves.

Every living being of the plant and animal kindoms are anywhere from 70% to 90% water.

We flow in the blood of every living creature, remember walking, burrowing, crawling, soaring.

We remember we have flowed in every living creature before them.

We have flowed in the blood of all our human ancestors, and we carry their memories. We remember.

We remember that our water will one day flow in the bodies of our children, our grandchildren.

We remember to honor every drop of the living water, for it is Who We Are.

In this moment, we remember we are ONE with all the waters of the universe, always connected to all.

Each droplet of our water has traveled over, under, and thru our world and our universe endlessly, as part of an ever-changing journey.

We remember we have been in the dirty snowballs called comets, and in oceans and seas, in rivers, lakes and streams.

We remember we live in the great glaciers, and the snow on the mountain tops.

We remember we have been to the bottom of the deepest ocean.

We remember we have risen as steam, evaporated into clouds, fallen as rain, snow, sleet, hail.

And we call upon the healing Waters to descend now upon the parched and burning lands, to douse the flames and quench the fires. May the rains come down! (Sprinkle a little water on the candle to extinguish it.)

And so we mingle the water carried in our current physical vessel with the water of life in our chalice. We drink of the waters of the Earth.

Water shared is Life shared. May you never thirst; Thou art God; Thou art Goddess!

(Drink deep. The ritual is complete.)

Conflict Resolution in CAW

By Brahn th' Blessed (Samm Dickens) *(August 28th, 2022)*

CONFLICT IS NOT MISCONDUCT; IT is beneficial to highlight this point at the start of this article. Conflict is only an aggravated disagreement among people, maybe even close friends who are not normally expected to display such hostility. Misconduct, on the other hand, typically involves inappropriate and possibly even criminal behaviour. The Church of All Worlds has a policy paper available regarding misconduct, entitled "**CAW Code of Behaviour.**" It recommends six positive steps toward exhibiting acceptable behaviour.

(1) Be Excellent to Each Other!
(2) Be Excellent to Yourself!
(3) Honor Diversity!
(4) Take Personal Responsibility!
(5) Consider the Consequences!
(6) Walk Your Talk!

The **Code of Behaviour** then delineates a longer and more detailed list of offensive actions and misbehaviours which *will not be tolerated by CAW*. These include:

Bullying and **harassment**, such as:
- Shaming
- Intimidation
- Physical or verbal threats of any kind
- Coercion of any person in any way (*this can be subtle at times and includes flattery and seduction, but the results are equally devastating*)
- Racial, religious, gender-based, sexual preference-based, ethnic, or any other kinds of slurs
- Brandishing a firearm or knife (*or any instrument that could be considered as a weapon*), or threatening anyone with bodily harm at CAW events
- Defacing, damaging or destroying property
- Fighting, or in any other way creating a disturbance which is disruptive or dangerous to others

Harassment includes, but is not limited to: Persistent verbal comments that reinforce social structures of domination [*related to gender, gender identity and expression, sexual orientation, disability, physical appearance, body size, race, age, or religion*].
- Deliberate intimidation, stalking, or following
- Harassing photography or recordings
- Sustained disruption of talks or other events
- Advocating for, or encouraging, any of the above behavior.

Sexual Misconduct includes, but is not limited to:
- Inappropriate physical contact
- Unwelcome sexual attention
- Intimidating with size or gender
- Stalking/following
- Constant "jokes" or innuendo
- Acting on the assumption of continuing consent (*just because there was consent once does not mean there is still consent*)
- Consistent pattern of Oversharing
- Taking pictures/recordings without consent (*especially if they could be used to shame/embarrass someone*)
- Manipulating/coercing to get sexual favors
- Any consistent pattern of harassment where one is made to feel physically unsafe because of the threat (stated or implied) of sexual violence.
- Advocating for, or encouraging, any of the above behaviors.

Finally, the CAW has a "Misconduct Committee to investigate and make recommendations to the CAW Board of Directors (BoD) regarding any individuals causing harm within the CAW community or Church. Such harm includes, but is not limited to: sexual misconduct, harassment, bullying, coercion, severe breaches of ethics, or any behavior that impactfully inhibits the safety and health of the Church of All Worlds, its community and the people in it."

If a conflict involves an accusation of wrong-doing, either misbehavior as described above or even a criminal act, the procedures of the **CAW Code of Behavior** shall take precedent AND a law enforcement agency shall be notified as necessary. If a conflict involves no actual wrong-doing, if it is only a disagreement, however hostile the proponents of opposing views have become, it can be resolved by communication, compromise, and compassion.

The Power of Ideas. Passion is welcomed in the CAW as it indicates a (sometimes fierce) conviction to an idea—a cause or a dream, a theory or a purpose, a personal goal or a group project. But passion can be misdirected; however certain we are in our conviction about some idea we cherish, that certainty does not necessarily correspond to infallible truth, and we are ill-served by passionate conviction to an unworthy idea. Nonetheless, we are seldom forced to recognize such errors; often we just lose our enthusiasm over time with our inability to share our passion with others. Consequently, we do not often confront our misjudgments, and do not realize fully how imperfect our human minds can be in committing to the various ideas that direct our lives. If we understood how often our actions are motivated by bad ideas, we might more humbly appreciate the dreamers who achieve their goals, and we might more carefully examine the ideas we hold dear before we commit to them.

Most interpersonal conflict is a conflict between conflicting ideas, so it is necessary that I discuss what I mean by "ideas." Our minds are loaded with hundreds of ideas of various kinds and powers. By *kind of idea* I mean that we may conceive an idea to be a thought, a concept, a notion or opinion, a word in any language, an article of faith, a theory or hypothesis, a simple conjecture, a supposition or assumption, a known fact, a deeply held religious conviction, a political viewpoint, propaganda, or any other fundamental or aggregate mental construct, however chronic or acute; kinds of ideas are myriad and general. They may be true or false, valid or invalid, positive or negative, all in varying degrees.

And ideas may be weak or mild, moderate and influential, or powerful and dominating. Martin Luther King's Dream was a very powerful idea of justice and equality in his life and in the lives of millions of other people, so powerful that it drove them to courageous and dangerous actions and sacrifice of their personal safety and security, even of their lives. At the bottom extreme, I have this notion: that my example of Dr. King and the civil rights movement was an effective example to illustrate the power of ideas. This notion is weak and insubstantial as ideas go; it may be accurate or not, it is a passing concern, but it illustrates the thousands of small ideas that contribute to larger ideas.

What you want for lunch is a small idea. *How you feel about a local political event* is a moderate idea. *Christianity, Islam, Hinduism, and all other such religious traditions* are massively powerful collections of ideas, although each of them is a single, massively aggregate idea as well. So I hope you get the idea about what all an idea can be and how powerfully motivational an influence it can exert in our lives. We all severely, and often disastrously, underestimate the influence of ideas in directing the course of human activity and history, and our personal lives and destinies.

The Heart is Master of Us All. I know one more very important thing about the ideas we have. I know that we don't get to believe just any ideas. There's a guardian at the gate of our minds. We have innate propensities to believe some ideas, and innate propensities to reject others. I'm a Pagan now, but I was a Christian as a child, raised by Christian family in a Christian world. Through all my teenage years, I was a Christian, but I encountered Pagan things in books and in nature. These encounters presented Pagan ideas that were easy for me to accept; my heart had ample room for Pagan ideas. At the same time, the ideas I read in my Bible did not all ring so true, did not all resonate with my inner self; I began internally to reject Christianity, piecemeal at first but in whole by the time I was a nineteen year old in the Air Force. After my service years, I never returned to the church. My heart—Don Juan Matus calls it my "innermost predilection"—lured me away from the Christian church and onto the Pagan path that I have followed ever since.

It is impossible to believe in an idea that your heart rejects or to reject an idea that your heart believes; no-one can make you believe an idea that your heart rejects, no-one can make you reject an idea that your heart cherishes. You can't do it, no-one else however ruthless can do it. The mind is not free to believe only for convenience, or to believe anything in the absence of sincere attachment; to try would only be pretense and folly.

Therefore when two ideas conflict, the two parties who hold those ideas also conflict, or at least tend to disagree. If the ideas are powerful, the conviction of the adherents will be passionate, the conflict will be heated, perhaps hostile. If one or more of the parties has an innately aggressive personality, the conflict can be greatly enhanced because conflict is not only engendered by ideas but by personalities as well.

Conflict Resolution in CAW

Step One: Talk it Out Between You. In the Church of All Worlds we encourage people in conflict to understand each other better and thereby reduce the conflict and hostility. For some of us, reducing hostility and resolving conflict comes easily, while for others of us it is an arduous process that leaves a bitter taste. CAW recommends that conflicting parties, as a first step, *try to resolve the conflict among themselves*, using the basic principles of conflict resolution:

(1) **two-way communication** (*speak your truth and listen intently*),
(2) **respect for the other persons** or the other party (compassion),
(3) **acceptance** of *the rights of other people to hold ideas contrary to your own*, and
(4) a **willingness to compromise** where possible and *seek a point of consensus* between all parties concerned.

Step Two: Advocacy. If the conflict between the two parties is too severe and they are unable to come to terms, they should carry the resolution effort to the second step and each acquire an **advocate** who has no vested interest in the issue of contention and allow those advocates to seek a resolution to the conflict. Bear in mind that a conflict is NOT resolved if acrimony continues between the parties in conflict, even if the conflicting ideas are brought by compromise to a consensus synthesis. It is better that the parties achieve an end to hostilities and leave the conflicting ideas unresolved; that is, if they "agree to disagree."

Step Three: Arbitration. As a final (third) step in resolving the conflict, when the advocates are unable to help the adversaries to resolve all the anger, disrespect, and hostility between them, the adversarial parties and/or their advocates may select a neutral **arbiter** to make a judgment on those issues that obstruct resolution of the conflict and restoration of amicable relations between the parties. The advocates must present to the arbiter each and every issue that seems to prevent a full resolution; then the advocates must argue the point of view of the parties they represent (the parties may also testify as witnesses under the direction of their advocates); and finally, the arbiter, having heard all arguments regarding outstanding issues, shall take up to one week to produce an *arbitration decision* on each issue (each *article of arbitration*) presented.

Each party in the conflict must either consent or object to each article of arbitration in the decision, by initial/signature on the arbitration document. Consent is not agreement; it is only acceptance of the arbitration. Objection is refusal to accept the arbitration. The arbiter must then decide if further discussion of any objectionable articles is warranted in order to achieve full consensus and resolution of the conflict. The arbitration procedure is repeated for any and all objected articles.

If *all issues in the dispute are resolved* to the point of mutual consent and if both parties exhibit an end to hostilities and a restoration of amicability and mutual respect, the conflict is considered to be **resolved**. If a number of issues, but less than a third of those presented to the arbiter, remain unresolved, the conflict may be considered **partially resolved**, as long as both parties are cordially agreeable to it. Else, the conflict is considered **unresolved** and outstanding.

If one or both parties are unable to overcome their hostilities even with arbitration, they may be **suspended from CAW** until they can show reasonable proof that they have put their negative feelings behind them; that decision would lie with the Board of Directors or with anyone they may appoint to direct conflict resolution for the church.

Conclusion and Summary. It is okay to get mad at a friend, to be mad at a friend, but not to stay mad at a friend. If you are angry with someone in the church, talk out your issues, speak your truth with calm sincerity. Passion for a cause is fine, but intemperance is not helpful. You cannot command respect when you are not showing respect, so listen intently to the truth spoken by your adversary; don't judge them, understand them. If you suppose that your adversary is wrong, then it must be clear that you may be wrong just as easily and may blindly believe you are right. Certainty after all is only an emotion. Your prolonged anger is wrong; subdue your anger and then cleanse it from your heart, for it is only a friction and an obstruction.

Sit with your adversary face to face, tear down any emotional walls you feel between you and build a bridge from your heart to theirs (*this meditation will help you communicate effectively*). Do not fear conflict; it is your ally. If you understand conflict, why it happens and how it can be domesticated for the mutual benefit of everyone, you can resolve conflict and grok yourself and your friends more deeply at the same time. This is the way of wisdom.

Suggestions for Conflict Resolution in CAW

by Anodea Judith and Oberon Zell

PERIODIC CONFLICT BETWEEN MEMbers of groups or organizations is unfortunately an inevitable risk of people working together in the creation of something new. These conflicts can undermine the success of all that you may wish to accomplish. Conflict can be poisonous. or it can be transformed into medicine.

In the Church of All Worlds, we do not necessarily advocate avoiding conflict at all costs, remaining forever in the safe zones of expected behavior, but instead try to see conflict as fruitful material for one's growth. This growth occurs through resolution of the conflict, as it forces change. It is important that attempts at resolution occur in as timely and respectful a way as possible.

The following guidelines are a distillation of various processes used by the CAW community to resolve conflict. We offer them as resources to fall back upon when conflict arises.

1. Avoid pouring gas on the flames.

Conflicts are emotionally charged issues. When we are involved in them, it is very tempting to discharge this energy by talking to others. Often this takes the form of malicious gossip, exageration of issues. and triangulated conversation. (Triangulation is talking to a third party about someone who isn't there.) Containment provides the hermetic seal that allows alchemical transformation. It requires discipline.

2. Write down your issues.

If you feel you are not ready to talk to the person with whom you have trouble, you can dissipate some of the charged energy by writing a fictious letter about how you feel. This letter would not be mailed or delivered but exists for you to validate your own feelings, get your thoughts in order, and discharge pent-up energy in a way that doesn't cause further harm.

In this private work-through of feelings, examine the patterns that may have existed elsewhere in your life. What part did you play in creating this conflict? Does this happen in other relationships? What are the particular triggers that are hardest for you to deal with? What is it about those triggers that has the most potential for your own growth? Learn to separate "what happened" from your *interpretation* of what happened. For example, what happened was that no one called you to inform you about the meeting. Your interpretation might be that "people are deliberately excluding me." Interpretations are the foundation of difficult feelings and may be wrong. Look for several different interpretations before drawing conclusions about someone else's behavior.

3. Attempt to talk to the person in question.

While this may seem utterly obvious. it happens all too seldom. Don't assume the person can't hear your objections until you have done the previous step and then attempted to communicate. You may be surprised. If the attempt fails, pay careful attention to where the communication breaks down. Things to try when communicating are:

A. Active listening. When the other person is speaking, listen closely, without judgment, and then repeat back to them what you think they said, whether or not you agree, whether or not it seems fair, accurate, or justified. This might take the form of "It sounds like you feel unappreciated and misunderstood." No editorializing!

Then ask the person to do the same for you. After you are both clear that what you have to say has been heard by the other person, then you can begin to talk about the differences in your viewpoints—still using the principle of active listening. "'So it sounds like you disagree with my statement that I do most of the housework and feel underappreciated when I say that."

Many problems result from misunderstandings, communication snafus, differing expectations, and over-commitments which can usually be resolved by clarifying things.

B. Use "I" statements and avoid "you" statements. "I" statements begin with the pronoun I; "you" statements with you. An "I" statement says, "I feel very misunderstood." A "You" statement says, "You never listen to anything I say." We can argue with accusations made of us, but we can't argue with how a person feels. "I" statements produce less resistance and antagonism.

C. Take a win-win approach. Try to avoid polarization of either/or, win/lose dynamics. Take the idea that a solution exists that will please both parties, and that otherwise, anyone's categorical win is by nature another's loss. Avoid having to be "right."

If attempts to communicate one on one are unsuccessful:

4. Restate the issues that need to be addressed, in writing.

5. Call for a mediation.

We have devised several approaches towards resolving disputes. What follows is a Procedure for interpersonal Conflict Resolution, approved by the CAW Board of Directors, deriving from Celtic. African, and Native American tribal custom and the authors' personal experience in mediation and counseling. It is most useful in dealing with disputes between individuals:

Interpersonal Conflict Resolution Procedure

I. Conditions.

A. **Agreement to Conflict Resolution Procedure.** *Membership in the Church of All Worlds implies an agreement to submit to a sanctioned procedure for Conflict Resolution.* Refusal to participate in a Conflict Resolution Procedure, and especially, refusal to attend a Conflict Hearing in which one is charged of wrongdoing, could be considered grounds for revocation of membership and/or privileges of membership in the Church.

B. **Parties.**
1. **Plaintiff** is the party making a complaint, charges or accusations of wrongdoing. Most commonly the Plaintiff is the one who will initiate a call for a Conflict Resolution Procedure.
2. **Accused** is the party charged with wrongdoing. Sometimes an Accused will seek to avoid a Conflict Resolution Procedure, particularly if the dispute is a serious manner, with serious charges. In other cases, one who feels unjustly accused may be eager for a Hearing, and may, in such a case, even be the one to initiate the Procedure.

II. Mediators, Advocates, Tribunal & Elders' Council.

A. **Mediator.** If both parties are able to talk with each other then they select a mutually-agreeable and willing Mediator to help them resolve the dispute. The Mediator makes arrangements with both parties for an acceptable time and place to hold a Hearing, as well as appropriate compensation for their time and trouble. The Mediator makes sure that both parties have a copy of this Procedure and agree to follow it.

B. **Advocates & Tribunal.** If the parties are not speaking to each other, then each party selects a willing Advocate, usually beginning with the Plaintiff, whose Advocate must then contact the Accused to select a Defense Advocate. The Advocates then select a mutually-agreeable and willing Mediator, thus creating a Tribunal. The Tribunal arranges with both parties for an acceptable time and place to hold a Hearing. as well as appropriate compensation for their lime and trouble.

C. **Elders' Council.** The disputing parties and/or their selected Mediator(s) may decide and agree to bring the matter before an Elders' Council. Such a Council may be composed only of Elders in the CAW, or it may comprise Elders in the wider Pagan community, such as the Grey Council, depending on the scale of relevance of the dispute. The Council makes arrangements with both parties for an acceptable time and place to hold a Hearing. as well as appropriate compensation for their time and trouble. It may be that the party initiating the Conflict Resolution Procedure will appeal directly to the Elders' Council. or a dispute may be referred to the Elders' Council by some other body of the Church, such as the Clergy Council, the Board of Directors, or a Nest Council. In such cases the Elders' Council must see to it that both parties have acceptable Advocates and a Mediator, or that either or both parties agree to waive Advocacy and/or Mediation.

III. The Hearing.

A. The Hearing may be open or closed, at the discretion of either of the disputing parties.

1. **A Closed Hearing** shall consist only of the disputing Parties, their Advocates, their Mediator (or Elders Council), and such Witnesses as either party wishes to bring forward. If either party wishes to present witnesses, this must be made known to the other party prior to the hearing. and with enough advance notice so that the other party may also present witnesses. If the parties are not on speaking terms, this communication shall be made by way of their Advocates.

2. **Open Hearing.** In addition to the above, either or both parties may invite other members of the community to attend and witness the proceedings, either by specific invitation, or by public announcement. If one of the parties intends to open the proceedings, the other party must be so informed prior to the Hearing. If the parties are not on speaking terms, this communication shall be made by way of their Advocates.

B. **The Mediator** (or Elder's Council) seeks a resolution based on **Truth** and **Justice.** The function of the Mediator is to balance the issues with as much fairness and objectivity as is humanly possible. It is important that the Mediator avoid judgments, condemnation, heady analysis, or biased support.

C. **Procedure.** The Mediator asks each party in turn: *"Let's hear your story."*

1. The first statement must be made by the one initiating the Procedure (for convenience here assumed to be the Plaintiff), who shall explain their case, charges and accusations as succinctly as possible. The Mediator must make sure that these three questions are addressed: *"What happened? Why did that happen? What happened as a result of that action?"* Upon conclusion of the Plaintiff's statement, the Accused's Advocate and/or the Media l or may ask questions for clarification.

2. The second statement must be made by the Accused, who shall explain their case as succinctly as possible. The Mediator must make sure that the same three questions are addressed: *"What happened? Why did that happen? What happened as a result of that action?"* Upon

conclusion of the Accused's statement, the Plaintiff's Advocate and/or the Mediator may ask questions for clarification.

3. Witnesses for the Plaintiff, if any, may then be brought forward by the Plaintiff's Advocate, and shall present their accounts. They may then be cross-examined by the Advocate for the Accused and/or the Mediator.

4. Witnesses for the Accused. if any, may then be brought forward by the Accused's Advocate. and shall present their accounts. They may then be cross-examined by the Advocate for the Plaintiff and/or the Mediator.

5. Addressing each in turn, beginning with the Plaintiff, the Mediator asks: *"What would you need to redress the grievances you have? What would you be willing to give in order to redress the grievances you caused? How do you feel Justice would be served here? What do you think would be fair?"*

The Mediator must listen attentively to all sides and then make suggestions and offer assistance towards redressing the issue in a way that takes the needs and offerings of both sides into account. It is most important that both panics feel that Justice has been served. There may be situations, however, in which Compassion may be a higher value than Justice... In any case, an agreement must be reached, even if it is an agreement to disagree, or to part company.

a. Moving from an individual assessment to a systemic viewpoint can take the pressure off individuals and decrease polarization. In other words, seeing the conflict arising out of a greater field of oppression, be it the dysfunctions of the whole group, the pressures acting upon the people in question at the time, or even the influence of the larger society, helps to diffuse the blaming and shaming that interferes with being receptive to difficult communication.

b. Sometimes a simple apology is sufficient to elicit forgiveness and healing. Since conflicts are seldom black-and-white, a mutual apology is ideal. A meaningful apology requires five steps:

i. **Acknowledgement** that a mistake was made and/or harm was done.

ii. **Repudiation** of the error or harm.

iii. **Apology.** (Forgiveness often follows.)

iv. **Commitment** to change ways or repair damage.

v. **Restitution:** "How can I make it up to you?"

c. If the Accused refuses to acknowledge wrongdoing and apologize for it, the Plaintiff may choose, for their own healing, to forgive the Accused anyway.

6. When an agreement has been reached, it shall be written up by the Mediator or a designated Recorder, and presented to both parties to sign and elate. If the agreement includes restitution, or actions to be taken in the future, these shall be so noted.

7. If the parties in dispute cannot be brought to an agreement, then the Mediator and the Advocates shall consult among themselves to reach an agreeable resolution. If such a resolution cannot be reached among the Tribunal. then the matter shall be referred to an Elders' Council for a resolution or judgment decision.

IV. Enforcement.

A. If one or both of the parties fails afterwards to abide by the agreement reached through this Procedure, the case shall be referred back to the original Mediator, who shall then turn to the local Nest Council, Elders' Council, Clergy Council, or Board of Directors (depending upon the Mediator's sense of which body should be addressing the issue). The appropriate governing body must then make a judgment decision.

B. Penalties for failure or refusal to abide by an agreement reached through mediation may range through the following degrees:

1. Banishment for a designated period from Church facilities or events.

2. Suspension of Church privileges for a designaled period.

3. Revoking of Church membership.

4. A legal restraining order placed against the offending party.

5. Other legal recourse (i.e. a lawsuit).

The CAW RINGS Cycle: Overview

NOW THAT YOU HAVE BECOME A member of the Church of All Worlds, you may be wondering what to do next. In truth, you don't have to do anything, but enjoy camaraderie with your new community, and pay your yearly dues. We are happy to be of service to you and to welcome you to our community.

Many people who join the Church are looking for a little more than that, however. They are seeking a way to expand their personal and spiritual growth, as well as a way to serve the community and to help CAW expand or maintain its services. Others feel a call to serve more deeply, as Teachers, Guides or members of the Clergy, and look to us for training and guidance along those lines.

The RING System is a fluid system created to answer these needs. It is a framework designed to create an interwoven network within the CAW community that supports both the individual and the Tribe, as well as contributing to the overall purposes of the Church, as stated in our mission statement.

The concept of life as an interconnected living web is the basis for our internal structure within the church. The RING web is an interconnected, egalitarian support network, utilizing our strengths and addressing our weaknesses. The term RING refers to rings in the labyrinth of the Divine, the Dearinth, a unique symbol of CAW which incorporates both the Goddess & the God, as well as the path of the Initiate. It is a system of nine concentric interconnected Circles, ever inward, towards the consciousness of the Goddess/God within. **RING** also stands for **R**equirements **I**nvoking **N**etwork **G**rowth.

The purpose of the RING System, like the Goddess we serve, is threefold:
1) to encourage personal growth,
2) to strengthen and deepen the individual's connection to and participation in the CAW Tribe,
3) to support the individual's ability to contribute positively and materially to the mission of CAW; i.e., to help equip the individual to contribute to our missions of responsible earth stewardship and a changing consciousness in the world psyche.

In following the labyrinth of the RING System inward, it is important to keep these three holistic goals in mind. It is important to remember that while the RING System _is_ a self-actualization program, it is not merely a program of personal growth. It is also designed to create community and to support CAW both as a Tribe and as an organization with a Mission.

The Church of All Worlds has evolved this network system to avoid the idea of climbing on a ladder of success to a hierarchical top, wherein one seeks power over others. As systems of hierarchy are the dominant paradigm in our society, it requires a radical change of thinking to set a net instead of a ladder, where each connection is equally vital to the whole. Together we make a flexible structure capable of holding things gently yet providing support.

Our community is tribal rather than hierarchical. An individual's evolution along this path requires a development of power _within_ and a dedication to service. While training and increased knowledge should naturally include growth and greater mastery of the chosen skill sets (in "guild" terminology, one might liken Seekers to Apprentices, Scions to Journeymen and Beacons to Masters in their chosen skill areas), we look to our Scions and Beacons as resources and guides, as advisors and teachers, not as models of "authority." We are prone to say that they are authori_tative,_ not authori_tarian._ Those who find their way to become Beacons will have more of a commitment to the community than the free agent who has just joined and they will carry commensurately more responsibility, but if they are expecting power and prestige, they will be sorely disappointed!

It is extremely difficult to set up a structure that is solid enough to hold us together and flexible enough to allow for the high level of individuality that we cherish in our members. There are those who resist any structure at all, yet others complain bitterly if things do not run smoothly. There are still others who want more structure, needing someone to give them very specific guidance. We are not gurus, and would rather foster someone's inner guidance than tell them what to do.

For this reason, we have tried to address

issues on many different levels. Some suggestions, such as books to read or tasks to accomplish, are relatively easy to achieve. Other levels, such as an individual's spiritual growth, creative abilities, and readiness to lead others, are much more subjective. While they may be harder to assess, we attempt to do so anyway; most often through the community's voice, but also through advisors and sponsors that connect with the individual along their pathway.

CAW also believes strongly in balanced self-actualization (as Heinlein said, "Specialization is for insects"). the RING System also balances requirements holistically and uses associations with the five Elements (Earth, Air, Fire, Water and Spirit) to emphasize this balance.

All members seeking to progress through the RINGS are encouraged to join the Mentoring Council and get to know their fellow journeymen and women, providing support and feedback for others and asking it for themselves. It is not just a matter of fulfilling tasks, but of growing closer and creating community. The Mentoring Council also puts in place a peer review and approval system that addresses challenges such as geographical isolation and an absence of sufficient Scions and Beacons to thoroughly oversee progression.

The emphasis is on the spirit of the RINGS, and flexibility is allowed in most criteria. If the seeker can show, to Lifeways as the supervisory body and to the Mentoring Council as the peer support network, that they have understood the purpose of the requirements and taken steps to fulfill them, it will usually be considered adequate.

When a member wishes to apply to move into the next Circle they should seek recommendation from the Mentoring Council to Lifeways. If someone leaves CAW or is directed to step down from their position, their return should be re-negotiated with Lifeways; i.e. if someone reaches Scion or Beacon status and resigns, they should have to re-connect with the community before resuming such a place

(Suggestion: The RINGS can seem overwhelming when taken all in one hit. Get a general overview, by all means, but also take it one step at a time. Which ring fits now? What is needed to move to the next one?)

FIRST RING – SEEKERS PURPOSE: GROWTH

The first ring section of the net is made up of those who are newest to us The purpose of this ring is to meet the Church of All Worlds with an open and inquiring mind; to find out if it is a Tribe that might suit you or that can help you in any way along your own individual path. We would like seekers to get to know us before becoming more involved. This means making personal contact with CAW members, attending events, reading CAW literature, subscribing to related magazines, learning about our history, sociology, and the practice of our religion.

Seekers are encouraged to pursue their own spiritual growth and to be well-informed before determining if the Church of All Worlds is for them. We want to make sure that you know what you are getting involved with, and that this is the right path for you.

Because of its emphasis upon new growth, this Ring is associated with the color green.

1st Circle (Kuiper Belt) Contact

The purpose of First Circle is to establish personal contact. Anyone who has been to any of our events, or attends any of our classes, is automatically in First Circle. Just as our Solar System is surrounded by the Kuiper Belt, with its many comets and planetoids of all sizes (including Pluto), this is our larger world community, of which only a portion are actual signed-up members of CAW, or "Waterkin."

2nd Circle (Neptune) Getting to Know Us

The purpose of Second Circle is getting to know us. It is made up of those individuals who have decided to join the Church of All Worlds. We would like these people to familiarize themselves further with the Church and to extend their connections to other members by attending events, working with their local Nest, and reading related literature. To demonstrate that they understand what we're all about, we ask them to write an essay or to create a presentation or composition on their impression of the Church of All Worlds and how they see themselves fitting in.

3rd Circle (Uranus) Growing

The focus in Third Circle is attending to your own personal growth and development while also growing closer to other CAW members. In this Circle you will be asked to read books, begin a spiritual practice, and begin learning manifestation skills and effective communication. You will also be asked to take a self-inventory to determine what steps are necessary for your holistic personal growth. This may entail things like entering therapy or taking classes.

As the actualization of human potential is an important goal for the Church of All Worlds, this Circle addresses the development of self as a later tool for service and social change. We do not want sheep, but people who understand their own strengths and purposes in the greater scheme of things.

A NOTE ABOUT WATER SHARING

To transition to 4th Circle, and from that point inward, Water Sharing becomes one of the requirements for movement. In harmony with the process of grokking, sharing the water that is essential to all life is the primary Sacrament of the Church of All Worlds. The intention of the Water Sharing ritual is to affirm bonds of kinship. Depending on the intimacy of the Circle, four levels of this bond are common:

1. Affirming our connection to each other and to all life;
2. Affirming belonging to a Tribe or tradition;
3. Affirming friendship;
4. A lifelong Commitment of deep communion, friendship, love, and compassion, which may or may not have an erotic component. (This is what we define as the deepest level – what we mean when we say "Waterkin," "Water-Siblings" or "Water Brothers.")

This Sacrament affirms our connection to each other strengthens the bonds of our Tribe and is important to the second goal of the RINGS program – "to strengthen & deepen the individual's connection to and participation in the CAW Tribe." As such, it is an integral part of the RINGS. To achieve this goal individuals progressing through the RINGS are expected to share water with more individuals and at deeper levels at each transition.

By the time an individual enters 3rd Circle, it is assumed that they will have shared water with members at the 1st and 2nd levels at festivals, nest meetings and other CAW events. To transition to the 2nd RING, the member is asked to begin sharing water at deeper levels and it is hoped that you will have at least one friend within CAW with whom you are intimate enough to share water at the deepest level, to become actual "water-siblings" with them. Likewise, it is expected that someone transitioning to the 3rd ring will have traveled, met many of our Tribe and have several individuals who are close enough to share water with at this level.

Since this requirement is such an integral part to connecting with our tribe, Water Sharing requirements are not as flexible as self actualization requirements.

SECOND RING – SCIONS PURPOSE: SERVICE

A Scion is a new shoot or living branch grafted onto another plant, or an extension on a family tree. Scions are the inheritors of their lineage, and are here accorded the color red to symbolize fertility. To become a Scion in the Church of All Worlds is to not only be a part of it, but also be committed to its further growth and expansion. Up until this point, membership in CAW may have been solely an exercise in your personal journey; but moving into the 2nd Ring indicates that your journey is now part of CAWs. Your purpose here is service and the Scion is expected to take an active role in CAW as a whole.

Scions are people who have been involved long enough to want to help run things, or create new aspects within the Church, such as a new Nest or a newsletter. It is not required that one enter this level, and it is better to remain in the First Ring than take this responsibility falsely, for others will count on you to carry through.

Before entering the Second Ring, you must contact the Scion Council, or speak to another person who has already transitioned inward through the Second Ring (an active Scion or Beacon) and request that they serve as your Scion Advisor. Initially you will simply have an informal chat with this person to discussion your desire to serve the Church as a Scion, but if you both agree that this is the appropriate path for you, this person will become your primary mentor and work closely with you, the Mentoring Council and the Scion Council to assist in your movement inward. Your Scion Advisor can help you navigate through your transition, as well as helping you to stay on track once you are in the 2nd Ring; s/he can help you connect with ways to serve and be served by the rest of the Net.

Once your decision to make this commitment is firm, we ask for references from members of your Nest (if you have one, or members of the Pagan community who know you if you do not), a Beacon and/or Clergy member and an essay (or presentation/composition) on comparative religion, to demonstrate your breadth of understanding, which compares your religion of origin, Paganism and another religion you have studied.

Scionhood and other progressions should, in principle, be conferred by the general membership of CAW. The Scion Advisor who has walked the journey with the applicant should ascertain if this support is available and, if so, recommend them for approval. This approval must be attained before any initiation/ordination ritual can take place.

4th Circle (Saturn) Serving

After your scion initiation you are expected to serve the community. This may involve mundane clerical or administrative duties, rudimentary tasks at gatherings, assisting in nest activities, leading rituals, offering classes, or donating time in your particular area of expertise.

TRACKS of Service

Recognizing that service can be conducted in many areas, depending upon interest, aptitude and the needs of the community, CAW includes specialized "tracks" of service and from the Fourth Circle inward makes specific recommendations for individuals interested in embarking upon specific tracks. As members enter the Second Ring, they may choose to focus upon an aspect that is most appealing to them.

One need not be restricted to just one track, and it is expected that most individuals will have interests in multiple tracks, but like a major and minor in college, people may choose to focus their service primarily in one or two tracks. It is intended that this recognition of different paths towards service will allow for the formation of track-oriented guilds and councils which will be responsible for making recommendations for making recommendations for service and growth in their individual area. Choosing a track does not preclude service in other tracks, rather pursuing a track is intended to allow individuals to focus more intensely upon their individual strengths and gifts, and provide a peer network focused on work within a specific area of concentration.

Currently the Lifeways Council recognizes the following Tracks of Service. Recommendations for other Tracks or Guilds may be submitted to the Lifeways Council for consideration.

Administrative & Support Services (Web Weaver's Guild)

This is the path of service through helping with administrative details: maintaining the mailing list, serving on the Board of Directors or administrative councils, keeping the books, editing newsletters, and just generally organizing things.

Technical Support Services (Web Builder's Guild)

This is made of people with technical expertise who enjoy figuring out how to make challenging puzzles *happen*. This may include computer networks, installation of water systems, building a stage for a festival, designing a building, solar panel system, audio system for ritual, lighting, stage design, etc.

Earth Stewards (Gaia's Guild)

This is a path of service focused on stewardship of the Earth. It involves hands-on work in the physical world: working on the land sanctuary, with gardening, farming, carpentry, or physical maintenance; also working in the world with eco-activism, tree-planting, pollution cleanup, etc.

Manifestation Studies (Wizard's Guild)

This track is for those who wish to focus on magic and other forms of manifestation work. It includes the study of magick and manifestation as a broad topic and includes studies such as magick and ritual, trance work, chakra work, mental disciplines such as meditation and the Silva method, political activism, Taiji practice, Prostrations, yoga, ecstatic, channeling, divination, and any magickal or energy work craft which helps one change consciousness, and change reality.

Healing Arts (Healer's Guild)

This track is for those members who are called to service in the various healing arts, both physical and mental/emotional. This includes therapists, body-workers, facilitators, mediators, herbalists, acupuncturists, doctors, medical technicians, nurses, etc. Service may be offered through practice and teaching of such skills as First Aid, CPR, Reiki, naturopathy, herbology, etc.

Academic Conclave (Scholar's Guild)

This track is for people who love to glean information from complicated books the rest of us don't have time to read, or who have put time and energy into special study of a subject related to CAW, such as Comparative Religion, History, Cosmology, Herbology, Nature Studies, etc.

The Scholar's Guild helps to evaluate the RINGS bibliography, creates research topics and papers of interest to CAW and the Pagan community, conducts and disseminates research, and helps to train teachers in academic areas such as Pagan history, physical & cultural anthropology, astrology/astronomy, physics/quantum physics, mythology, mythoarcheology, etc. They may be called upon to research or provide information to others who may be writing rituals, papers or creating classes.

Artistic Guilds (Various Guilds)

Some people seek to make their contribution through creativity, through serving in Artistic Guilds such as the Bardic Guild, the Guild of Visual Artists, the Fine Arts Guild, or Home Arts. Service through guilds involves adding your creativity to the body of lore that we are developing and helping to coordinate others within your chosen guild. Guild members are drawn upon for contributions at major events.

Religious Life & Spirituality Studies (Hestia's Guild & Clergy Council)

This track is for people who feel a calling specifically to the religious life and spiritual studies, and for those interested in pursuing training towards becoming CAW Clergy. The training in this track focuses on spiritual training and development of counseling and leadership skills. The path of service here involves counseling, leading rituals, developing spiritual practice, researching and learning and personal development and actualization.

Those who wish to become CAW Clergy members should also note that CAW Clergy are expected to serve in multiple tracks as part of their training and development, and that their Clergy training and application is separate from their RINGS training. Members interested in pursuing this track towards preparing for ordination in CAW should contact the Clergy Council as early as possible and seek out a Clergy Advisor to assist them in their path.

5th Circle (Jupiter) Creation

After serving for some time, people begin wanting to create new threads within the Church. In the 5th Circle, we encourage you to create rituals, new services, projects, infrastructure changes, and new Nests. You become involved by working creatively with others.

6th Circle (Mars) Dedication

This Circle is for people who feel an even stronger calling to serve by dedicating their life to the mission of CAW. Individuals who enter 6th Circle feel a deep connection to the Tribe of CAW, a strong desire to serve their community fully, and an overwhelming desire to promote responsible Earth stewardship and the evolution of consciousness. The 6th Circle is both a Circle of intensive service and a Circle of study & reflection. Most members who enter the 6th Circle are interested in becoming Beacons and the time spent in 6th Circle gives the Dedicant an opportunity to connect more deeply, to serve more intensely, and to reflect on whether s/he wishes to make the life time commitment required of Beacons.

A person enters the 6th Circle through proven accomplishment in the more outer Circles, a demonstration of wide-ranging leadership skills in creative and practical spheres, acceptance by the community, recommendation by their Nest or Circle, and a consensus vote of confidence by the existing 3rd ring. At 6th Circle, Dedicants spend a minimum of a year and a day working with their Third Ring Sponsor to complete any remaining areas that need focus or attention and learning through experience and service what lifelong commitment to the third ring entails.

THIRD RING – BEACONS PURPOSE: LEADERSHIP

The third Ring is made up of long-time members of the Church, who have undergone spiritual training and extensive training in their particular Track of Service, and who desire to commit fully to CAW & the CAW Mission. Many Beacons also serve as members of CAW's Priesthood, though this function is independent, with its own criteria. To become a member of the Third Ring, you first need to have learned to serve and create, have been approved and initiated by the community, and have dedicated your life to the gods, to CAW as a Tribe, and to the Mission of CAW. The role of the Inner Circles is to offer leadership, guidance, teaching, ritual creation, and to accept final responsibility (the buck stops here).

Additionally, Beacons are encouraged to create subsidiary Orders to manifest various aspects of the greater Vision of CAW for world transformation. Some examples of these are:

> *Green Egg*
> Nemeton
> Annwfn
> Forever Forests
> Holy Order of Mother Earth (HOME)
> Lifeways

Entering the Third Ring is a complex process requiring fulfillment of all the previous levels, as well as a level of personal development that is worthy of setting an example for others. Once you have been approved by Lifeways and have undergone your initiation ritual, your purpose now is to foster the growth and development of the Pagan movement and community, and help the return of the Goddess to the world at large. This is achieved in numerous ways: through ritual, leadership, workshops and teaching, writing, traveling, conducting interviews, creating works of art, and just getting in there and doing it.

This Ring uses the color violet to signify spirituality.

7th Circle (Earth) Leading

Once initiated, the Beacon is now asked regularly to lead rituals, coordinate activities and major events, reach out to the larger community, conduct interviews, write articles, counsel, vision, and create. They become an integral focal point in the net, supporting and guiding others along the path.

8th Circle (Venus) Fostering

The next level addressed is to interface with the larger Pagan community and to foster the philosophy of the Church and the Pagan movement in general within the larger world. This involves travelling and teaching workshops, writing books, recording music, creating major events and otherwise making a noticeable mark outside the Tribe.

9th Circle (Mercury) Grokking

Grok is a term found in *Stranger in a Strange Land*, which means to fully and totally comprehend something—literally, "to drink." Those who enter Circle nine have attained a recognized spiritual mastery and are free to do as they choose, trusting that their level of development will dictate that they choose well.

The prime criterion for recognition as 9th Circle is having a particular positive impact on the dominant paradigm, in fulfillment of Atl's original Mission Statement: "To make the world safe for people like us."

NOTE: As of 2024, only four people have been recognized as 9th Circle, and each of these for a particular positive impact on the dominant paradigm. We expect there will be more in the future. These four individuals—and their paradigm-changing achievements to qualify—are:

Richard Lance Christie: Atl; Church of All Worlds; Association for the Tree of Life (ATL); Earth First!; The Renewable Deal.

Oberon Zell: Atl; Church of All Worlds; Neo-Paganism; *Green Egg;* TheaGenesis (the Gaea Thesis); Living Unicorns; The Millennial Gaia; The Grey School of Wizardry.

Morning Glory Zell: Shamanic Witchcraft; Holy Order of Mother Earth (HOME); Ecosophical Research Association (ERA); Living Unicorns; Mythic Images; Polyamory; The Goddess Collection.

Anodea Judith: Lifeways; Sacred Centers; Wheels of Life (Chakra paradigm).

So, having waded through our general plan, what you find on the following pages is a list of suggestions and/or requirements for progression into the web, should you still desire to proceed. Do remember that this progression is not a requirement for membership in the Church or the community. Also remember that through obtaining an advisor or sponsor at the different levels, you may be able to substitute experience of your own for some of the requirements. This is available on a case-by-case basis only, through the discretion of your advisor or sponsor.

It is important to note that this is not designed to be particularly easy, nor should it be overly difficult. We do want to have a standard which requires more intimate involvement in and connection to the Tribe as one moves inward. We do want to emphasize that service to the community, both within CAW and outside of CAW, is important to moving inward. We do want to have holistic standards of self-actualization that foster a sense of accomplishment as one grows, without promoting hierarchical thinking or dogma.

We are constantly evolving this structure as people weave their way through it and we find out what works and what doesn't, and how it fits the needs within the community. We are open to feedback in the form of suggestions and constructive criticism.

AT A GLANCE

FIRST RING: **SEEKERS**
PURPOSE: **GROWTH**

Circle One:	Contacting
Circle Two:	Participating
Circle Three:	Growing

SECOND RING: **SCIONS**
PURPOSE: **SERVICE**

Circle Four:	Committing
Circle Five:	Creating
Circle Six:	Dedicating

THIRD RING: **BEACONS**
PURPOSE: **LEADERSHIP**

Circle Seven:	Leading
Circle Eight:	Fostering
Circle Nine:	Grokking

Requirements Invoking Network Growth System (RINGS)
Personal Check List: First Ring

(This check list is intended for your personal use in applying for Circle progression. It encapsulates in a simple form the more detailed information listed in the RINGS Cycle—see CAW website. Please note that, while checking off your accomplishments here is a useful way to keep track of your progress in training, you will still need to present the written materials to the RINGS Coordinator along with a copy of this check list.)

Name_______________________________________

FIRST RING—"Seekers" (Circles 1-3)
Color: Green; Purpose: Growth

☐ Become involved with CAW: attend one or more CAW events (festivals, workshops, nest meetings), correspond, subscribe to CAW-Phoenix elist, subscribe to *Green Egg*, etc.

This brings you into FIRST CIRCLE (Kuiper belt)
Your purpose here is <u>Contact</u>.
To progress to the 2nd Circle, you must:

☐ Fill out a membership application (online) and send us the current annual dues for 2nd Circle. Date_________

☐ Receive CAW membership packet. You may join our members-only Google Group, and access our "members only" forums at www.CAW.org. In addition you are eligible for a discount on a subscription to our online e-zine, *Green Egg,* and a 10% discount on all classes and events sponsored by the Church or its subsidiaries.

This brings you into SECOND CIRCLE (Neptune)
Your purpose here is <u>Getting to know us.</u>
Minimum time in this Circle: 1 year.
To progress to the 3rd Circle, you must:

☐ Read *Stranger in a Strange Land*, by Robert Heinlein (1961 edition, **not** the "original uncut"--or unedited--1991 version).

☐ Read *Radiant Circles,* by Alder Moonoak

☐ Read *GaeaGenesis: Conception & Birth of the Living Earth,* by Oberon Zell

☐ Read *Green Egg* magazine (quarterly)

☐ Read one other book from the CAW Bibliography
Title_________________________________

☐ Attend your local Nest meetings if available.

☐ Take classes that are offered.

☐ Attend further CAW events.

☐ Seek out other Waterkin with questions and comments.

☐ Write a short essay (1-2 pages) or record an oral presentation describing your understanding of CAW, and how you see yourself fitting in.

☐ Submit 3rd Circle application and dues to RINGS Coordinator. Date____________

This brings you into THIRD CIRCLE (Uranus)
Your purpose here is <u>Growing.</u>
Minimum time in this Circle: 1 year.
To progress to the 4th Circle, you must:

☐ Read *Drawing Down the Moon*, by Margot Adler (at least read the chapter on CAW)

☐ Read *Creating Circles & Ceremonies* by Oberon & Morning Glory Zell.

☐ Read *Grimoire for the Apprentice Wizard* by Oberon Zell.

☐ Read two more books from two different categories of the CAW Bibliography.
Title_________________________________
Title_________________________________

☐ If you haven't already done so, begin some form of training in magick, energy work, or miracle manifestation.

☐ Develop your social and relationship skills both within CAW and within the wider community. If possible, join a Nest or magickal Circle in your area.

☐ Begin to identify personal issues from your past experience (childhood and otherwise); take steps to address any recurrent problems.

☐ Meet at least one self-set goal aimed towards improving your overall social skills and psychological well-being.

☐ Actively associate with the other members of the CAW outside of formal group functions. Organize at least one group social function on your own initiative.

☐ Attend and actively participate in nest meetings and give your input in a constructive manner.

☐ Take steps to address any issues of conflict with other members in CAW making use, when appropriate, of the CAW Conflict Resolution Policy.

☐ Reduce your imposition on Mother Nature by reducing your consumption and waste (reduce, re-use, recycle.)

☐ Spend time in intimate contact with Mother Nature; e.g. gardening, hiking, camping

☐ Meet at least one self-set goal aimed towards improving your overall health.

☐ Learn and use skills to earn a livelihood and support yourself and your family in reasonable comfort.

☐ Perform a cleansing and blessing ceremony in your home, ward it properly, and create a home or personal altar.

☐ Learn basic first aid and begin to study a healing technique of your choice (herb craft, massage, Reiki, etc.)

☐ Participate in at least one Community Service project in your area.

☐ Learn to perform the following life skills:
   o Change a diaper.
   o Build a fire

- o Use a compass
- o Find North by the stars
- o Sew a seam
- o Swim without aid
- o Perform CPR
- o Cook a meal
- o Change a tire
- ☐ Establish a regular spiritual practice to enhance your own state of being, strengthening mind, body, and spirit.
- ☐ Begin a spiritual journal. Write a paper on your own personal religious worldview, beliefs and ethics. Design your own "Credo" and include this in your spiritual journal.

Transition to Second Ring (Becoming a Scion)

- ☐ Contact Membership Coordinator to find a Scion Advisor, and call the advisor up and have a chat about CAW, being a Scion, etc.
- ☐ Obtain two letters of recommendation from members of your local Nest.
- ☐ Share water and become water-siblings with another member.
- ☐ Create a Curriculum Vitae (CV), a sort of academic resume detailing the ways in which you have met the requirements of the previous Circle, why you believe that you're prepared to move further inward and how your moving inward will be of service to CAW as a community, to include with your Scion application.
- ☐ Write essay comparing the religion you were brought up in (or the absence of such), Neo-Paganism, and a third religion that you have studied on your own. Submit it to your advisor for review; who will then pass it on to the RINGS Coordinator.
- ☐ Submit 4th Circle application and dues to RINGS Coordinator. Date____________
- ☐ Undergo Scion Initiation ritual. Date__________
- ☐ Receive Scion Certificate, vows, and red ID card.

SECOND RING—"Scions" (Circles 4-6)
Color: Red; Purpose: Service

This brings you into FOURTH CIRCLE (Saturn) Your purpose here is <u>Service</u>. Minimum time in this Circle: 1 year.

As a Scion, you are expected to:
- ☐ Make a tithing pledge for the equivalent of one hour's wage per month to the Church, (minimum $5 per month) which may be earmarked toward an area chosen by the Scion, such as website development, publishing projects, computer equipment, subsidiaries, Sanctuary maintenance and improvements, etc. All contributions are tax-deductible.
- ☐ Attend CAW festivals at cost (usually half price) and continue to receive 10% discount on classes.
- ☐ Take on an active role in CAW affairs (form or help run local Nest, serve on committees or projects, attend CAW meetings, take on organizing or reporting tasks, or help to run festivals or events).
- ☐ Continue your magical & spiritual training, studies & practice training.
- ☐ Read more books from the CAW Bibliography.
- ☐ Continue contact with Mother Nature (camping, hiking, rafting, climbing, diving, spelunking, etc.)
- ☐ Become familiar with CAW's literature, history, and internal structure. Be able to discuss our thealogy, ethics, vision, historical perspective, goals, etc.

The Five Tracks of the Second Ring

Continuing service and progression through the Second Ring will be conducted in one or more of the following Elemental Tracks:

- **Educational and Mental Growth (Air)**
- **Magickal Growth and Will (Fire)**
- **Group Dynamics and Emotional Growth (Water)**
- **Personal and Community / Environmental Growth (Earth)**
- **Spiritual and Religious Growth (Spirit)**

Requirements Invoking Network Growth System (RINGS) – In Detail

The Church of All worlds (CAW) is concentric Circles (see Stranger in basis for training, growth and grouped into three basic RINGS of and Beacons (see overview, above.) This system is designed to create a and focus, a process of ever- Tribe, and a foundation for service

organized in a structure of nine a Strange Land) which provide a commitment. These Circles are three Circles each: Seekers, Scions (Yes, the CAW is a 3-ring Circus!) sense of spiritual accomplishment deepening connection to the CAW to promote the CAW's primary

mission. Each Circle assumes incorporation and completion of previous levels. It should be emphasized that there is absolutely no expectation or requirement that you, as a member of CAW, need to progress into the Circles at all, unless you yourself so desire. Many members are perfectly content to remain in 2nd Circle indefinitely, and only a very few feel called to become Beacons. But if you should wish to become more involved in the workings of CAW, and to help evolve a network of Pagans interested in changing themselves and the world around them, here's how:

FIRST RING: SEEKERS

(CIRCLES 1-3) RING COLOR: GREEN
PURPOSE: GROWTH

Circle One: Contacting

If you are reading this, you have already come into contact with us, and this automatically puts you in Circle One. The purpose of this phase is to -make-contact-. Ways to accomplish this are:

- attend one or more CAW events (festivals, workshops, nest meetings etc)
- talk or correspond with CAW members about the Church
- subscribe to a CAW publication
- study CAW literature
- Decide whether you like us well enough to want to join CAW

We recommend that you spend at least 6 months in 1st Circle getting to know us before applying to become a member of 2nd Circle.

Transition to Circle Two

If you decide to join, then you simply fill out a membership application and send us the current annual dues for second Circle.

Joining the Church automatically puts you in:
Circle Two: Participating

(Minimum 1 year)

Once you join, you will receive a members' fulfillment package with membership card, a frame-worthy PDF of your Membership Pledge, and a 3rd Circle application. You will receive an invitation to our members-only Google Group, and are eligible for access to our "members only" forums at www.caw.org. In addition you are eligible for a discount on a subscription to our online e-zine, *Green Egg,* and a 10% discount on all classes and events sponsored by CAW or its subsidiaries.

The purpose of this phase is to get to know the people, the philosophies of the Church, our religious practices, and the movement of which we are a part. Ways to accomplish this are:

Read the following books:

- ***Stranger in a Strange Land***, by Robert Heinlein (1961 edition—*not* the "original uncut"—actually unedited—1991 version). While this wonderful science fiction classic is a bit outdated by now, it was the seminal book out of which the Church of All Worlds, in its original form, was conceived. From this book, we got our concept of grokking, the ritual of water sharing, and the "waiting-is" that will remind you of why everything takes so long.

- ***Radiant Circles,*** by Alder Moonoak. This germinal and definitive book on the Church of All Worlds is by Alder Moonoak, recently deceased editor of *Green Egg* magazine: *Radiant Circles* is an examination of both Ecospirituality and the Church of all Worlds. The book ranges widely in its historical, cultural and theological exploration of the Church and discusses its role and place as both as a unique Neo-Pagan and futurist New Religious Movement.

• *GaeaGenesis: Conception & Birth of the Living Earth*, by Oberon Zell. Oberon was the first to propose and publish the radical idea that the total biosphere of Earth is a single living organism. His initial article on the subject electrified the emerging modern movement of Earth-based spirituality. *GaeaGenesis* culminates five decades of work developing Zell's thesis: that the entire evolution of life on Earth is the literal embryology of a single vast living being—one replicating continuum of DNA and protoplasm. Mother Earth is a living, sentient being with a "soul" that humans can perceive. In essence, the living beings that populate the Earth are cells within a greater macro-organism we call "Gaea."

We also encourage you to read further Pagan publications, including at least one other book from the CAW bibliography

In addition to reading we ask that you:

- Attend your local Nest meetings.
- Take classes that are offered.
- Attend further CAW events
- Seek out other Waterkin with questions and comments.
- Take time to smell the roses during this phase of getting to know us.

Transition to Circle Three

Once you feel certain that this is the right place for you and that your own ideas are complementary to ours, we ask you to write a short essay (1-2 pages) or record an oral presentation describing your understanding of the Church of All Worlds, and how you see yourself fitting in. You might include special skills you'd like to offer, pertinent ideas that sing to your soul, or what you hope to get out of your affiliation with us. This enables us to better know how to serve our members, and to make sure people do not have the wrong impression of us. Acceptance of the essay puts you in:

Circle Three: Growing

(minimum 1 year from acceptance of essay)

Now that you have placed your feet firmly upon the path, we request that you turn your attention to personal growth and education. At this point we also introduce the 5 Elemental associations into our program to better help you balance your program of self-actualization holistically.

Recommended steps to achieve your personal self actualization goals are:

Educational and Mental Growth (Air):

- Read *Drawing Down the Moon*, by Margot Adler. This book chronicles the Neo-Pagan revival and describes the movement of Goddess-oriented worship and the people that are part of it. This is a sizable tome; and for those who may feel daunted, we ask that you at least read the chapter on the Church of All Worlds. It gives you some idea of our past history and development.
- Read *Creating Circles & Ceremonies* by Oberon & Morning Glory Zell. This comprehensive "Book of Shadows" details 40 years of CAW liturgy and lore from numerous contributors from within the CAW tradition.
- Read *Grimoire for the Apprentice Wizard* by Oberon Zell. This essential handbook is profusely illustrated with original art by Oberon and friends, as well as many woodcuts from medieval and alchemical manuscripts--plus many detailed charts, tables, and diagrams.
- Do further reading from two different categories of the CAW Bibliography.
- Be prepared to add further books which you consider relevant and worthwhile to the Bibliography with annotations.

Magickal Growth and Will (Fire):

- If you haven't already done so, begin some form of training in magick, energy work, or miracle manifestation. This can come from classes, correspondence course, private teacher, and in some cases where a lengthy time period is allowed, simple osmosis. Some people come to us having already completed this level prior to their contact with us. If so, simply continue, and you will be credited for previous experience.

Group Dynamics and Emotional Growth (Water):

- Develop your social and relationship

skills both within CAW and within the wider community. Where possible, join a Nest or magickal Circle in your area.

• Begin to identify personal issues from your past experience (childhood and otherwise); take steps to address any recurrent problems (e.g. drug dependencies, abusive relationships); and develop a means of support for your psychological health and further growth. This may involve entering therapy, a 12-step growth group, co-counseling, bodywork, or other group experiences, such as Anodea Judith's Chakra Intensive.

• Learn to take responsibility for your emotions and how you express and transform them. . Demonstrate your progress by meeting at least one self-set goal aimed towards improving your overall social skills and psychological well-being.

• Actively associate with the other members of the CAW. Establish and maintain warm, positive relationships with others in your Nest, within CAW and within your local NeoPagan community. Socialize with members of CAW outside of formal group functions. Organize at least one group social function on your own initiative.

• Enhance your empathy and learn to respond constructively to the feelings of others. Demonstrate that you can work in harmony and cooperation with others by participating in the group consensus process within your nest.

• Attend and actively participate in Nest meetings and give your input in a constructive manner. If your Nest has a Nest Council, attend any open meetings.

• Take steps to address any issues of conflict with other members in CAW making use, when appropriate, of the CAW Conflict Resolution Policy.

Personal and Community / Environmental Growth (Earth):

• Reduce your imposition on Mother Nature by reducing your consumption and waste (reduce, re-use, recycle).

• Get into intimate contact with Mother Nature; e.g. gardening, hiking, camping.

• Learn to take care of your physical health through proper diet, exercise, releasing addictions, etc. Demonstrate your progress by meeting at least one self-set goal aimed towards improving your overall health.

• Learn and use skills to earn a livelihood and support yourself and your family in reasonable comfort.

• Perform a cleansing and blessing ceremony in your home, ward it properly, and create a home or personal altar.

• Learn basic first aid and begin to study a healing technique of your choice (herb craft, message, Reiki, etc.)

• Participate in at least one Community Service project in your area.

• Perform the following life skills:
  o Change a diaper.
  o Build a fire
  o Use a compass
  o Find North by the stars
  o Sew a seam
  o Swim without aid
  o Perform CPR
  o Cook a meal
  o Change a tire

Spiritual and Religious Growth (Spirit):

• Establish a -regular- spiritual practice. This can be meditation, Tai Chi, exercising, a daily ritual of some kind, establishing a home altar, daily meal blessings, prayers, puja, yoga, or taking care of animals. It should enhance your own state of being, strengthening mind, body, and spirit.

• Begin a spiritual journal. Write a paper on your own personal religious worldview, beliefs and ethics. Design your own "Credo" and include this in your spiritual journal.

Transition to Second Ring:
(Becoming a Scion)

After spending a minimum of one year from your previous essay, and a minimum of two years from date of joining (though we suggest much longer), you may feel you are ready to work within the organization by offering service in the form of time, energy, or other skills that are needed. If so, you may wish to become a Scion. (This does not mean that we do not accept help from those who are not Scions, but that Scions are formalizing their commitment to service.)

If you wish to do this, we ask that you contact Lifeways to find a "Scion Advisor," and call the advisor up and have a chat about CAW, being a Scion and what it's all about from the perspective of someone who's doing it.

If you remain interested, then we ask you to obtain two letters of recommendation from members of your local Nest, or the equivalent if no Nest exists yet (responsible, adult Pagan associates). These letters should attest to your organizational skills, your general character, your communicative abilities, and your ability to inspire confidence in others. We also ask that you chat with a clergy member and get them to make a verbal or written recommendation.

Share Water:

To transition to Second Ring, you must share water and become water-siblings with another member. Where possible, this should be done with a member further inward and should be at the deepest level. If this is not feasible, other Waterkin are acceptable, preferably longer-term members, so long as they have a demonstrated commitment to CAW. Both parties need to demonstrate their understanding of the water-bond.

CV, Scion Essay and Application

From 3rd Circle inward, you will create a Curriculum Vitae (CV), a sort of academic resume detailing the ways in which you have met the requirements of the previous Circle, why you believe that you're prepared to move further inward and how your moving inward will be of service to CAW as a community, to include with your application. It is strongly recommended that you submit your CV to your advisor and to the Mentor Council before submitting your application to Lifeways.

In addition, we ask for a piece of writing or a presentation that demonstrates your ability to think critically and express yourself knowledgably about Comparative Religion by writing the following essay: "Compare the religion you were brought up in (or the absence of such), Neo-Paganism, and a third religion that you have studied on your own." If you need more guidelines about this essay, contact Lifeways. (Lifeways@caw.org) Submit it first to your advisor, and if he or she feels it addresses the issue, and that you have satisfactorily completed the above suggestions, they will pass your essay/ presentation and a note of recommendation on to Lifeways for final approval, and the setting up of your Scion Initiation Ritual.

Undergo Scion Initiation Ritual--preferably in the company of other CAW members. Ideally, CAW Clergy should officiate at the initiation, but where this is not practicable, other CAW members may fill in, for the ritual.

Receive Scion Certificate and vows.

SECOND RING: SCIONS
(*CIRCLES 4-6*) *RING COLOR: RED*
PURPOSE: SERVICE

In addition to committing to service, a Scion tithes the equivalent of one hour's wage per month to the Church, (minimum $5 per month) which can be earmarked toward an area chosen by the Scion, such as Lifeways, Forever Forests, publishing projects, computer equipment, or Sanctuary improvements. All contributions are tax-deductible. Work trades are seldom acceptable.

For this the Scion gets to attend festivals at cost (usually half price) and will continue to receive 10% discount on classes.

The Scion is expected to take on an active role in CAW affairs. This might mean forming a proto-Nest if there is not one in your area, or helping to run it if there is. It also means serving on committees or projects, attending CAW meetings, taking on organizing or reporting tasks, or helping to run festivals or events. There are always things that need to be done, and some people have skills such as carpentry, word-processing, fund-raising, legal or medical skills that are especially helpful at their appropriate times.

In addition, the Scion is expected to:
- continue your magical training
- read more books from the bibliography
- continue contact with Mother Nature, and
- become familiar with CAW's literature, history, and internal structure....

All in your copious spare time!

The minimum length of service to spend in each Circle from Circle four inward is "a year and a day." You must, therefore, spend a minimum of 3 years and 3 days in Second RING before transitioning to Third RING, should you choose to progress that deeply inward.

Circle Four: Serving

Educational and Mental Growth (Air):

• Become familiar with the broad history of Paganism, including the development of Goddess religions and various pathways such as Druidism, Gardnerian, Alexandrian, Norse, etc.

• Read at least ten books from the Bibliography in at least five different categories.

• Recommend at least two books to the Bibliography and submit annotated recommendations to the Library Council.

• Be prepared to act as a Scion Advisor for other members, giving feedback and encouragement in their progression

• Familiarize yourself further with CAW literature, history and internal structure. Be able to discuss our theology, ethics, visions, historical perspective, goals etc.

Magickal Growth and Will (Fire):

• Continue your magickal/manifestation training, studies and practice.

• Be active in a Nest or magickal Circle. If there is not one readily accessible to you, find some like-minded people and create one.

Group Dynamics and Emotional Growth (Water):

• Serve as Nest Coordinator for your Nest, or start a Nest in your area.

• Take on an active role in CAW affairs by attending gatherings, meetings, helping to run rituals, taking on specific projects.

• Make and deepen personal connections with other members.

Personal and Community/ Environmental Growth (Earth):

• Make a tithing pledge, which can be earmarked to your own interests

• Explore and establish patterns of healthy living, physically, emotionally and psychologically

• Continue spending time in intimate contact with Mother Nature and extend your skills and understanding in this sphere.

• Become informed and politically active concerning environmental and social justice issues.

Spiritual and Religious Growth (Spirit):

• Continue your spiritual training, studies and practice

• Make a study of comparative mythology and ancient or indigenous religions; choose a specific mythology and study it in depth

• Visit other religious centers and services. Engage in interfaith dialogues.

Tracks of Service Recommendations:

Specific recommendations for service based on the individual tracks are:

Administrative & Support Services

• **Take on** one or more of the rudimentary tasks that need doing, such as producing a Nest newsletter, doing bookkeeping, helping with membership, etc. Ideally this should be at least one hour per week, but most find themselves doing more and some tasks are irregular in their time requirements.

• Take some steps to **study related topics**, such as Organizational Development, Public Relations, Recordkeeping, Management of time, persons, offices or budgets, Business in general, Grant writing, Mediation, or Marketing.

• **Read** at least three books from the Bibliography listed under the Administrative/Support/Organization category.

• **Recommend** at least one book for the Administrative/Support/Organization category for the Bibliography..

• Join the Web Weaver's Guild *and help to create resources, guidelines and RINGS recommendations for your track.*

Technical Support Services

• Volunteer to help with needed tasks which use your specific technical skill; join the Web Spinners, help build a new system for CAW central, help your nest coordinator or administrative volunteers repair, upgrade or maintain their system, help with design or support at festivals.

• Sharpen your technical skills; take a new programming class, catch up on the newest

• **Read** at least three books from the Bibliography listed under Technical & Other Skills category

• **Recommend** at least one book for the Technical & Other Skills category for the Bibliography.

• Join the Web Builder's Guild *and help to create resources, guidelines and RINGS recommendations for your track.*

Earth Stewards

- **Keep a garden,** orchard or house plants if a garden is impossible.
- **Subscribe** to at least two environmental journals, such as *Earth Island Journal, Earth First!, EDF* (Environmental Defense Fund newsletter) or other informational journals dealing with environmental issues.
- **Help others** to reduce their imposition on Mother Nature, volunteer to set up recycling at work or work to establish a curbside recycling program in a neighborhood that doesn't have one, volunteer to help an elderly or disabled neighbor recycle.
- **Build an outdoor altar** somewhere that enables you to maintain an Earth Mother shrine.
- **Write letters to Congresspeople** concerning environmental issues.
- **Inform other members** in the Tribe about issues they should be aware of and what they could do about it (without being obnoxious about it.)
- **Read** *Earth in the Balance,* by Al Gore, and two other environmental books from the Bibliography.
- **Recommend** at least one book for the Environmental/Earth Stewardship category of the Bibliography
- Join Gaia's Guild *and help to create resources, guidelines and RINGS recommendations for your track.*

Manifestation Studies

- **Volunteer** at, organize or lead at least 1 major group ritual or event focused on manifesting change in an area related to the mission statement. This could include creating a transformational ritual for your nest, leading a community building ritual at a festival, or helping to organize a political rally for environmental activism or social justice.
- **Establish** a daily manifestation ritual which is aimed at creating real change in your personal life and the world around you.
- **Watch** "The Secret" & "What the Bleep Do We Know" (preferably the Quantum edition.)
- **Read** *Real Magic* by P.E.I. Bonewits and at least two other books in the Manifesting Reality section of the Bibliography.
- **Recommend** at least one other book for the Manifesting Reality section of the Bibliography.

- Join the Wizard's Guild *and help to create resources, guidelines and RINGS recommendations for your track.*

Healing Arts

- **Volunteer** your healing services (where legally and ethically appropriate) at festivals and Nest events. An example is to volunteer at the grounding or first aid tents.
- **Work with** your Nest mates to help them meet their physical & mental health growth goals.
- **Read** at least three books in the Healing Arts section of the Bibliography.
- **Recommend** at least one other book for the Healing Arts section of the Bibliography.
- Join the Healer's Guild *and help to create resources, guidelines and RINGS recommendations for your track.*

Academic Conclave

- **Help** other members to research areas that will contribute to advancing their paths of self actualization or which contribute to advancing the CAW mission.
- **Pursue** at least one focused area of research which will contribute to the rituals, lore and/or knowledge of CAW. Present your interest in the form of an article suitable for publication or a class which can be presented to other CAW members or the general public.
- **Read** at least five **additional** books from the Bibliography (above the 10 book requirement for this Circle.)
- **Recommend** at least three other books to be added to the Bibliography. Give preference to areas not covered by other guilds.
- Join the Scholar's Guild) *and help to create resources, guidelines and RINGS recommendations for your track.*

Artistic Guilds (Various Guilds)

- **Find out who Guild members are** in your area and join the guild, or establish a guild for your area of study.
- **Take on some of the tasks of the Guild,** such as organization, compiling song books, information, etc.
- **Make contributions** to rituals, lore, newsletters, or help resolve problems that exist.
- **Read** at least 3 books relevant to studies

in your Guild.

• **Recommend** at least one other book for the section of the Bibliography most relevant to studies in your Guild.

Religious Life & Spirituality Studies (Clergy Council)

• Assist in the rituals of your local Nest.

• Student-teach classes in religion & spiritual studies

• Help present Clergy in their duties, and assist in the ritual planning and execution at major events.

• Studies should include development in the following areas:

> o **Counseling:** Take courses in counseling techniques, and learn as much as you can about 12-step programs, crisis counseling, addiction recovery, family systems, mediation techniques, bodywork, diet and nutrition, death and dying, co-dependence, and group facilitation.

> o **Drama and liturgy:** Study basic acting techniques and liturgical construction. Develop skills in presentation, voice projection and holding an audience.

> o **Religion:** Study the ancient Greeks, Egyptians, Celts, Native Americans, Hindu, African, or Oriental pantheons and magical systems. (not limited to this list.) Visit local Buddhist temples, Christian churches, synagogues or other religious services. Sit in on Interfaith dialogues.

• Become familiar with the history of the Craft, the development of the Goddess religion, its downfall and resurgence. Become familiar with the various sects and styles within Paganism, such as Druids, Gardnerians, or Contraries.

• **Read** at least five **additional** books from the Bibliography (above the 10 book requirement for this Circle) taken from the Religion or Mythology sections of the Bibliography. Alternately, these books may be in an area which adds to leading a spiritual life or enhances religious experience.

• **Recommend** at least three other books to be added to the Bibliography for the Religions or Mythology sections. Alternately, these books may be in an area which adds to leading a spiritual life or enhances religious experience.

Share Water

To transition to 5th Circle, you should expand your family of water-siblings by at least one and share water with at least one more person on the deepest level. Where possible, this should be done with a member further inward and should be at the deepest level. It is also hoped that you will deepen your connection to tribe by sharing water with several other members on the first three levels (community, nest & friendship) of watersharing.

CV and Application

Create a Curriculum Vitae (CV), detailing the ways in which you have met the requirements for 4th Circle, why you believe that you're prepared to move further inward and how your qualifications and participation will be of service to CAW as a community, to include with your application. It is strongly recommended that you submit your CV to your advisor and to the Mentor Council before submitting your application to Lifeways.

Circle Five: Creating

After serving for some time, people begin wanting to create new threads within the Church. In the fifth Circle, we encourage you to create rituals, new services, projects, infrastructure changes, and new nests. You become involved by working creatively with others.

In 5th Circle you are expected to continue your tithing pledge and to maintain all requirements from previous while increasing your active involvement in community and CAW and advancing your personal growth.

Educational and Mental Growth (Air):

• Read at least six more books from the Bibliography from different categories and recommend at least one additional book to a category on the list not covered by your "track".

• Continue your personal training program and develop teaching skills to assist others.

• Subscribe to Pagan, environmentalist, and religious publications.

• Develop and submit your own program for further progression, ensuring that requirements are balanced. Add at least one self-determined goal to each of the five Elemental areas (Air, Fire, Water, Earth, Spirit.) Include study, training and preparation in all areas:

intellectual, emotional, physical, psychic, eco-psychic, manifestation, spiritual, social, psychological, experiential etc.

Magickal Growth and Will (Fire):

• Take on a personal artistic and creative short term project and share results with CAW

• Take on at least one manifestation project (magickal, political or practical) focused on advancing the CAW Mission. This could include taking on a role in the administrative running of CAW, participating in the RINGs council, helping with editing a newsletter, organize a gathering or a political rally, taking an active part in a political campaign, working with a like-minded or affiliated organization.

Group Dynamics and Emotional Growth (Water):

• Establish a guild or specialist interest group; start a Nest or magickal Circle

• Create and lead rituals or group activities at Nests and CAW events.

• Become a Scion advisor for at least one other CAW member.

Personal and Community / Environmental Growth (Earth):

• Become involved in community development groups and events (e.g. local councils, boards of management, hobby groups).

• Create new events in your community which advance the CAW Mission.

• Spend time in the outdoors. Learn to feel at home with Mother Nature in her untamed state. Barring physical impairments, be able to guide and support others on a nature walk or expedition into the wilderness or to teach others about Nature and the environment.

Spiritual and Religious Growth (Spirit):

• Explore your own religious path. Create at least one goal focused on developing self knowledge and deepening your connection to the Divine both Within and Without.

• Explore at least two other religious paths in more depth. Create at least one goal focused on developing knowledge and understanding of a religious path with which you have less experience.

• Read *Wheels of Life* by Anodea Judith.

Share Water

To transition to 6th Circle, you should expand your family of water-siblings by at least 1one and share water with at least one more person on the deepest level. Where possible, this should be done with a member further inward and should be at the deepest level. It is also hoped that you will deepen your connection to Tribe by sharing water with several other members on the first three levels (community, Nest, and friendship) of watersharing.

CV and Application

Create a Curriculum Vitae (CV), detailing the ways in which you have met the requirements for 5th Circle, why you believe that you're prepared to move further inward and how your qualifications and participation will be of service to CAW as a community, to include with your application. It is strongly recommended that you submit your CV to your advisor and to the Mentor Council before submitting your application to Lifeways.

Tracks of Service Recommendations:

Recommendations for individual tracks of service are created by their respective councils or guilds. The following areas are left open for those Councils/Guilds to include recommendations once established.

In addition to the goals established by their respective Council or Guild, members are expected to read at least 3 additional books to advance knowledge in their track(s) and to recommend at least one book to the Bibliography for their track. Members following multiple tracks should do this for each track; request Guild Requirements.

Administrative & Support Services
Technical Support Services
Earth Stewards
Manifestation Studies
Healing Arts
Academic Conclave
Artistic Guilds)
Religious Life & Spirituality Studies
Sixth Circle members of this track comprise the Ministry and postulants to the ordained Priesthood of CAW, therefore 5th Circle requirements for this track prepare one for a life of religious service and the guidelines for conduct and movement through 5th Circle for this track are contained within the *Clergy Handbook.*

Circle Six: Dedication

This Circle is for people who feel an even stronger calling to serve by dedicating their life to the CAW Mission and the CAW community. When you enter this Circle, you undergo dedication and become a Postulant to the Beaconate. The CAW term "Beacon" is adapted from the Christian term "Deacon," which is derived from the Greek word *diakonos* (διάκονος), which means "servant." Beacons in CAW are both servants of the Tribe as well as the larger Neo-Pagan community, and a source of enlightenment and inspiration. Dedication to the 6th Circle gives the Postulant an opportunity to work closely with a Beacon sponsor to determine whether or not the Postulant wishes to commit fully to this life of service.

A Postulant enters the Sixth Circle through proven accomplishment in the former Circles, a demonstration of wide-ranging leadership skills in creative and practical spheres, acceptance by the community, recommendation by their Beacon sponsor, the Mentoring Council, and their Nest or Circle, and a consensus vote of confidence by the existing Third Ring. A Postulant spends a minimum of a year and a day working with their sponsor to complete any remaining areas that need focus or attention before they are initiated into the 7th Circle, should there be a mutual decision to proceed inward.

Beacon Sponsor and Curia preparation

The first step required to transition into Sixth Circle is to obtain a Beacon sponsor. One of the major responsibilities of the Beaconate is to "hold the center" of our web… to act as the communication conduit between the Leadership of CAW and the entire membership through our open membership forums, the Curia. This ensures that our organization, while relying on the experience and guidance of our Elders and those members most firmly connected to the vision and the community, does not ever become a hierarchy of "power over" but remains a consensus-focused tribe.

To fulfill this crucial function, each Beacon takes vows to hold Curia whenever opportunity and need arise and to listen to each and every member, from 1st Circle inward, with an open mind and heart. Such a responsibility requires both a sound level of emotional maturity and well-developed group dynamics and communi-

cation skills. If the postulant is lacking in these areas, special focus must be given to growth in the "Group Dynamics and Emotional Growth (Water)" area before the postulant can proceed inward to the 3rd RING. Postulants are advised to attend and assist with as many Curias as possible as part of their preparation.

Educational and Mental Growth (Air):

- Continue personal training program.
- Read at least 7 more books from bibliography and be able to discuss the concepts they convey. Demonstrate a basic level of scholarship in the areas relevant to Pagan leaders (e.g. psychology, religion, history, sociology etc.).
- Write an in-depth research paper or create a substantive and influential presentation or project relevant to your area or expertise and to the CAW Mission which demonstrates intelligent insights.
- Submit, in writing, your qualifications for service and plan for further enrichment of the Church, including a statement of your particular interest.
- Submit to oral examination and evaluation by the 3rd RING examination panel (which is composed of Clergy members, Beacons and members of the Curia approved by the Mentoring Council.)

Magickal Growth and Will (Fire):

- Coordinate and/or initiate CAW projects
- Be politically active about your concerns with regard to local environmental and social issues.

Group Dynamics and Emotional Growth (Water):

- Continue involvement in CAW activities and groups.
- Develop / foster strong, ongoing, healthy relationships with other members of your Nest and those within the larger tribe of CAW.
- Demonstrate the ability to lead rituals and/or events, to work well with others, and to serve the community
- Working with your Beacon sponsor, learn to facilitate a Curia. Be open and receptive to the ideas of others, regardless of RING, Circle or membership status. Learn to inspire and foster the participation of others. If necessary, take classes and workshops in public speaking, small group communication and consensus

process to allow you to effectively fulfill this role as a Beacon.

• Be accountable to the CAW membership for your personal actions and behaviors which reflect upon the general membership. Address any issues of conflict that may exist with other CAW members making use of the Conflict Resolution Policy.

• Take responsibility for addressing personal issues from past or present experience and undergo therapy when appropriate. Be prepared to discuss problems with clergy advisors and accept criticism, mediation and problem-solving processes.

• Seek nomination from sponsoring Beacons and Clergy, your nest or Circle, and members of the Curia. Provide at least five recommendations, including one Clergy recommendation and the recommendation of one Beacon besides your sponsor to the examining panel.

Personal and Community / Environmental Growth (Earth):

• Demonstrate that you have established personal relationships with animals and plants or that you provide ongoing environmental support to Gaia, (e.g. gardening, raising animals, recycling, etc.)

• Get your life reasonably together emotionally, financially, physically, spiritually.

Spiritual and Religious Growth (Spirit):

• Demonstrate your ability to represent the Divine (Within/Without) to the mainstream world in a way that commands respect.

• Go on a solitary vision quest, minimum of seven days, under the guidance of your Beacon sponsor. (If necessary this requirement may be modified by your sponsor to accommodate health issues.)

• Create and design your own initiation ritual to enter the third ring. (You may seek the assistance of a member of the Religious Life & Spirituality Studies track or a Clergy member to complete this requirement if you do not have expertise in that track.)

Share Water

To transition to the Third Ring (7th Circle) you must share water with at least one more person on the deepest level and this must be a person within the Third Ring. By now you should also have deepened your connection to Tribe by sharing water with several other members on the first three levels (community, nest & friendship) of watersharing.

CV, Beacon Project and Application.

Create a Curriculum Vitae (CV), detailing the ways in which you have met the requirements for 6th Circle, why you believe that you're prepared to move further inward and how your qualifications and participation will be of service to CAW as a community.

In addition to your CV, you must also create a Beacon Project – a project in your primary area of expertise which you accept responsibility to foster and promote. Your Beacon Project should be something which in some provides a major, positive impact on CAW and significantly and perceptibly advances the CAW Mission.

This project can be anything which promotes the Mission of CAW, but must be a substantial work and something which you are willing to dedicate yourself to long term. Examples of past projects have been the establishment of CAW subsidiaries such as E.R.A., Lifeways and H.O.M.E. and the establishment of ministries to serve special populations such as the Women's, Prison and Handicap Ministries. It is also possible to resurrect an abandoned project or ministry if one exists. To transition to third ring you **must** submit your CV along with your Beacon Project proposal to your Beacon sponsor for review rather than to Lifeways. Once your Beacon sponsor reviews your application s/he will submit it to the Beacon Council for approval. If approved, the Beacon Council will forward your approved application to Lifeways to notify them of your progress inward into the Third Ring.

Once accepted into the 3rd RING, you will undergo a Beacon Initiation Ritual in the company of other CAW members. Ideally, CAW Clergy should officiate at the initiation but where this is not practicable; another CAW Beacon may fill in for the ritual.

Receive Beacon Certificate & vows.

Tracks of Service Recommendations:

Recommendations for individual tracks of service are created by their respective councils or guilds. The following areas are left open for those Councils/Guilds to include recommendations once established.

In addition to the goals established by their respective Council or Guild, members are expected to read at least 3 additional books to advance knowledge in their track(s) and to recommend at least one book to the bibliography for their track. Members following multiple tracks should do this for each track. Request Guild Requirements.

> **Administrative & Support Services**
> **Technical Support Services**
> **Earth Stewards**
> **Manifestation Studies**
> **Healing Arts**
> **Academic Conclave**
> **Artistic Guilds)**
> **Religious Life & Spirituality Studies**

Sixth Circle members of this track comprise the Ministry and postulants to the ordained Priesthood of CAW. Further guidelines for conduct and movement through the 3rd RING for this track are contained in the *Clergy Handbook*.

THIRD RING: BEACONS
(CIRCLES 7-9) RING COLOR: VIOLET
PURPOSE: LEADERSHIP

To become a member of the Third Ring, you first need to have learned to serve and create, have been approved and initiated by the community, and to have dedicated your life to the Mission of CAW. The role of the Beacon is to offer leadership, guidance and teaching, to "hold the center" of the tribal web of CAW, and to accept final responsibility (the buck stops here).

Entering the Beaconate is a complex process requiring fulfilment of all the previous levels, as well as a level of personal development that is capable of leading and worthy of setting an example for others. Requirements for entering the Beaconate are developed on an individual basis by the Dedicant and his/her Beacon sponsor and completion of the Beacon project is a major requirement.

Once you have been approved by the 3rd RING Council and have undergone your Beacon initiation ritual, you are considered a Leader within CAW. Your purpose now is to foster the growth and development of the Pagan movement and community, and to advance the Mission of CAW. This is achieved in numerous ways: through ritual, leadership, workshops and teaching, writing, travelling, conducting interviews, creating works of art, and just getting in there and doing it.

Movement further inward once one is in the Third RING involves creating something, or doing something which in some way significantly shifts or at significantly impacts the dominant paradigm in the greater world outside of CAW. Thus Beacons who wish to move inward beyond 7th Circle are required to develop at least one (and generally multiple) Advanced Beacon Project(s).

Examples of projects which qualified their creators for the innermost Circles of CAW Leadership were the founding of CAW itself; instigating the Pagan movement by the adoption of "Pagan" as a self-identification; articulating the Gaea Thesis (all of which were done by Oberon); Morning Glory's Goddess workshops, which have advanced Goddess education; and publication of major works such as Anodea Judith's Chakra system materials which have promoted energy work among the general population.

This ring uses the color violet to signify spirituality.

Tracks of Service Recommendations:

Since Beacons most often work in multiple tracks of service, from 7th Circle inward, recommendations for individual tracks of service become less important than they are in 2nd RING and thus these requirements are optional at 7th Circle inward. Where desired, such requirements are created by their respective councils or guilds and approved by the Beacon Council.

In addition to the goals established by their respective Council or Guild, members are expected to continue reading to advance knowledge in their track(s) and to recommend at least one book to the bibliography for each track they are involved in.

Religious Life & Spirituality Studies

Third RING members of this track form the ordained Priesthood of CAW. Further guidelines for conduct and movement through the 3rd RING for this track are contained within the *Clergy Handbook*.

Circle Seven: Leading
Educational and Mental Growth (Air):

- If you have not already done so, begin some level of formal, apprenticed or credentialed training in your primary area(s) of service. For a Minister this might be attending seminary or taking formal classes in religion; for a Wiccan Priest/ess it might be completing 3rd degree training under another Priest/ess; for a person in the Administrative /Technical services it might be completing an Associates or Bachelor's degree; and for someone in the Earth Stewards track it might be enrolling in the forestry service or completing a year of stewardship on sacred lands. The program should be appropriate to the track or tracks the individual has been pursuing and should be easily recognizable as imparting the expertise necessary to provide leadership in your chosen track(s).

- Teach what you know.

- Think on your feet and be able to wing it when necessary.

Magickal Growth and Will (Fire):

- Take responsibility for making things happen.

- Create original material, projects and activities which advance the Mission of CAW.

- Maintain clarity of vision for the community.

Group Dynamics and Emotional Growth (Water):

- Whenever possible, facilitate or assist with Curia. Communicate with and listen to members of all Circles with an open heart and mind. Encourage the participation of members on all levels.

- Effectively demonstrate respectful communication and model the principle "Be excellent to each other."

- Put out fires effectively.

- Have a sense of presence that is inspiring to others.

- Have personal credibility through lack of hypocrisy.

- Effectively lead others without using power over.

- Evoke a sense of affection and respect

Personal and Community / Environmental Growth (Earth):

- Demonstrate the ability to take a clear and honest self-inventory, to accept constructive criticism from others, and to be able to give constructive feedback which will help others in their personal growth.

- Be able to deal with administrative issues effectively and appropriately, within a required time-frame.

- Demonstrate a visible connection to Gaia and the ecosphere and inspire others to strengthen their connection to our Mother Earth and all her living biospheres.

Spiritual and Religious Growth (Spirit):

- Establish a link between the Divine and community, and help people make that link themselves.

- Be able to clearly articulate the body of lore and doctrine of the Church to anyone.

- Show respect for and understanding of people from other faith communities and demonstrate the ability to work effectively in interfaith affinity groups.

Share Water

To transition to 8th Circle, you should expand your family of water-siblings and share water with at least three more people on the deepest level. Deepen your connection to tribe by sharing water with as many other members on the first three levels (community, nest & friendship) of watersharing as possible.

CV and Application

Create a Curriculum Vitae (CV), detailing the ways in which you have met the requirements for 7th Circle, why you believe that you're prepared to move further inward and how your qualifications and participation will be of service to CAW as a community, to include with your application. Submit your CV to the Beacon Council for approval before submitting your application to Lifeways.

Circle Eight: Fostering

Educational and Mental Growth (Air):

- If you have not yet completed the formal, apprenticed or credentialed training in your primary area(s) of service, continue to advance in that training program.

- Assist other members in your areas of expertise to advance in their training. Teach others about your field(s) of expertise, mentor or sponsor one other individual seeking formal training in at least one of your areas of expertise.

• Design, facilitate, teach and organize CAW classes and workshops.

Growth and Will (Fire):

• Walk your talk and help others to do the same. Also talk your walk!

• Learn to clearly visualize and manifest those community and social changes which will contribute to the CAW Mission.

Group Dynamics and Emotional Growth (Water):

• Continue to model and foster respectful, consensus building communication.

Personal and Community / Environmental Growth (Earth):

• Continue creatively to foster the connection of others to the tribe of CAW, the extended community and to the Divine Within and Without.

Spiritual and Religious Growth (Spirit):

• Do everything in your power to creatively foster the evolution of "a network of information, mythology and experience that provides a context and stimulus for reawakening Gaia and reuniting Her children through tribal community dedicated to responsible stewardship and the evolution of consciousness."

Share Water

To transition to 9th Circle, you should expand your family of water-siblings and share water with at least three more people on the deepest level. Deepen your connection to tribe by sharing water with as many other members on the first three levels (community, Nest & friendship) of watersharing as possible.

CV, Advanced Beacon Project and Application

Create a Curriculum Vitae (CV), detailing ways in which you have met the requirements for 8th Circle, why you believe that you're prepared to move further inward and how your qualifications and participation will be of service to CAW as a community, to include with your application.

In conjunction with the Beacon Council create an Advanced Beacon Project by creating something or doing something which in some way significantly shifts or at least significantly impacts the dominant paradigm in the greater world outside of CAW, and which by so doing significantly and perceptibly advances the CAW Mission. Submit your CV and application to the Beacon Council for approval.

Circle Nine: Grokking

• The primary and ultimate criterion for 9th Circle is having a significant and recognized positive impact on the dominant cultural paradigm.

Educational and Mental Growth (Air):

• If you have not already done so, complete the formal, apprenticeship or credentialed training in your primary area(s) of service. 9th Circle members are expected to have recognized expertise in multiple tracks of service.

• Assist and inspire others in your areas of expertise. Teach others about your field(s) of expertise. Mentor, guide and sponsor others.

Magickal Growth and Will (Fire):

• Be a shining example of diverse ways to contribute to and manifest the CAW Mission. Create Miracles.

Group Dynamics and Emotional Growth (Water):

• Demonstrate the consistent ability to inspire confidence in "Self" in others and to inspire open and honest communication.

• Consistently communicate caring, respect and consideration to others.

• Inspire others to participate and contribute.

Personal and Community / Environmental Growth (Earth):

• Minimize your impact on Mother Earth.
• Be a positive example of healthy living.

Spiritual and Religious Growth (Spirit):

• Seek always your "True Will".
• Model "Thou Art God/dess".
• Recognize and ennoble Divinity in others.

CV and Application

• No Curriculum Vitae or Application are necessary for progression into Ninth Circle.

RINGS of Oz

Requirements Invoking Network Growth System (RINGS)
Personal Check List

[This is a draft proposal for a revised RINGS to operate in Australia]

THE RING SYSTEM IS A FRAMEWORK designed to create an interwoven network within the CAW community that supports the individual as well as the overall purposes of the Church. The concept of life as a living web is the basis for our internal structuring within the Church. The RING web is an interconnected egalitarian support network, utilizing our strengths and addressing our weaknesses. The term RING refers to rings in the labyrinth of the God and Goddess that, as the *Dearinth,* has become the symbol for the Church of All Worlds.

Within the system there are three rings, with three circles within each of those rings, corresponding to the nine planets. Movement through the rings indicates personal and spiritual growth, a deepening connection to the church, a strengthening commitment towards its well-being, and a contribution to a changing consciousness in the world psyche. It is intended as a non-hierarchical system and each individual determines their own rate of progress. Some may choose to stay in the same ring level and never progress further; their place is as important as that of the clergy in the inner circle.

The Church of All Worlds has evolved this network system to avoid the idea of climbing on a ladder of success to a hierarchical top, wherein one seeks power over others. It requires a radical change of thinking to create a net instead of a ladder, where each connection is equally vital to the whole. Together we make a flexible structure capable of holding things gently, yet providing support.

Our community is tribal rather than hierarchical. An individual's evolution along this path requires a development of power within and a dedication to service. Those who find their way to become clergy will have more of a commitment to the community than the free agent who has just joined. If they are expecting power and prestige they will be sorely disappointed!

It is extremely difficult to set up a structure that is solid enough to hold us together and flexible enough to allow for the high level of individuality that we cherish in our members. There are those who resist any structure at all, yet others who complain bitterly if things do not run smoothly. There are still others who want more structure, needing someone to give them very specific guidance. We are not gurus, and would rather foster someone's inner guidance than tell them what to do.

For this reason we have tried to address issues on many different levels. Some suggestions, such as books to read or tasks to accomplish, are relatively easy to achieve. Other levels, such as an individual's spiritual growth, creative abilities, and readiness to lead others, are much more subjective. While they may be harder to assess, we attempt to do so anyway, most often through the community's voice but also through advisors and sponsors that connect with the individual along their pathway.

All members seeking to progress through the RINGS are encouraged to join the Vortex and get to know their fellow journeymen and women, providing support and feedback for others and asking it for themselves. It is not just a matter of fulfilling tasks, but of growing closer and creating community. The Vortex also puts in place a peer review and approval system that addresses challenges such as geographical isolation and an absence of sufficient scions and clergy to thoroughly oversee progression.

The emphasis is on the spirit of the RINGS, and flexibility is allowed in all criteria. If the seeker can show, to Lifeways as the supervisory body and to the Vortex as the peer support network, that they have understood the purpose of the requirements and taken steps to fulfil them, it will usually be considered adequate.

When a member wishes to apply to move into the next circle they should seek recommendation from Vortex to Lifeways. If someone leaves CAW or is directed to step down from their position, their return should be re-negotiated with Lifeways i.e. if someone reaches scion or clergy status and resigns or leaves through other avenues, they need to re-connect with the community before resuming such a place. Which does not mean having to write essays again!

(Suggestion: The RINGS can seem overwhelming when taken all in one hit. Get a general overview, by all means, but also take it one step at a time. Which ring fits now? What is needed to move to the next one?)

First Ring – SEEKERS (Circles 1-3) – Getting to Know Us

The purpose of this ring is to meet the Church of All Worlds with an open and inquiring mind; to find out if it is a tribe that might suit you or that can help you in any way along your own individual path. We would like seekers to get to know us before becoming more involved. This means making personal contact with CAW members, attending events, reading CAW literature, subscribing to related magazines, learning about our history, sociology and the practice of our religion. Seekers are encouraged to pursue their own spiritual growth and be well-informed before determining if the Church of All Worlds is for them.

Because of its emphasis upon new growth, this ring is associated with the colour green.

1st Circle (Kuiper Belt) Contact

The purpose of first circle is to establish personal contact. Anyone who has been to any of our events, or attended any of our classes, is automatically in First Circle. This is our larger community, of which only a portion are actual members.

- ❑ attend one or more CAW events (festivals, workshops, nest meetings etc)
- ❑ talk or correspond with CAW members about the Church
- ❑ subscribe to the CAW newsletter or magazine
- ❑ study CAW literature
- ❑ Decide whether you like us well enough to want to join CAW

2nd Circle (Neptune) Getting to Know Us

The purpose of second circle is getting to know us. It is made up of those individuals who have decided to join the Church of All Worlds. We would like these people to familiarize themselves further with the Church and to extend their connections to other members.

- ❑ Submit CAW Membership Application and annual dues
- ❑ Receive CAW Membership Certificate, ID card and Membership Handbook
- ❑ Sign the CAW Affirmation
- ❑ Read *Stranger in a Strange Land* by Robert Heinlein
- ❑ Read *Drawing Down the Moon* by Margot Adler, or at least the chapter on CAW
- ❑ Read *The Fifth Sacred Thing* by Starhawk
- ❑ Read further pagan publications, including another book from the CAW bibliography
- ❑ Attend further CAW events
- ❑ Seek out other waterkin with questions and comments
- ❑ If you want to progress further, join the Vortex, a peer review and support network that produces a regular newsletter with member's ideas, opinions and feedback
- ❑ Write/record and submit, to Vortex and Lifeways, a short essay describing your understanding of CAW and how you see yourself fitting in
- ❑ Submit application for 3rd circle to Lifeways.

3rd Circle (Uranus) Growing

The focus in third circle is attending to your own personal growth and development while also growing closer to other CAW members. As the actualisation of human potential is an important goal for the Church of All Worlds, this circle addresses the development of self as a later tool for service and social change. We do not want sheep, but people who understand their own strengths and purposes in the greater scheme of things.

- ❑ Undertake some form of magickal training
- ❑ Establish a regular spiritual practice e.g. home altar, meal blessings, daily meditation

- Reduce your imposition on Mother Nature by reducing your consumption and waste (reduce, re-use, recycle)
- Develop your social and relationship skills both within CAW and within the wider community. Where possible, join a nest or magickal circle in your area.
- Take training in communication and group dynamics
- Begin to identify personal issues from your past experience (childhood and otherwise); take steps to address any recurrent problems e.g. drug dependencies, abusive relationships; and develop a means of support for your psychological health and further growth
- Find a scion advisor to mentor you through this process and nominate them to Lifeways. The scion advisor should be someone from a circle further inward, but if this is not practicable, then it may be someone who has been in the church longer and/or has more experience in CAW
- Consult with your scion advisor about your personal growth and development, and the deepening of your connections with CAW
- Spend time in intimate contact with Mother Nature e.g. gardening, hiking, camping
- Do further reading from at least 3 different categories of the CAW bibliography
- Be prepared to add further books which you consider relevant and worthwhile to the bibliography with annotated summaries
- Continue your active involvement in the peer support/feedback network of Vortex
- Take steps to address any issues of conflict with other members in CAW making use, when appropriate, of the CAW Conflict Resolution Policy.
- Share water and become water-siblings with another member. Where possible, this should be done with a member further inward. If this is not feasible, other waterkin are acceptable, preferably longer-term members, so long as they have a demonstrated commitment to CAW. Both parties need to demonstrate their understanding of the water-bond.

- Be a financial member of CAW for at least a year, and in the 3rd circle for at least 6 months.
- Research and write/record an essay comparing the religion you were brought up in (or the absence of same), paganism or a particular path therein, and a third religion you have studied on your own.
- Write a resume of the ways in which you have met the criteria of third circle
- Submit essay and resume to Vortex for peer review and feedback
- Seek nomination from Vortex to Lifeways for progression into second ring
- Submit your essay, resume and application to Vortex and Lifeways, with at least two letters of recommendation. At least one from a Vortex member and the other from your scion advisor. If you are a member of a nest/circle, then it would be appropriate to also have one from there.

Second Ring – SCIONS (Circles 4-6) – Service

A scion is a new shoot or a piece grafted onto another plant, or an extension on a family tree. It is accorded the colour red to symbolise fertility. To become a scion in the Church of All Worlds is to not only be a part of it but also be committed to its further growth and expansion. Up until this point, membership of CAW may have been solely an exercise in your personal journey, but moving into the second ring indicates that journey is now part of CAW's. Your purpose here is service and the scion is expected to take an active role in CAW as a whole.

Scions are people who have been involved long enough to want to help run things, or create new aspects within the church, such as a new nest or a newsletter. It is not required that one enter this level, and it is better to remain in the first ring than take this responsibility falsely, for others will count on you to carry through.

Scionhood and other progressions should, in principle, be conferred by the general membership of CAW. The Scion advisor who has walked the journey with the applicant should ascertain if this support is available and, if so, recommend them to Lifeways for approval.

This approval must be attained before any initiation/ordination ritual can take place.

4th Circle (Saturn) Serving

After your scion initiation you are expected to serve the community. This may involve mundane clerical or administrative duties, rudimentary tasks at gatherings, assisting in nest activities, leading rituals, offering classes, or donating time in your particular area of expertise.

- ❏ Undergo Scion Initiation Ritual preferably in the company of the other CAW members. Ideally, CAW clergy should officiate at the initiation but where this is not practicable, other CAW members may fill in, for the ritual.
- ❏ Receive scion certificate, vows, red ID card and copper Thearinth
- ❏ Make a tithing pledge, which can be earmarked to your own interests
- ❏ Take on an active role in CAW affairs by attending gatherings, meetings, helping to run rituals, taking on specific projects
- ❏ Make and deepen personal connections with other members
- ❏ Continue magickal and spiritual training, studies and practice
- ❏ Be familiar with the broad history of paganism, including the development of Goddess religions and various pathways such as Druidism, Gardnerian, Alexandrian, Norse etc.
- ❏ Read at least ten books from the bibliography in at least five different categories. Make further annotated recommendations to the bibliography.
- ❏ Be active in a nest or magickal circle. If there is not one readily accessible to you, find some like-minded people and create one.
- ❏ Study ancient traditions such as Greek, Egyptian, or local indigenous.
- ❏ Visit other religious centres and services. Engage in interfaith dialogues.
- ❏ Undertake some training in counselling and other areas of healing
- ❏ Be prepared to act as a scion advisor for other members. Play an active role in Vortex, giving feedback and encouragement to other members.

- ❏ Undertake drama training or equivalent to develop skills in presentation, voice projection and holding an audience
- ❏ Explore and establish patterns of healthy living, physically, emotionally and psychologically
- ❏ Continue spending time in intimate contact with Mother Nature and extend your skills and understanding in this sphere.
- ❏ Become informed and politically active concerning environmental and social justice issues.
- ❏ Familiarise yourself further with CAW literature, history and internal structure. Be able to discuss our theology, ethics, visions, historical perspective, goals etc.
- ❏ Share water and become water-siblings with other waterkin
- ❏ Spend a minimum of six months in 4th circle
- ❏ Apply for 5th circle, seeking recommendations from the Vortex and members of your nest or circle to Lifeways

5th Circle (Jupiter) Creating

After serving for some time, people begin wanting to create new threads within the church. In the fifth circle, we encourage you to create rituals, new services, projects, infrastructure changes, and new nests. You become involved by working creatively with others.

- ❏ Continue tithing pledge and maintain all requirements from previous circles e.g. outdoor altar, active involvement in community and CAW, magickal training
- ❏ Take on a personal artistic and creative short term project and share results with CAW
- ❏ Establish a guild or specialist interest group; start a nest or magickal circle
- ❏ Create and lead rituals at nests and other festivals
- ❏ take on a role in the administrative running of CAW e.g. NMC, editing newsletter, organising a gathering
- ❏ Read at least 6 more books from the bibliography from different categories in the bibliography and add your own recommended publications to the same
- ❏ Subscribe to pagan and/or environmental publications

❑ continue personal training program and develop teaching skills to assist others

❑ become a scion advisor for other CAW members

❑ create and conduct rituals for a group

❑ become involved in community development groups and events e.g. local councils, boards of management, hobby groups

❑ create new events in your community

❑ spend time in the wilderness. Learn to feel at home with Mother Nature in her untamed state. Be able to guide and support others on a bushwalk or expedition into the wilderness.

❑ Seek out present members of the clergy for sharing of wisdom and general advice.

❑ Develop and submit your own program for further progression and, if desired, eventual ordination. Include study, training and preparation in all areas: intellectual, emotional, physical, psychic, eco-psychic, magickal, spiritual, social, psychological, experiential etc.

❑ Be part of 5th circle for at least 6 months.

❑ Obtain recommendation from Vortex and clergy to Lifeways for movement into 6th circle.

6th Circle (Mars) Dedication

This circle is for people who feel an even stronger calling to serve by dedicating their life to this path. When you enter this circle, you become either a Minister or a Postulant for the priesthood.

Ministers are those who do not feel they want to make the commitment to becoming CAW Priests or Priestesses, but feel a strong desire to serve their community in a very particular way, such as in prison work or hospices. Ministerial credentials are awarded on a case-by-case basis, by the Priesthood, through the recommendation of their Priesthood sponsor and Vortex. The criteria is based on whether they have completed the previous circles, and whether they are adequately trained for the Ministry they have chosen. A proposal in writing should be made stating desires and qualifications, and the duties to which ones wants to be supported. Upon acceptance, a Minister may choose to create a ritual for themselves to commemorate this passage, though this is not required. Ministers remain in sixth circle unless they decide to become Postulants.

A Postulant enters the sixth circle through proven accomplishment in the former circles, a demonstration of wide-ranging leadership skills in creative and practical spheres, acceptance by the community, recommendation by the Clergy sponsor, the Vortex, and their nest or circle, and a consensus vote of confidence by the existing third ring. A postulant spends a minimum of a year and a day working with their sponsor to complete any remaining areas that need focus or attention before they become fully ordained.

❑ continue tithing pledge and maintain all requirements from previous rings

❑ secure sponsorship of clergy for personal training towards ordination

❑ Continue personal training program.

❑ Continue involvement in CAW activities and groups

❑ Coordinate and/or initiate CAW projects

❑ Demonstrate the ability to lead rituals, work well with others, and serve the community

❑ Be accountable to the CAW membership for actions/behaviours that reflect upon the general membership. Address any issues of conflict that may exist with other CAW members making use of the Conflict Resolution Policy.

❑ Share water and become water-siblings with another member, preferably in a circle further inward.

❑ Demonstrate ability to represent the God or Goddess to the mainstream world in a way that commands respect.

❑ Be politically active about your concerns with regard to local environmental issues.

❑ Develop personal relationships with animals and plants e.g. gardening, raising animals

❑ Read "Wheels of Life" by Anodea Judith.

❑ Read at least 7 more books from bibliography and be able to discuss the concepts they convey. Demonstrate a basic level of scholarship in the areas relevant to pagan clergy e.g. psychology, religion, history, sociology etc.

❑ Write an in-depth research paper, or equivalent, on a relevant aspect of the pagan religion which demonstrates intelligent insights.

- ❏ Study and demonstrate competence in a divinatory skill e.g. tarot, astrology, scrying
- ❏ Take responsibility for addressing personal issues from past or present experience and undergo therapy when appropriate. Be prepared to discuss problems with clergy advisors and accept criticism, mediation and problem-solving processes.
- ❏ Get your life reasonably together emotionally, financially, physically, spiritually
- ❏ Go on a solitary vision quest, minimum of seven days, under the guidance of clergy sponsor.
- ❏ Be a CAW member for at least three years and part of sixth circle for at least 6 months
- ❏ Undergo, and pass, a police check as required by Australian law.
- ❏ Seek nomination from sponsoring clergy, your nest or circle, and Vortex to Lifeways. Lifeways should take steps to determine your acceptability to the membership of the Church.
- ❏ Submit, in writing, your qualifications for service and plan for further enrichment of the Church, including a statement of your particular interest.
- ❏ Submit to oral examination and evaluation by a group of clergy members and/or others nominated by Vortex and approved by Lifeways
- ❏ If approved by Lifeways, create and design your own ordination ritual to enter the third ring.

Third Ring – BEACONS (Circles 7-9) – Leadership

To become a member of the third ring, you first need to have learnt to serve and create, have been approved and ordained by the community, and to have dedicated your life to the gods. The role of the Priesthood is to offer leadership, guidance, teaching, ritual creation, and to accept final responsibility (the buck stops here).

Entering the Priesthood is a complex process requiring fulfilment of all the previous levels, as well as a level of personal development that is worthy of setting an example for others. Once you have been approved by Lifeways and have undergone your ordination ritual, you are considered a priest or priestess within CAW. Your purpose now is to foster the growth and development of the Pagan movement and community, and help the return of the Goddess to the world at large. This is achieved in numerous ways: through ritual, leadership, workshops and teaching, writing, travelling, conducting interviews, creating works of art, and just getting in there and doing it.

This ring uses the colour purple to signify spirituality.

- ❏ Establish a link between gods and community, and help people make that link themselves
- ❏ administer sacraments, meaning be able to perform the rituals of the religion
- ❏ clearly articulate the body of lore or doctrine of the Church to anyone
- ❏ teach what you know
- ❏ take responsibility for making things happen
- ❏ put out fires effectively, in a real and a metaphorical sense
- ❏ have a sense of presence that is inspiring to others
- ❏ create original material
- ❏ have personal credibility through lack of hypocrisy
- ❏ think on your feet and be able to wing it when necessary
- ❏ effectively lead others without using power over
- ❏ evoke a sense of affection and respect
- ❏ maintain clarity of vision for the community
- ❏ be able to deal with administrative issues effectively and appropriately, within a required time-frame
- ❏ be able to raise power magically
- ❏ lead regular services
- ❏ be water-siblings with several other CAW members, including those further inward

Further guidelines for conduct and movement through the rings are contained within the Clergy Handbook.

Church of All Worlds Bibliography

by Anodea Judith & Oberon Zell

IT IS IMPOSSIBLE TO CATEGORICALLY SEPARATE THESE BOOKS APPROPRIATELY to each Ring, so they are here followed when possible by the letters A, B or C, indicating texts recommended for basic, intermediary or advanced studies. Of course, no one is expected to read all or even most of these books; rather, we intend to offer here a selection of the best-recommended.

The goal is for everyone coming into CAW to be oriented in our basic identity and worldview. So we have attempted to include only those books that express and teach the worldview that is our ground, at varying levels of complexity. We have attempted to include in each category fiction and nonfiction books, tapes, and films that make the same basic point. (Special thanks to Wendy Hunter-Roberts, D.J. Hamouris, Anna Korn, Firebird, Sam Webster, Fathom Hummingbear, Jon DeCles, Nancye Kirtley, James Assad, Nybor, Jordan Gruber, Gail Slocum.)

SPECIAL NOTE: Many of these books are available as audiobooks and recordings for the blind. Whenever known, such will be indicated by the following codes: Recordings for the Blind [RFB], 20 Roszel Rd., Princeton, NJ 08540; Womyn's Braille Press [WBP], POB 8475, Minneapolis, MN 55408; Nat'l Library Service [NLS] for Blind & Physically Handicapped.

CAW Course Outline

I. THE CONTEMPORARY PAGAN MOVEMENT
- A. THE NEW PAGANISM
- B. INSPIRATIONS & VISIONS OF COMMUNITY
- C. MODERN WITCHCRAFT

II. PAGAN HISTORY
- A. ANCIENT HISTORY/ARCHAEOLOGY
- B. GODDESS HYSTORY
- C. MEDIEVAL WITCHCRAFT

III. MYTHTHEOILOGY
- A. GENERAL MYTHOLOGY
- B. GODDESSES
- C. THE GOD

IV. EARTH & NATURE
- A. ECOSOPHY
- B. COSMOLOGY & METAPHYSICS
- C. EMERGENT EVOLUTION

V. MIND, PSYCHE & BEHAVIOR
- A. PSYCHOLOGY & PERSONAL GROWTH
- B. SEXUALITY & RELATIONSHIPS

VI. THE EVOLUTION REVOLUTION
- A. CONSCIOUSNESS
- B. PARADIGM SHIFT
- C. PSYCHEDELIA
- D. THE FRINGES OF SCIENCE

VII. WOMEN'S & MEN'S MYSTERIES
- A. WOMEN'S SPIRITUALITY & FEMINIST THEALOGY
- B. MEN'S MYSTERIES

VIII. SOCIAL CHANGE
- A. FEMINISM
- B. GREEN POLITICS & R/EVOLUTION
- C. FUTURISM

IX. COMPARATIVE RELIGION & WORLD MYTHOLOGY
- A. THE CELTS
- B. BRITISH ISLES
- C. GREECE
- D. ROME
- E. EGYPT
- F. SHAMANISM
- G. NATIVE SOUTH AMERICA
- H. NATIVE NORTH AMERICA
- I. AFRO-CARRIBEAN RELIGION
- J. NORTHERN EUROPE
- K. EASTERN RELIGIONS
- L. FAERIE
- M. CULTS & SECRET SOCIETIES
- N. CHRISTIANITY

X. METAPHYSICAL PRACTICES
- A. BASIC MAGIC & RITUAL
- B. DIVINATION

I. THE CONTEMPORARY PAGAN MOVEMENT

A. THE NEW PAGANISM

1. RADIANT CIRCLES: ECOSPIRITUALITY & THE CHURCH OF ALL WORLDS, Alder Moonoak, 2022. Wide-ranging historical, cultural and theological exploration of the CAW, discussing its role and place as both as a unique Neo-Pagan and futurist New Religion.(C)
2. DRAWING DOWN THE MOON, Margot Adler, 1979; revised 1986. The most comprehensive, essential book ever written on the modern Neo-Pagan movement. (A)[RFB]
3. THE TRIUMPH OF THE MOON: A HISTORY OF MODERN PAGAN WITCHCRAFT, Hutton, Ronald. 2000. The first full-scale study of modern Pagan Witchcraft. (B)
4. THE SPIRAL DANCE, Starhawk, 1979. The most basic, readable, and concise book on Neo-Pagan premises and practice. (A)[RFB]
5. SHARING WATER: CHURCH OF ALL WORLDS MEMBER HANDBOOK, Oberon Zell, Ed. 2024. Fundamental writings on CAW for members and other Pagans. (A)
6. CHURCH OF ALL WORLDS CLERGY HANDBOOK, Oberon Zell, Ed. 2024. Good resource for any Pagan clergy. (B)
7. PEOPLE OF THE EARTH: THE NEW PAGANS SPEAK OUT, Ellen Evert Hopman & Lawrence Bond, 1996. Interviews with many major Pagan leaders. (A)
8. TRUE MAGICK, Amber K, 1990. Practical, cheap, complete, humorous. A good companion to *Spiral Dance.* (A)
9. SIRENS, 1994. Beautiful movie centered on the great Australian Neo-Pagan artist of the early 20th century, Norman Lindsey. (A)
10. THE ENCYCLOPEDIA OF WITCHES & WITCHCRAFT, Rosemary Guiley, 1989. Excellent entries on people, groups, history, of both Witchcraft and Neo-Paganism. (ref.)
11. THE SABBATS: A NEW APPROACH TO LIVING THE OLD WAYS, Edain McCoy, 1994. Origins, modern practice, rituals. (A)
12. MODERN PAGANS, Sulak, John & Vale, V, 2001. (A)
13. PAGAN AND WITCH ELDERS OF THE WORLD: PAST AND PRESENT, Von Forslun, Tamara. 2020. (B)
14. WHEN, WHY…IF: AN ETHICS WORKBOOK, Wood, Robin. 1996. (A)

B. INSPIRATIONS & VISIONS OF COMMUNITY

1. STRANGER IN A STRANGE LAND, Robert A. Heinlein, 1961. (NOT the 1991 unedited release!) Germinal in the original CAW vision, this prophetic novel still has some important ideas for new members. (A)[NLS]
2. DAS ENERGI, Paul Williams. Poetic and visionary revelation of How It Is. (A)
3. ISLAND, Aldous Huxley, 1962. This antithesis to *Brave New World* is a Pagan paradise with which we can strongly identify. [NLS]
4. THE THREE SIRENS, Irving Wallace, 1963. Sacred sexuality in a utopian island paradise. (fiction)(B)

C. MODERN WITCHCRAFT

1. THE WAXING MOON: A GENTLE GUIDE TO MAGIC, Helen Chappell. 1974. (A)
2. WICCA: A GUIDE FOR THE SOLITARY PRACTITIONER, Scott Cunningham, 1988. A good introductory guide. (A)
3. THE FAMILY WICCA BOOK, Ashleen O'Gaea, 1992. Witchcraft for families. (A)
4. BUCKLAND'S COMPLETE BOOK OF WITCHCRAFT, Raymond Buckland, 1986. The most comprehensive book on Wiccan teachings and practices. (B)
5. THE REBIRTH OF WITCHCRAFT, Doreen Valiente, 1989. Valuable history of 20th century revival of Witchcraft from Gardner in the 1930s, through popularization in the '60s, to feminist Craft. (B)
6. WITCHES U.S.A., Susan Roberts, 1971. Early American Witchcraft in the late 1960s, and some key personalities involved. (B)
7. AN A-B-C OF WITCHCRAFT, Doreen Valiente, 1973; 1986. It's all here! (ref.)(B)
8. A WITCHES BIBLE COMPLEAT, Janet & Stewart Farrar 1984. First published as EIGHT SABBATS FOR WITCHES (1981) and THE WITCHES' WAY (1981). The Farrars joined CAW in 1995. (B)
9. WITCHCRAFT TODAY, Gerald Gardner, 1954; 1982. The book that introduced the modern Witchcraft revival. (C)
10. CRAFTING THE ART OF MAGICK, Aidan Kelly, 1991. A scholarly but controversial investigation into the origins of Gardnerian Witchcraft. (C)

II. PAGAN HISTORY

A. ANCIENT HISTORY/ARCHAEOLOGY

1. GOD AGAINST THE GODS: THE HISTORY OF THE WAR BETWEEN MONOTHEISM AND POLYTHEISM, Jonathan Kirsch, 2005. Kirsch observes that monotheistic religions have too often used the worship of one god as a way to persecute those who do not share similar beliefs. (B)

2. THE ALPHABET AND THE GODDESS: THE CONFLICT BETWEEN WORD AND IMAGE, Leonard Shlain, 1998. This groundbreaking book proposes that the rise of alphabetic literacy reconfigured the human brain and brought about profound changes in history, religion, and gender relations. (B)

3. THE CHALICE AND THE BLADE, Riane Eisler, 1987. How patriarchy took over through the acceleration of militarism. True female/male partnership as the direction for the future. (A)[RFB]

4. A CHRONICLE OF THE LAST PAGANS, Pierre Chuvin, 1990. A history of the triumph of Xianity in the Roman Empire as told from the perspective of the Pagans of the time. (A)

5. THE CREATION OF PATRIARCHY, Gerda Lerner, 1986. A brilliant analysis of the earliest law codes that legislated the new patriarchy. (B)

6. THE ROOTS OF CIVILIZATION, Alexander Marshack, 1972. The cognitive beginnings of our first art, symbol and notation. (C)

7. THE SECRET OF CRETE, Hans Wunderlich, 1983. Brilliant analysis of the "Minoan" civilization, refuting many of the popular notions regarding the "palace" of Knossos. (C)

8. THE MYSTERY OF THE ORACLES, Philipp Vandenburg, 1979; 1982. World-famous archaeologists reveal the best-kept secrets of antiquity. (C)

B. GODDESS HYSTORY

1. WHEN GOD WAS A WOMAN, Merlin Stone, 1976. Stone's story points us to a time when all worshipped the Goddess, reminding us that patriarchal religion is not natural or inevitable. (A)[RFB]

2. WHENCE THE GODDESSES: A SOURCEBOOK, Miriam Robbins Dexter, 1990. An essential reference. (B)

3. THE ONCE AND FUTURE GODDESS, Elinor Gadon, 1989. Art historian and scholar Gadon uses well researched art history, archeological speculations, and current artistic trends to reconstruct goddess-based culture and world view in past, present, and future. Readable. (art/religions history)(B)

4. GODDESSES AND GODS OF OLD EUROPE (1982), THE LANGUAGE OF THE GODDESS (1990), THE CIVILIZATION OF THE GODDESS (1991), Marija Gimbutas. Bold and imaginative scholarly reconstruction of earliest religious symbols. (C)

C. MEDIEVAL WITCHCRAFT

1. WITCHES AND PAGANS: WOMEN IN EUROPEAN FOLK RELIGION, 700-1100 (Secret History of the Witches) Max Dashu, 2017.

2. SORCERESS. Beautiful French film of an historical encounter between a village Witch and an Inquisitor. (video from Mystic Fire, POB 1092, Cooper Stn., New York, NY 10276. 800-292-9001)(A)

3. THE HEART OF THE FIRE, Cerridwen Fallingstar, 1990. Powerful story of a coven during the Burning Times, told by a practiced, skilled Witch, with lots of examples of how it's done. (fiction)(A)

4. ANCHORESS, Judith Stanley-Smith & Christine Watkins, writers; Chris Newby, dir. 1993. A Pagan lens on the 14th century, seen through the eyes of the 14-yr-old daughter of the village Wise Woman. (video)

5. ARADIA, OR THE GOSPEL OF THE WITCHES, Charles G. Leland, 1889. Essential scriptural material of 19th century Tuscany Witches, or Strega. (scripture)(A)

6. COWS, PIGS, WARS & WITCHES: THE RIDDLE OF CULTURE, Anthony Harris, 1989. A brilliant and insightful analysis of Medieval history and what shaped it. (B)

7. WITCHCRAFT & THE GAY COUNTERCULTURE, Arthur Evans, 1978. A radical view of Western Civilization and some of the people it has tried to destroy. (B)

8. WITCHCRAFT IN THE MIDDLE AGES, Jeffrey Burton Russell, 1972. Comprehensive history of European Witchcraft from the 5th to 15th century, and its social and religious implications. (C)

III. MYTHEOILOGY

A. GENERAL MYTHOLOGY

1. SMALL GODS, Terry Pratchett. Hilariously funny and painfully brilliant theology on the origin and nature of gods and religion; in the Discworld series. A must read! (fiction)(A)

2. THE GODS ABIDE, Thomas Burnett Swann, 1976. Swann's final novel, telling of the retreat of the Pagan gods and all their retinue. A beautiful and moving story. (fiction)(A)

3. MYTHS & LEGENDS OF ALL NATIONS, Herbert Spencer Robinson & Knox Wilson, 1950; 1961. Synopses of the essential stories from virtually every culture on Earth. (A)

4. A COMPREHENSIVE DICTIONARY OF THE GODS, Anne S. Baumbgartner, 1984. A virtual biographical dictionary of every god or goddess known from every culture. (ref.) A)

5. MYTHS TO LIVE BY, Joseph Campbell, 2011. Readable theory of mythology. What are myths? What do they contribute to our lives? (B)[NLS]

6. HISTORICAL ATLAS OF WORLD MYTHOLOGY, Joseph Campbell, 1988. Multivolume magnum opus. Giant books, profusely illustrated. Each book in this series is a complete work. (ref.)(B)

7. THE POWER OF MYTH, Joseph Campbell, 1988. Conversations with Bill Moyers, transcribed from the six-hr. PBS TV series. (interview available on video from PBS)(B)

8. THE MASKS OF GOD: TRANSFORMATIONS OF MYTH THROUGH TIME, Joseph Campbell, 2018. Excellent for a grounding in myth and archetype. (4 volumes)(B)

B. GODDESSES

1. ANCIENT MIRRORS OF WOMANHOOD, Merlin Stone, 1979 (2 volumes). A fine selection of important Goddess legends, artfully presented. (mythology)(A)[WBP]

2. THE WITCHES' GODDESS: THE FEMININE PRINCIPLE OF DIVINITY, Janet & Stewart Farrar, 1987. Overview of Goddess from ancient Near East, Western Europe, Celtic and Meditetrranean, with rituals to invoke each one, and a list of Goddesses of the world. By CAW members. (A)

3. INANNA, QUEEN OF HEAVEN AND EARTH, Diane Wolkstein, Joseph Noel Kramer, 1983. Mytho-poetic, readable reconstruction of most ancient Sumerian scriptures of the Goddess that still speak to us today. Beautiful poetry, good scholarship. (A)

4. THE HEART OF THE GODDESS, Hallie Eagleheart, 1990. Brief, well-told myths of the Goddess in all her aspects from around the world. Profusely-illustrated coffee table book. (mythology)(A)

5. THE BOOK OF GODDESSES AND HEROINES, Patricia Monaghan, 1981; revised 1997. You can find any goddess from any pantheon here. (ref.)(B)

6. GODDESS: MOTHER OF LIVING NATURE, Adele Getty, 1990. Profusely illustrated coffee-table book of Goddess imagery. (B)

7. THE GREAT MOTHER, Erich Neumann, 1963. Voluminous investigation of the archetype, with substantial photo section. ©

8. THE WHITE GODDESS, Robert Graves, 1948; revised 1966. Enormous work exploring the depth and scope of True Poetry as Muse-inspired, underpinning Druidic teachings and the Celtic Tree Calendar. (C)

9. IN ALL HER NAMES: EXPLORATIONS OF THE FEMININE IN DIVINITY, Joseph Campbell & Charles Musés, eds. 1991. Brilliant essays on the Goddess by Joseph Campbell, Charles Musés, Marija Gimbutas & Riane Eisler. (essays)(B)

C. THE GOD

1. THE WITCHES' GOD, Janet & Stewart Farrar, 1989. Companion to *The Witches' Goddess,* with invocations and list. (A)

2. THE GREEN MAN: ARCHETYPE OF OUR ONENESS WITH THE EARTH, William Anderson, photos by Clive Hicks, 1990. Thorough examination of the archetype. (A)

3. THE GOD OF THE WITCHES, Margaret Murray, 1933. Legendry but controversial thesis of Medieval Pagan Witchcraft that inspired Gerald Gardner. (B)[RFB]

4. THE GOLDEN BOUGH, James Frazier, 1890; 1981. Classic compendium of worldwide customs regarding the cycle of the sacrificed Year-King. (ref.)(C)[NLS]

IV. EARTH & NATURE

A. ECOSOPHY, GAEA/GAIA

1. GAEAGENESIS: CONCEPTION & BIRTH OF THE LIVING EARTH, Oberon Zell, 2022. The definitive compilation of Gaean theology, history and philosophy from ancient times to now, by CAW's Founder. (A)

2. WAKING THE GLOBAL HEART, Anodea Judith, 2010. Will we survive into the next age? If so, what will it look like and what will it take for us to get there? (B)

3. THE GLOBAL HEART AWAKENS: HUMANITY'S RITE OF PASSAGE FROM

THE LOVE OF POWER TO THE POWER OF LOVE, Anodea Judith, 2013. A CAW Priestess explores mythic themes in various historical eras to explain the past, present, and future of the human experience. It suggests that the world is facing a rite of passage into adulthood and that a time of cooperation, stabilization, and sharing is approaching. (B)

4. SONG OF GAEA, Kirsten Johnson, Oberon Zell, Pratima Sarkar (illustrator), 2021. Gorgeous full-color children's book. (A)

5. LIVES OF A CELL, Lewis Thomas, 1974. Brilliant essays on the nature of Life. (A)

6. LIFETIDE, Lyall Watson, 1979. The awareness that "we are all one" examined from a biological and evolutionary perspective. (A)

7. GAIA: AN ATLAS OF PLANET MANAGEMENT, Norman Myers, ed. 1984. The definitive guide to a planet in critical transition. Profusely illustrated, with over 100 contributors. Extraordinary. (B)

8. SACRED LAND, SACRED SEX, RAPTURE OF THE DEEP, Dolores LaChappelle, 1988. A brilliant, multi-disciplinary examination of how ritual works. Demands deep concentration, and well worth it! (C)

9. GAIA: THE GROWTH OF AN IDEA, Lawrence Joseph, 1990. (B)

10. GAIA: A NEW LOOK AT LIFE ON EARTH (1979), THE AGES OF GAIA (1988), HEALING GAIA (1991), James Lovelock. Implications of Gaia Thesis. (B)

11. THE RECOVERY OF CULTURE, Henry Bailey Stevens, 1963. Classic. (B)

B. COSMOLOGY & METAPHYSICS

1. COSMOS, Carl Sagen, 1980. Superb! (non-fiction book & TV series)(A)

2. COSMOS: A SPACETIME ODESSEY, Neil DeGrasse Tyson, 2014. Fabulous sequel to Sagan. (TV series)(A)

3. COSMOS: POSSIBLE WORLDS, Neil De Grasse Tyson, 2020. Another awesome sequel. (TV series)(A)

4. THE UNIVERSE IS A GREEN DRAGON, Brian Swimme & Thomas Berry, 1984. (A)

5. THE SELF-ORGANIZING UNIVERSE, Erich Jantsch, 1980. (C)

6. THE TAO OF PHYSICS, Fritjof Capra, 1975. [NLS, RFB]

C. HUMAN EVOLUTION

1. STAR MAKER, Olaf Stapleton. 1937; 1972. One of the most far-reaching SF books ever written. An evolutionary projection from humanity to Gaia to the galaxy and beyond! (A)

3. THE DESCENT OF WOMAN, Elaine Morgan, 1972. Presents the radical thesis that human evolution included a significant phase as an aquatic ape. (A)

4. SO HUMAN AN ANIMAL, René Dubos, 1968. 1969 Pulitzer Prize winner on our emergence and nature. (essays)(A)

7. MORE THAN HUMAN, Theodore Sturgeon. A vision of the possible future evolution of group consciousness. (fiction)(B)

8. ODD JOHN, Olaf Stapleton. 1935? A classic science fiction novel of *Homo Novus*. (B)

V. MIND, PSYCHE & BEHAVIOR

A. PSYCHOLOGY & PERSONAL GROWTH

1. WHEELS OF LIFE: A USER'S GUIDE TO THE CHAKRA SYSTEM, Anodea Judith, 1987; and THE SEVENFOLD JOURNEY, Selene Vega & Anodea Judith, 1993. A carefully wrought and readable synthesis of the ancient chakra system and modern psychology in two books by CAW High Priestess that provide keys to our own selves and lives. (A)

2. THE SEVEN HABITS OF HIGHLY EFFECTIVE PEOPLE, Stephen Covey, 1989. Powerful lessons in personal change. (A)

3. TOWARD A PSYCHOLOGY OF BEING, Abraham Maslow, 1962. Grandaddy of Transpersonal Psychology gives us the basics of a psychology of self-actualization. (C)

4. CARE OF THE SOUL, Thomas Moore, 1992.

B. SEXUALTY & RELATIONSHIPS

1. FIFTY YEARS OF POLYAMORY IN AMERICA: A GUIDED TOUR OF A GROWING MOVEMENT, Glen Olson & Terry Lee Brussel-Rogers, 2022. (A)

2. LOVE WITHOUT LIMITS, Debora Annapol, ed. 1992. First book specifically exploring the option of polyamory. (essays)(A)

3. COURTSHIP RITE, Donald Kingsbury, 1982. Brilliant novel of group marriage and religion in a SF cannibal society. (fiction)(A)

4. THE REBELLION OF YALE MARRAT, Robert Rimmer, 1964. A non-science-fiction analog of Heinlein's SISL, including a new Goddess religion. (fiction)(B)

5. SACRED PLEASURE, Rhiane Eisler, 1995. A sequel to *The Chalice & the Blade,* addressing all aspects of sexuality and pleasure through the ages, including suppression. (B)
6. MARRIAGE AND MORALS, Bertrand Russell, 1929. Amazing insights! (essays)(B)
7. LOVING MORE: THE POLYFIDELITY PRIMER, Ryam Nearing. Excellent on structuring multiple relationships. (B)

VI. THE EVOLUTION REVOLUTION

A. CONSCIOUSNESS
1. THE ORIGIN OF CONSCIOUSNESS IN THE BREAKDOWN OF THE BICAMERAL MIND, Julian Jaynes, 1977. Very important theory of consciousness as a function of hemispheric laterality, with the "gods" inhabiting the right hemispheres of humanity. (B)
2. THE TANGLED WING: BIOLOGICAL CONSTRAINTS ON THE HUMAN SPIRIT, Melvin Konner, 1982; 2003. How consciousness is shaped by biology. If we continue to ignore our animal nature and heritage, we will never move forward into a world of peace and justice. (socio-biology)(C)
3. THE COSMIC TRIGGER, 1978; and PROMETHEUS RISING, 2016. Robert Anton Wilson (C)

B. FUTURISM & PARADIGM SHIFT
1. THE SYNTELLECT HYPOTHESIS: FIVE PARADIGMS OF THE MIND'S EVOLUTION, Alex Vikoulov, 2020 Envisioning the future integration and synthesis of humanity and technology, with many predictions of things to come. (C)
2. THE FOURTH TURNING:AN AMERICAN PROPHECY, William Straus & Neill Howe, 1997. An analysis of American history in 20-year generational cycles. (B)
3. THE POSSIBLE HUMAN, Jean Houston, 1982. Based on extensive consciousness research, Houston gives us a look at what we might be, if we truly realized our potential. Includes some practices for self-realization.
4. THE BRIDGE BETWEEN MATTER & SPIRIT IS MATTER BECOMING SPIRIT, Paulo Soleri, 1973. An impassioned plea for a new religion of the Earth, by the architect of Arcosanti. (essays)(B)
5. LET ME EXPLAIN (1970) and BUILDING THE EARTH, Pierre Teilhard de Chardin.

The best general explanations of Chardin's vision of future evolution to the Omega Point of planetary awakening. (B)
6. THE PHENOMENON OF MAN, Pierre Teilhard de Chardin, 1965. One of the most significant and influential books of all time, embracing the entirety of evolution from Alpha to Omega. (C)
7. NEW AGE & ARMAGEDDON: THE GODDESS OR THE GURUS?. Monica Sjöö, 1992. A feminist Pagan critique of the New Age, and a vision for the future. (B)
8. THE FINAL EMPIRE: THE COLLAPSE OF CIVILIZATION & THE SEED OF THE FUTURE, William H. Kötke, 1993. 10,000 years of civilization brilliantly analyzed, with a prescription for planetary salvation. (B)
9. THE GLOBAL BRAIN AWAKES, Peter Russell, 1982; 1995. A vision of the immanent emergence of collective planetary consciousness. (also available as a video) (A)
10. THE TIME FALLING BODIES TAKE TO LIGHT, William Irwin Thompson, 1981. Mythology, sexuality and the origins of culture at the threshold of our future evolution. Superb! (A)
11. THE TURNING POINT, Fritjof Capra, 1982. Evidence leading to the immanent emergence of a new phase in the evolution of human consciousness. (A)[NLS, RFB]
12. GLOBAL MIND CHANGE, with Juanita Brown, Rachel Naomi Remen, MD, & Willis Harman. Three leading thinkers discuss the emergence of a new world view based on interconnectedness. (New Dimensions audiotape interview #2314)

C. PSYCHEDELIA
1. THE ARCHAIC REVIVAL, 1991, and FOOD OF THE GODS, 1993, Terence McKenna. The evolution of human consciousness catalyzed by magic mushrooms; also addresses UFOs, the rebirth of the Goddess, and the "end of history." (Available as audiotape and video)(A)
2. HALLUCINOGENS & SHAMANISM, Michael J. Harner, 1973. (B)
3. CEREMONIAL CHEMISTRY, Thomas Szaz, 1975. A significant overview of the long history of the war against psychotropic plants and those who use them. (B)
8. THE PSYCHEDELIC EXPERIENCE, Tim Leary, Ralph Metzner, Richard Alpert, 1964.

A manual based on the *Tibetan Book of the Dead.* Metzner was a member of CAW. (C)

D. THE FRINGES OF SCIENCE

1. THE EDGES OF SCIENCE, Richard Morris, 1990. Crossing the boundary from physics to metaphysics. An excellent introduction to the borderline territory. (A)
2. PASSPORT TO MAGONIA, Jacques Vallée, 1969; 1993. A comparison of the UFO phenomena with historical reports and legends of encounters with Fäerie. Provocative! (A)
3. STALKING THE WILD PENDULUM, Itzak Bentov, 1977. A creative and holistic view of human consciousness and the universe. Fun!
4. THE CRACK IN THE COSMIC EGG, Joseph Chilton Pearce. Classic. (B)
5. A WIZARD'S BESTIARY, 2nd Edition. Oberon Zell, 2022. With more than 1,500 illustrations and details of creatures and cryptids mythical, legendary and mysterious. (A)
6. THE WORLD'S MOST INCREDIBLE STORIES, Adam Sisman, ed. 1992. Mind-boggling news reports selected from 20 years of the *Fortean Times*. Will definitely give you something to think about! Over 200 photos and drawings. (news clips)(A)
7. NO WAY: THE NATURE OF THE IMPOSSIBLE, Philip Davis & David Park, ed. 1987. Essays on the "impossible" by 20 writers. (B)
8. INCREDIBLE COINCIDENCE, Alan Vaughn, 1979. The first major collection of synchronicity case histories. (B)
9. FORBIDDEN SCIENCE, Jacques Vallée, 1992. Personal journal of the 1960s by the world's foremost researcher of the UFO phenomenon. (journal)(B)
10. BOOK OF THE DAMED (1919) and LO! (1931), Charles Fort. Reports of the Weird.

VII. WOMEN'S & MEN'S MYSTERIES

A. WOMEN'S SPIRITUALITY & FEMINIST THEALOGY

1. MOTHER WOVE THE MORNING, Carol Lynn Pearson, 1992. An incredible one-woman stage performance of 16 women throughout history, searching for The Mother. (video & book available)(A)
4. GODDESSES IN EVERY WOMAN, Jean Shinoda-Bolen, 1984. (A)
5. THE GREAT COSMIC MOTHER: REDISCOVERING THE RELIGION OF THE EARTH, Monica Sjöö & Barbara Mor, 1987; 1992. (new edition has color plates)[WBP]
8. THE POLITICS OF WOMEN'S SPIRITUALITY, Charlene Spretnak, 1982. Just what it sounds like! Coherent, powerful arguments for a feminist spiritual ground for healing our world. Readable and basic. (B)[WBP]
9. DESCENT TO THE GODDESS, Sylvia Perera, 1981. Relationship to the Goddess/feminist spirituality takes us on a journey down into our depths. Perera describes and illuminates this journey and its meaning. (A)
10. BEYOND GOD THE FATHER, Mary Daly, 1985. [WBP]
11. WOMEN'S MYSTERIES, ANCIENT & MODERN, M. Esther Harding, 1971. (B)
12. MOTHERWIT, Diane Mariechild, 1981; 1988. Important handbook of feminist spiritual practice, "co-creating our own reality."
13. THE WOMEN'S SPIRITUALITY BOOK, Diane Stein, 1986. Summarizes historical shift from matriarchy to patriarchy and growth of women's spirituality in '70s and '80s, then instructs in practices. Useful. (A)

B. MEN'S MYSTERIES

1. BLINDFOLD ON A TIGHTROPE: MEN'S MYTHS & MEN'S MYSTERIES, Ramfis Firethorn, 1993. By a CAW member. (A)
2. THE FLOWERING ROD: MEN, SEX & SPIRITUALITY, Kenny Klein, 1991. Written by a CAW member and a founder of Blue Star Witchcraft tradition. (A)
3. CELEBRATING THE MALE MYSTERIES, R.J. Stewart, 1991.
4. THE HORNED GOD: FEMINISM & MEN AS WOUNDING AND HEALING, John Rowan, 1987. Where do men fit into feminist spirituality? Psychologist Rowan gives us a powerful answer, affirming both male and female power in his redefinition of masculinity. (B)
5. HERO OF A THOUSAND FACES, Joseph Campbell, 1956. Classic. (C)

VIII. SOCIAL CHANGE

A. FEMINISM

1. BACKLASH: THE UNDECLARED WAR AGAINST AMERICAN WOMEN, Susan Faludi, 1991. Important analysis of the anti-women forces and their programs. (A)[WBP]
5. THE HEROINE'S JOURNEY, Maureen Murdock, 1990. Life journey of Everywoman

towards a sense of self in connection with the Goddess. A healing book. (A)

2. WOMEN'S REALITY: AN EMERGING FEMALE SYSTEM, Ann Wilson Schaef, 1992. Schaef shows us how the "normalcy" we take for granted is a system that subjugates and exploits, by virtue of its every assumption of thought and habit. (B)

3. MASCULINE AND FEMININE: THE NATURAL FLOW OF OPPOSITES IN THE PSYCHE, Gareth S. Hill, 2001. A Jungian analyst provides a new model for understanding the masculine and feminine principles that exist in everyone, providing insight into the events of daily life and the themes of entire lifetimes. (B)

B. GREEN POLITICS & R/EVOLUTION

1. EARTH IN THE BALANCE: ECOLOGY & THE HUMAN SPIRIT, Al Gore, 1992. A rationale and blueprint for saving the planet, by the Vice President of the US! And there is even mention of The Goddess! (B)

2. DREAMING THE DARK: MAGIC, SEX AND POLITICS, Starhawk, 1982. Good ideas about female/male relations, power, sex, spirituality, and of course, the Goddess and the God. [WBP, RFB]

3. SPIRITUAL DIMENSION OF GREEN POLITICS, Charlene Spretnak, Fritjof Capra, 1985-6. Shows Green politics to be compatible with ancient Goddess religion yet adaptable to needs of modern society.

4. ANTAGONISTS IN THE CHURCH; HOW TO IDENTIFY AND DEAL WITH DESTRUCTIVE CONFLICT, Kenneth C. Haugk, 1988. Firm yet caring steps for dealing with dissension in the church. An essential book for Pagans as well as Christians! (A)

5. RULES FOR RADICALS: A PRACTICALMPORIMER FOR REALISTIC RADICALS, Saul Alinsky, 1989. Simply the best political organizing book ever written. (B)

IX. COMPARATIVE RELIGION & WORLD MYTHOLOGY

A. THE CELTS

1. CELTIC GODS, CELTIC GODDESSES, R.J. Stewart, 1990. Beautifully-illustrated legends and lore of Celtic mythology. (A)

2. CELTIC MYTH & LEGEND, Charles Squire, 1975. The most comprehensive compilation of Celtic legends and poetry ever written. It's all here. (mythology)(B)

3. THE LIFE & DEATH OF A DRUID PRINCE, Ann Ross & Don Robins, 1989. The story of Lindow Man, found in an English peat bog in 1984, and the implications of the find. (A)

B. BRITISH ISLES

1. THE CRYSTAL CAVE (1970); THE HOLLOW HILLS (1974); THE LAST ENCHANTMENT (1979); THE WICKED DAY (1983), Mary Stewart. Terrific novelization of the whole Arthurian mythos, seen through the eyes of Merlin. (fiction)(A)

2. THE MABINOGION: PRINCE OF ANNWN (1974); CHILDREN OF LLYR (1971); SONG OF RHIANNON (1972); ISLAND OF THE MIGHTY (1936; 1964), Evangeline Walten. The Welsh national epic in novelized form. (4 volumes mythology)(B)

C. GREECE

1. THE BULL FROM THE SEA, Mary Renault, 1962. Great telling of the legend of Theseus and the Minotaur. (fiction)(A)

3. HERCULES, MY SHIPMATE, Robert Graves, 1966. Splendid telling of the Argossy. (A)

4. THE LAST VOYAGE OF ODYSSEUS, Karen Carey, 1983. What happens after Odysseus returns home? (fiction)(A)

5. THE AMBER PRINCESS, Henry Treece, 1963. The story of the Trojan War and its aftermath, seen through the eyes of Electra, daughter of Agamemnon. (fiction)(A)

6. JASON AND THE ARGONAUTS, Ray Harryhausen, 1963. Movie of the Quest for the Golden Fleece. (film)(A)

7. THE GREEK MYTHS, Robert Graves, 2012. Classic. (A)

C. ROME

1. THE GOLDEN ASS, Lucius Apuleius (translated by Robert Graves) 2009. (scripture)(B)

2. METAMORPHOSIS, Ovid, David Raeburn, et al, 2004. Beginning with the creation of the world, Ovid interweaves many of the best-known myths and legends of ancient Greece and Rome. Classic. (A)

E. EGYPT

1. EGYPTIAN RELIGION, E.A. Wallis Budge, 1900; 1959.

2. EGYPTIAN MYTHOLOGY, Veronica Ions, 1965. Paul Hamlyn series. (mythology)(B)
3. EGYPT BEFORE THE PHARAOHS, Michael A. Hoffman, 1979. The prehistoric foundations of Egyptian civilization. (C)
4. THE EGYPTIAN BOOK OF THE DEAD, translated by E.A. Wallis Budge, 1895; 1967.

F. SHAMANISM
1. THE WAY OF THE SHAMAN, Michael J. Harner, 1982. Accurate, comprehensive, and readable book on the shamanic path. [RFB]
2. WIZARD OF THE UPPER AMAZON, F. Bruce Lamb, 1993.
3. FACES IN THE SMOKE, Douchan Gersi, 1991. An eyewitness account of Voodoo, shamanism, psychic healing and other amazing human powers over a lifetime of experiences among tribal peoples. (B)
4. SHAMANISM: ANCIENT TECHNIQUES OF ECSTASY, Mircea Eliade, 1974. (C)

G. NATIVE SOUTH AMERICA
1. THE EMERALD FOREST, 1985. Great movie about the world of the Amazon. (A)
2. RAUNI: THE FIGHT FOR THE AMAZON, Jean-Pierre Dutilleux, 1979. An Amazon chieftain accompanies a video crew back to civilization in an attempt to save his people and forest. (video documentary from Mystic Fire)(B)
3. FROM THE HEART OF THE WORLD: THE ELDER BROTHERS' WARNING, Alan Ereira, 1991. The only outside contact with the Kogi; the last surviving pre-Columbian civilization of South America. (video documentary from Mystic Fire)(B)

H. NATIVE NORTH AMERICA
1. BLACK ELK SPEAKS: THE COMPLETE EDITION, John G. Neihardt, 2014.
2. NATIVE AMERICAN MYTHS & MYSTERIES, Vincent H. Gaddis, 1976; 1991.
3. BOOK OF THE HOPI, Frank Waters, 1977.

I. AFRO-CARRIBEAN RELIGIONS
1. DIVINE HORSEMEN: THE LIVING GODS OF HAITI, Maya Deren, 1983. First published in 1953, this is widely recognized as a primary source book on the culture and spirituality of Haitian Voudoun. (B)
2. ORISHAS, GODDESSES, AND VOODOO QUEENS, THE DIVINE FEMININE IN THE AFRICAN RELIGIOUS TRADITIONS, Lilith Dorsey. 2020. An exploration of the goddesses of West Africa and their role in shaping Yoruba (Ifa), Santeria, Haitian Vo-doun, and New Orleans Voodoo. (A)
3. JAMBALAYA: THE NATURAL WOMAN'S BOOK OF PERSONAL CHARMS & PRACTICAL RITUALS, Luisah Teish, 1985; 2021. Neo-African religion by a Yoruba priestess of Oshun. Since its original publication in 1985, *Jambalaya* has become a classic among Women's Spirituality Educators, practitioners of traditional Africana religions, environmental activists, and cultural creatives. (A)
4. THE SERPENT AND THE RAINBOW:, Wade Davis. 1985. A Harvard scientist's astonishing journey into the secret society of Haitian voodoo, zombis and magic. (B)

J. NORTHERN EUROPE
1. NORSE MYTHOLOGY, Niel Gaimon, P. Craig Russell, et al. 2023. Graphic novel, 3 volumes. Wonderful! (A)
2. THE WELL OF REMEMBRANCE, Ralph Metzner, 1995. Rediscovering the Earth Wisdom myths of Northern Europe. Ralph was a CAW member. (A)
3. SEX SONGS OF THE ANCIENT LETTS, Bud Berzing, trans. 1969. 1,000 annotated short songs from the Pagan Latvians going back 4,000 years. Important historical material on the last Europeans to be Christianized. (B)

K. EASTERN RELIGIONS
1. AN INTRODUCTION TO ORIENTAL MYTHOLOGY, Clio Whittaker, 1990. (B)
2. TAO TE CHING: A NEW ENGLISH VERSION, trans. Stephen Mitchell, 1988. Taoism is the Paganism of China. This is a definitive translation for our time. (scripture)

L. FÄERIE
1. THE WORLD GUIDE TO GNOMES, FAIRIES, ELVES AND OTHER LITTLE PEOPLE, Thomas Keightley, 1880; 1978. (C)
2. THE UNDERWORLD INITIATION, R.J. Stewart, 1985. Celtic shamanism and folklore are analyzed to plot a guided journey into Fäerie. (nonfiction)(B)
3. THE FAIRY-FAITH IN CELTIC COUNTRIES, W.Y. Evans-Wentz, 1911; 1966. (C)

M. ALTERNATIVE RELIGIONS, CULTS & SECRET SOCIETIES

1. ENCYCLOPEDIA OF MAN, MYTH & MAGIC, Richard Cavendish, ed, 1983. An amazing encyclopedia covering every conceivable topic in these areas, replete with full-color illustrations. (24 volumes, ref.)(A)
2. GLOBAL RITUALISM: MYTH & MAGIC AROUND THE WORLD, Denny Sargent, 1994. Common themes and archetypal symbols. Denny is a CAW member. (B)
3. THE SACRED FIRE, B.Z. Goldberg, 1932. Experience attending rites and rituals in the ancient world. (B)
4. A HISTORY OF SECRET SOCIETIES, Arkon Daraul, 1962. Fascinating! (B)
5. THE ANCIENT MYSTERIES: A SOURCE-BOOK, Marvin W. Meyer, ed.1987. Sacred texts of the Mystery religions of the ancient Mediterranean world. (scripture)(C)
6. SECRET TEACHINGS OF ALL AGES, Manly Palmer Hall, 1925; 1977. (ref.)(C)

N. CHRISTIANITY

1. GOODBYE JESUS, I'VE GONE HOME TO MOTHER, Oberon Zell, 2021. A rear-view look at Christianity from people who've left it. (A)
2. WHY I AM NOT A CHRISTIAN, Bertrand Russell, 1957. Brilliant! (essays)(A)
3. THE DARK SIDE OF CHRISTIAN HISTORY, Helen Ellerbe, 1995. Documents in detail the tragedies, sorrows and injustices inflicted upon humanity by the Church. (A)
4. JESUS DOESN'T LIVE HERE ANYMORE, Skipp Porteous, 1991. His personal journey from Fundamentalist preacher to Director of the Institute for First Amendment Studies. (A)
5. EUNUCHS FOR THE KINGDOM OF HEAVEN: WOMEN, SEXUALITY, AND THE CATHOLIC CHURCH, Uta Ranke-Heinemann, 1988-90. Brilliant analysis of the centuries-old oppression of women by the Catholic Church, translated from German. (B)
6. THE BOOK YOUR CHURCH DOESN'T WANT YOU TO READ, Tim C. Leedom, ed., 1993. An anthology of freethinkers and others examining the beliefs and history of Christianity from its Pagan origins to now. (B)
7. DECEPTIONS AND MYTHS OF THE BIBLE, Lloyd M. Graham, 1975. As it says. (B)
8. THE VIRGIN: MARY'S CULT AND THE RE-EMERGENCE OF THE GODDESS, Geoffrey Ashe, 1976; 1988. Important! (B)
9. HOLY BLOOD, HOLY GRAIL, Henry Lincoln, Richard Leigh, Michael Baigent, 1982. Was Jesus married? Did he have kids? (B)

X. MAGICK & METAPHYSICAL PRACTICES

A. BASIC MAGIC & RITUAL

1. PROMETHEA, Alan Moore (author), J.H. Williams III & Mick Grey (Illustrators), 3 vols. 2001-2003. Brilliant and gorgeous metaphysical journey. Most highly recommended! (Graphic novel) (A)
2. GRIMOIRE FOR THE APPRENTICE WIZARD, Oberon Zell & the Grey Council. 2004. Foundational textbook for the Grey School of Wizardry. (A)
3. COMPANION FOR THE APPRENTICE WIZARD, Oberon Zell & the Grey School of Wizardry. Things to make and do. 2006 (A)
4. CREATING CIRCLES & CERERMONIES: RITUALS FOR ALL SEASONS & REASONS, Oberon & Morning Glory Zell. 2006. (A)
5. REAL MAGICK, P.E.I. Bonewits, 1971; revised 1979. Theory of magic and ritual by one of the founders of the contemporary Neo-Pagan movement. Superb! (A)
6. RITUAL BODY ART: DRAWING THE SPIRIT, Charles Arnold, 1997. A grimoire extraordinaire for any magickal library! (A)
7. MASTERING WITCHCRAFT, Paul Huson, 1970. Basic how-to introduction to practical Witchcraft and magick. (practice)(A)
8. THE MAGICIAN'S COMPANION, Bill Whitcomb, 1993. A practical and encyclopedic guide to magical and religious symbolism. Tables of Correspondence. Intended as a supplement to *Real Magic.* (ref.)(B)
9. MAGICAL RITES FROM THE CRYSTAL WELL, Ed & Janine Fitch, 1984. A book of basic rituals for solitary Pagans. (rituals)(A)
10. MAGICAL RITUAL METHODS, William Gray, 1971. (practice)(C)

B. DIVINATION

1. THE ART OF DIVINATION, Scott Cunningham, 1993. A comprehensive book with detailed instructions for practicing over 100 divinatory techniques. (A)
2. PICTORIAL KEY TO THE TAROT, Arthur Edward Waite, 1959. The basic book. (A)
3. THE TAROT, Paul Foster Case, 1947. (A)

Questions & Answers On Paganism & CAW

By Oberon Zell

Q: What is Neo-Paganism?

A: Neo-Paganism is a revival and reconstruction of ancient Nature religions adapted for the modern world. It is a religion of the living Earth—a religious motif especially appropriate to the Aquarian Age, as Christianity was the dominant religious motif of the Piscean Age. Neo-Paganism is a natural religion, viewing humanity as a functional organ within the greater organism of all Life, rather than as something special created separate and "above" the rest of the natural world. Neo-Pagans seek not to conquer Nature, but to harmonize and integrate with Her. Neo-Paganism should be regarded as "Green Religion," just as we have "Green Politics" and "Green Economics."

Q: Doesn't "Pagan" mean irreligious or heathen?

A: The word "Pagan" comes from the Latin *Paganus,* meaning peasant or country dweller. As a religious term, it is correctly used by anthropologists to designate the indigenous folk religions of particular r regions and peoples, and by classical scholars to refer to the great ancient pre-Christian civilizations of the Mediterranean area (as in the phrase, "Pagan splendor," often used in reference to classical Greece). Thus all traditional native tribal religions are Pagan, such as those of the American Indians, Polynesians, Africans, Norse, Celts, Gauls, Australian Aborigines, Hindus, etc.

Heathen is not a specifically religious term at all, but simply referred to the people who lived on the heaths (where the heather grew), as in the British Isles. Since such people were usually Pagans, the two terms became regarded as synonymous as far as Christians were concerned.

Q: Don't Pagans worship the Devil?

A: Of course not. "The Devil" is a specifically Christian concept, and no one outside of Judaism, Christianity or Islam recognizes him at all. Indeed, the very notion of a supreme God of Evil is entirely peculiar to Jahvistic monotheism, and utterly alien to most Pagan theology (though it is largely derived from the dualism of Persian Zoroastrianism, wherein Ahura-Mazda, the Lord of Light, is opposed to Ahriman, the Lord of Darkness). The popular confusion arose as a result of the 1486 publication of the *Malleus Malificarum,* or "Hammer of the Witches" by Dominicans Kramer and Sprenger, wherein they gave the first physical description of the Devil as he is commonly depicted today, based on a demonization of the Greek horned God, Pan. As Pan and other horned Gods, such as the stag-horned Cernunnos and Herne, were popular deities of the hunt and the animal kingdom, and widely worshipped by European Pagans, Kramer and Sprenger's equation of that imagery with the Christian's Satan was able to be used to justify the centuries of terrible persecution inflicted by the Church upon those who clung faithfully to their worship of the old gods.

"Satan" of the Old Testament was never described by such imagery, but was rather referred to as a fallen angel, a serpent, or a dragon. The word Satan is merely Hebrew for "adversary," and is related to the Egyptian Set and the Roman Saturn. The word "devil," interestingly enough, is Sanscrit in origin and means "little-god." The root word, devi, is also the root of our words "divine" and "divinity." During the Witchcraft persecutions of the late Middle Ages and on through the 17th century, whenever the defendant spoke of the Horned God being present at the Sabbats (which he was in the person of the High Priest, who costumed himself appropriately and assumed the role) the court recorder would substitute the word "Satan" or "Devil," to have written the word "God" as spoken by the accused would have been considered blasphemous by the Christian court.

The most universal deity worshipped by Pagans worldwide is not a God, but a Goddess: Mother Earth. She is called by many names in many cultures, such as Hertha, Terra, Pachamama, and the familiar Greek name, Gaea. In a greater expansion of Her identity, She is Mother Nature, the All-Mother, the Great Mother, and we, the animals and plants, and the Gods themselves, are all Her children.

Q: What is the relationship between Paganism and Witchcraft?
A: The spiritual leaders in Pagan tribal cultures are the shamans, or medicine men and women, who are both gifted and learned in talents and skills of augury, herbalism, hypnosis, psychic work and sorcery. They are the village teachers, magicians, spirit guides, healers and midwives. Among the Celtic tribes of western Europe, such shamans were known as Wicce—an Anglo-Saxon word meaning "shaper"—from which we derive our present term "Witch." During the centuries of persecution at the hands of the Christian churches, many of these shamans were martyred, along with many of the people they served. Lately there has been a revival of The Craft, based on scholarly reconstructions and some inherited traditions, in which the arts of the shaman are being taught to all members of the "covens." Thus Witchcraft is now emerging as a distinct religion and way of life for entire religious communities, rather than the specialized craft of the village shamans, as it once was. Today, The Craft in many diverse traditions is a flourishing Neo-Pagan religion, but while all Witches are thereby necessarily Pagans, all Pagans are not necessarily Witches!

Q: What do you feel most Pagans have in common regardless of their tradition?
A: We're all children of the same Mother. Most of us work in a Circle, call upon the four directions as Elemental Sprit Beings, and celebrate a seasonal round (the Wheel of the Year) of eight main Festivals (Sabbats), aligned with the Solstices, Equinoxes and cross-quarters. We also tend to celebrate at the full Moon, and we're not afraid of the dark! Most of us regard Divinity as immanent ("Thou art God/dess") and our thealogy tends towards polytheistic pantheism. We honor and value women as Priestesses (only Pagan religions have priestesses!). We draw our values from Nature, we regard life as sacred, and we believe in and practice Magic (probability enhancement). We regard sex as a sacrament, and rape in all forms as the primal "sin." We are a part of a seamless whole with all of Nature, and we believe in a living cosmos, as opposed to the inanimate

clockwork of the Christian worldview. We are brought together by our innate longing for tribal community; reverence for all life; celebration of diversity; intellectual curiosity and honesty; magic; feminism; environmentalism; recognition of non-human sentience; good stories; great parties; much love; noble friends and worthy companions; splendid rituals; wondrous festivals; magnificent Priestesses and Priests.

Q: What is the distinction between Pagan "magickal" and "religious" practices?
A: It is impossible to separate out the magickal from the religious, as it all seems a continuum. Magickal practices run the gamut from simple "Kitchen Witch" spells and charms—mostly concerned with individual healings, blessings, transformations, and other small workings; through "Circle Work" involving raising group energy for healings, community service, weather working, etc.; to larger group workings to save the planet—protecting endangered forests, peoples and species, etc.

The religious aspects include maintaining household altars and shrines (in a Pagan household, every horizontal flat space becomes an altar, just as every wall becomes a bookcase!), meditations, conversations with the Gods, to rituals and celebrations, especially those of the great Sabbats of the Wheel of the Year. These latter often include great theatrical productions, with sets, costumes, props and music, wherein people take on the personas of Gods, Elementals, and other Archetypal Beings. Much of our Festivals include the revival of various ancient traditional customs and rites, such as the May Games, May Queen and King, Maypole Dance, Morris Dancing, Mummers Plays, Ostara Egg Hunt, Yule Tree & Log, and acted-out storytelling.

There is also a lot of political Paganism, especially in the area of environmental activism, as with Earth First!. This involves going out into the wilderness, holding circles in sacred groves, and perhaps chaining ourselves to trees to thwart the loggers; or blockading a nuclear power plant with circles and chants...

Q: How do Pagans worship?
A: Pagans, like persons of other faiths, gather for times of worship. Most Pagans view worship as a time of connection and interaction between themselves, their concepts of Deity, and

the material and spiritual world. This interaction is possible because most Pagans believe that all things are interconnected and interdependent. Emphasizing this continuity, most Pagan worship services take place in a circle.

Pagan worship tends to be experiential. This means that Pagan worship emphasizes the involvement of the participants, and can include singing, dancing, movement, drumming, energy work, meditation and healing. Since the Pagan movement in general does not promote any one dogma, many view Paganism as a religion that emphasizes experience. Pagans are encouraged to explore and test the ideas they encounter, and to adopt ideas or beliefs as their own only when validated by personal experience. Such experience helps Pagans achieve personal and spiritual growth. Pagans, therefore, design their times of worship--which may be called circles or rituals--to foster their growth through a variety of religious experience.

Pagan worship is also intended to promote spiritual maturity. Many Pagans believe that all life, including humanity, is naturally propelled toward its greatest growth, potential and fulfillment. This natural urge needs attention and care. When properly cultivated, it leads to a development of conscience, ethics, and personal responsibility—which are vital for true spiritual maturity.

Q: When do Pagans worship?
A: Many religions establish their yearly observances around the historical actions of prophets, holy men or women, or miraculous acts. In contrast, the Pagan liturgical year follows the seasonal cycle of the Earth, often referred to as "The Wheel of the Year." This seasonal round is commemorated by eight great festivals (called "Esbats" in Witchcraft). In the northern hemisphere, these include Spring Equinox (Ostara) (March 21), Summer Solstice (Litha) (June 21), Fall Equinox (Mabon) (September 21), and Winter Solstice (Yule) (December 21). These are known as the "quarter points." The "cross-quarters" are the dates that fall directly between each of the quarter points. These are Imbolc (February 2), Beltane (May 1), Lughnasadh (August 1), and Samhain (October 31). In the Southern hemisphere, many Pagans reverse these dates.

In addition to the Solar-based Wheel of the Year, many Pagans (especially Witches) also follow the Lunar cycles, gathering for "Sabbats" at the full Moons, and sometimes also at the dark of the Moon. Other Pagan festivals and holidays dedicated to various deities and Mysteries (such as the Eleusinia) may also be celebrated in various traditions, and at various times.

Each Pagan tradition, and each group or circle within a tradition, observes Pagan holidays in its own fashion. Some traditions provide detailed instructions and forms for worship, while others do not.

Q: Where do Pagans worship?
A: Pagans may worship in their homes, in nature, or in churches, although Pagan worship is not limited to specific times or places. Any moment or activity can be an opportunity for worship.

Some Pagan groups have formally organized into churches which are recognized by the Internal Revenue Service as tax-exempt organizations. Certain Pagan traditions have been recognized by the United States Military, and Federal case law specifically affords Wiccans and other Pagans First Amendment Constitutional status and protection.

Q: What are the Pagan sacraments?
A: A "sacrament' is something regarded as holy, or sacred. Ordinary acts or substances may be elevated to the status of Sacraments in a ritual context, thereby becoming gateways into a greater awareness of the beauty and power of the Cosmos and our part in it. Sacraments may be grouped into three categories: Actions, Rituals and Substances. The most universal sacramental substance is water!

Life passages, called "Rites of Passage," ritually mark significant periods in life, movements between life-stages, and personal transformations. They are a public acknowledgment and recognition of growth. Just as the seasons pass in order, so do the stages of life. The inner and outer worlds mirror each other, so Rites of Passage provide a further link with the Earth and the Cosmos. Rites of Passage include coming of age, marriage, pregnancy, birth, gender transitions, welcoming of new members to the community, dedications to a path or course of study, ordination, *croning* and *saging* (passage into elderhood), separations, and death.

Q: What advice would you give to newcomers?

A: Cherish diversity! Find fascination in the strange and unusual. Live passionately. Explore everything, especially things forbidden. Read voraciously. Grow a garden. Establish and maintain altars in your home. Go camping and hiking in the wilderness. Work on yourself.

The great strength of our evolving community is in the love and dedication of Her people, as She calls forth from each of us our best and highest service. This service can unite us all, children of the same Mother, that we might finally find our long-elusive unity through diversity!

Q: What do you see as Paganism's role in modern society?
A: To heal the alienation between humanity and Nature, between man and woman, between spirit and matter, between the Darkness and the Light. Thus shall we save the Earth, and ourselves as well. This is, after all, what religion is supposed to do, isn't it?

Q: What are the most important issues facing Paganism in the coming years?
A: How to deal with our exponential growth: we have vastly more neophytes coming in now than we have teachers to guide and instruct them. How to deal with an increasing public awareness of our existence: will we be hailed as a viable alternative to the crumbling madness, or perceived as a threat? How to deal with the increasing Fundamentalist backlash. How to deal with legal and political systems that have been put in place to outlaw much of what we are and stand for. How to come together in a worldwide religious community with power and influence. How to handle our inevitable success: we have been so used to being outsiders and underdogs that we will have to undergo a major attitude change as our basic paradigms become more mainstream.

Q: What does the Church of All Worlds believe?
A: The Church of All Worlds is not a belief-based religion, but a religion of experience. CAW members, or "Waterkin," try to avoid speaking of "belief" or "faith." We are committed to honoring each other's unique individual experiences and perspectives. We are not trying to become "true believers," but people of knowledge. "Belief" is generally an expression of wishful thinking rather than true understanding, and positions of belief far too often form a basis for the persecution of unbelievers. If anything, CAW is a religion of heretics!

Q: What does the CAW teach about God?
A: CAW embraces the theology of pantheism, as we experience what has been called "God" as an immanent quality inherently manifest in every living Being, from a single cell to an entire planet—and likely the universe Itself. We define Divinity as the highest level of aware consciousness accessible to each living being, manifesting itself in the self-actualization of that Being. Divinity is a function of emergent evolution. Thus, every man, woman, tree, cat, snake, flower or grasshopper IS "God." We express this in the phrase, "Thou Art God," which was used by Robert Heinlein in his germinal novel, Stranger in a Strange Land, but may also be found in the Bible (Psalms 82:6; John 10:34), and in much basic thinking of Hinduism and Buddhism. At the macrocosmic level, we recognize that the entire Earth is a vast living Entity: Mother Earth, Mother Nature, The Goddess. We also recognize that groups of living Beings organized into various ecosystems may manifest psychically as a single collective Entity; hence the local Spirits of particular places, and even tribal deities such as Jahveh. However, Gods, Goddesses and Spirits are personae with their own agenda, and should not be considered merely as aspects of human psychology, as the Jungians would have it.

Q: Does CAW accept the divinity of Jesus?
A: Certainly. Why should he be left out? We accept the Divinity of every living Being in the universe! Thou art God(dess).

Q: Is Paganism really a religion?
A: Absolutely. The word *religion* means "re-linking." A religion is a body of sacred myths, metaphors, observances and practices in a cultural context, which are designed to connect individuals with Divinity and heal the rift between dichotomized aspects of existence. We observe that the great dilemma of present-day human society seems to be the alienation caused by splitting apart man and woman, humanity and Nature, matter and spirit, light and dark, good and evil. The basic commitment of the

CAW—and of modern Paganism—is to the re-integration or re-linking of people with ourselves, our fellow humans, and with the whole of living Nature around us. There are many religions, and they are not all of the same mold. Modern Pagans have little in common with the religious mold as found in monotheistic or philosophical religions (Judaism, Christianity, Islam, Buddhism, etc.), but a very great deal in common with the Pagan religions of all peoples. Pagans create no artificial demarcation between the sacred and the secular. To a Pagan, religion is ultimately a whole way of life, not some acts performed once a week in a ritual. In this sense, Paganism *is* religion; the foundation, ground and source of all we may term "religious" and "spiritual. And the CAW is essentially and profoundly Pagan.

Q: Why must you create another religion?
A: Pagan religions, unlike philosophical religions, are not exactly "created," but swell up from the hearts of a people to fulfill a need. Paganism is re-emerging today but because natural religion is a spontaneous evocation of the spirit of Life, and will inevitably find expression in human cultures. The practices of the ancient Pagans occurred during a different era in culture, when we lived closer to the land and were more directly connected with farming. Much of what was practiced has been lost, due to the thousands of years of persecutions, from the onset of the Bronze Age, through the Inquisition and Witch-burnings, to the present day. Therefore, we cannot accurately say we practice ancient Paganism, but a form we are "remembering and inventing" together. The particular orientation of the CAW requires a new religious vehicle for its expression simply because the values, knowledge, and experience we hold in common are found in no other integrated system currently in existence.

Q: What's different about CAW?
A: CAW may be the first religion to draw as much of its inspiration from the future as from the past, embracing science fiction as mythology with the same enthusiasm as we embrace the classical myths of ancient times. We are future-oriented, meaning we care about how we evolve and change, not only about how we got here and how we will come to an end. We embrace evolution, and in embracing the planet as a living organism, we embrace the evolutionary changes of the planet by bringing human consciousness into direct contact with the growing web of planetary consciousness through such things as the worldwide computer Internet. Unlike nearly all other religions, we are not focused on nostalgia for a Paradise Lost; we are actively involved in helping to save the present world as well as working to actualize a visionary future. With roots deep in the Earth and branches reaching towards the stars, we evoke and create myths not of a Golden Age long past, but of one yet to come...

Q: Is Neo-Pagan religion less dogmatic than others?
A: The dogmatic nature of the practitioners of any religion vary from person. We have met dogmatic and non-dogmatic Christians from the same church. The same goes for Pagans. Some may be dogmatic about the form of their practice, while others are not. Some believe that magic is stronger when actions are repeated the same way each time. Others make their rituals completely new each time. The general structure of Neo-Paganism, however, is so varied as to be impossible to dictate to any large number of people. As the saying goes, ask two Pagans a question and get three different answers. We generally believe the world is to be discovered, not dictated. We are not arrogant enough to think we have all the answers, and believe flexibility is essential in reflecting an organic, Nature-based religion. Dogmatism stagnates. Only flexibility allows evolution to occur. Neo-Paganism is not a "cult." We do not have a messianic leader, follow prescribed patterns of activity, nor stick to closed communities.

Q: What does the CAW teach about sin and atonement?
A: Rather than focusing on "right" and "wrong," whose definitions will vary from person to person, religion to religion, and from one cultural phase to another, we look at the world in terms of cause and effect. If you hurt someone, you have damaged a relationship that will not be as viable for you in the future. If you abuse the planet, you will live in a damaged environment. We are responsible for our actions. It is not our role to pass judgment on one

another. We believe that everything is interconnected and the events that occur in one's life as a result of ignorant or harmful action are usually judgment or "punishment" enough. If someone comes to bring harm into our own sphere, we will do what we can to stop them and teach them something different. We do not believe punishment has a lot of value in changing behavior, but teaching does. The Wiccan Rede, "If it harm none, do what thou wilt," means that we are responsible for our own wills, and our responsibility includes avoiding harm to self and others.

Q: What does CAW teach about good and evil?

A: We define "Good" in terms of Nature—that which is pro-life, pro-choice, pro-actualization, pro-evolutionary, pro-diversity, pro-enlightenment; counter-entropy. "Evil" would be that which is anti-Nature, anti-life, anti-choice, anti-actualization, anti-evolutionary, anti-diversity, ignorance; entropy. Good is that which enhances and maximizes options; evil is that which reduces them. Specifically, evil is malice, malevolence: deliberate intention to cause harm to others. We do not see these in terms of dualism, imagining that there are two antagonistic forces in the universe, but rather we perceive a continuum moving always in a direction towards greater manifestation of evolutionary actualization and increasing consciousness; i.e. Divinity.

Q: What does the CAW teach about life after death?

A: We have no certain knowledge about life after death, and therefore cannot teach about it. We feel it is more appropriate to be concerned with life after birth. Our orientation is towards living, not dying, and we hold no official dogma regarding an afterlife. We do have many interesting speculations and opinions on the matter, however, and the range of opinions held by our people runs the gamut from nihilism to reincarnation, with many of us tending to feel that whatever you personally believe in is possibly what you get. Overall, we tend to view life, death and rebirth as a continuum in an infinite spiral dance, recycling both matter and energy into ever more complex forms in the endless Circle of Life. In this view, those of us who are bound to this living world by strong ties of love have returned time and time again to reunite with our loved ones in the unfolding of our collective Destiny, and we will continue doing so.

We do observe that "death" as experienced by human beings in Western culture does not normally occur in Nature. That is, seldom does a plant or animal just "die" and become inert for all time. Rather, under normal circumstances, plants and animals are killed and consumed as food by other plants, animals, or bacteria while their component cells are still alive Thus the life-energy force becomes assimilated into whatever eats them, and is not actually terminated or destroyed. Humans have attempted to remove themselves from the Circle of Life by killing all the cells in our food through cooking, and by embalming our dead and sealing the corpses in life-proof vaults. Thus people are the only beings on Earth that do not normally partake of immortality! Some ancient Pagans customarily buried their dead, coffinless and unembalmed, under a young tree, or with the seed of a tree on their chest, so that their life-energy would be recycled into the growing tree. Many CAW Waterkin identify strongly with that practice.

Q: Neo-Paganism is close to the Earth. Does this include the rest of the cosmos? Regardless of how good we now treat the Earth, we must eventually leave for other worlds, if the species is to survive. Will Pagan religion follow us from its root planet to other worlds?

A: Paganism is Nature-based religion, and Pagans revere the Earth as a living Mother Goddess. The essential goal of any living organism is to reproduce; indeed, that is the prime criterion for defining "life." For a living planet, such reproduction must necessarily manifest in the seeding of other worlds with life to produce other planetary biospheres as offspring. Our future terraforming of sterile worlds such as Mars, Luna, Venus, and the Jovian moons will be, in effect, Gaea reproducing Herself. She can only do this through us, as only we, as a technological species, can construct the spacefaring arks to convey Her fragile protoplasm into the void beyond Her atmospheric shell and hatch Gaea's chicks out into the starry realm of the cosmos:

And we who reach for the stars in the heavens,
Raising our gaze from the hedges and rows,
Still live in the love of the Lord and the Lady;
The greater the Circle, the more the love grows...
~Ann Cass, Circles

Moreover, other planets will also have their seasonal cycles, from Sostices to Equinoxes, and the cross-quarters between. Many have their own moons—sometimes several—and the stars in their skies may be configured into constellations, forming signs of an alien Zodiac. Mountains, valleys, seas and rivers of other worlds too will have their sacred places, and their spirits thereof. And stories will come to be told of all this, and how it all came to be, and where it is all going. Paganism is universal!

Q: What is the political affiliation and structure of your community? Where does CAW stand in regard to radical environmentalism?

A: Politically, CAW is basically Green. Many of us tend toward some form of Anarcho-Libertarianism, and some of us are actively involved with Earth First! CAW's aim is to make a connection to the Holy Biosphere of our Mother Earth: to protect Her, and to heal the rift between Wo/man and Nature. We do advocate protecting that which we worship, in whatever way feels right to you. If that means writing your Congressperson and signing petitions; if that means getting involved with tree planting and picking up litter; if that means having a sit-down at a nuclear power plant or chaining yourself to a tree; then do what thou wilt. All of these things are effective. All have their place. You have to take responsibility for your own actions. We support all levels of political action, and have an excellent relationship with our local Congressman and other government officials.

Q: Where does your community stand on sexuality issues?

A: The kind of sexuality that we support is the Goddess's charge: "All acts of love and pleasure are my rituals." We sanction all loving and responsible relationships between informed and mutually consenting adults, whatever their gender, number, or practice. We have many diverse life- and love-styles in CAW, with various folk gravitating towards their own preferred choices in such matters as sacraments; sexual practice, preference and orientation; politics, beliefs, etc. We are united by our love of our Mother, the Living Earth, of each other as Waterkin, and of all living beings as brothers and sisters; all children of the same Mother. We accept Robert Heinlein's definition of "love" as stated in Stranger in a Strange Land: "That condition wherein another person's happiness is essential to your own."

This means we honor and welcome all sexual orientations, genders and practices into our Nests and circles; we perform handfastings (weddings) for heterosexual, gay, bisexual, or transsexual couples, triples, and group marriages; and we support all aspects of personal and mutual choice. This absolutely includes the choice to have an exclusive, monogamous nuclear family; or even to be celibate; if that's what everybody concerned wants to do. We absolutely do not expect or require that others should engage in practices, sexual or otherwise, that they do not wish to, just because someone else does. Our informal motto is: "If you don't like it, you can't have any!"

And, in these days of AIDS, we fanatically advocate Safe Sex, whomever you do it with!

Q: How does Neo-Paganism view the role of the male?

A: Female and male are the two partners in the cosmic Dance of Life. Both are essential to the creation of new life, and neither should be denigrated or subordinate to the other. There can be no Mother without a Father (at least among mammals!), and there can be no Father without a Mother (even among Gods). Female and male, Goddess and God, Priestess and Priest; partners and consorts, our fates entwined like the double helix of the DNA molecule.

And incidentally, this view of equality between the sexes should not be construed to preclude all-female or all-male working groups, or same-sex lovers. These things too are part of the great Balance, and it is the Balance itself which we honor, holding neither side above or below the other.

Q: What is the CAW position on birth-control and abortion?

A: It is ecologically, psychologically, spiritually and politically indefensible to bring unwanted children into the world. We are pro-life, regarding the quality of life for all beings to be of utmost importance. The CAW unconditionally supports the right of every woman to make her own decisions regarding her desire and ability to bear and responsibly raise a child. We declare and defend a woman's right to safe, effective, affordable and acceptable methods of fertility regulation of her choice, including a timely abortion if and when she should deem it necessary. We support the right of all women to access to appropriate health-care services that will enable them to go safely through pregnancy and childbirth and provide them with the best chance of bearing and raising healthy children. We work for the rights of women to maintain and expand their reproductive options.

Q: Do you welcome children and allow them full freedom of expression?

A: We are nearly always delighted to have our wonderful children participate in our rituals. The only exceptions to this are explicitly sexual rites, such as the Beltane May Games. While our children are encouraged to explore a great range of personal expression, we do teach them ethics and responsibilities of freedom. Violent and destructive behavior, for instance, is not tolerated. We expect them to exercise considerable responsibility, and the older kids take a good deal of responsibility towards the younger ones. All the adults in the community pretty much relate parentally to the kids, and vice versa.

Q: What is the CAW position on mind-altering drugs?

A: Various psychotropic chemicals have been used as sacraments in virtually every culture on the planet: b beer among the Sumerians and Egyptians, wine among the Greeks and Romans, mead for the Northern Tribes of Europe, fly agaric mushrooms for the Vikings and Tungusik shamans, tobacco for the North American Natives, Coca for the Inca, betel nut for the Melanesians, Cannabis for the Indo-Europeans, rye ergot for the Eleusinian Mysteries of Greece, "Flying Ointment" (datura and other psychotropic plants) for the Witches of Medieval Europe, peyote for the Huitchol and the Indians of the Mexican deserts, opium for the Mediterranean and Chinese cultures, ayahuasca for the natives of Brazil, magic mushrooms and toads for the Mayans and Aztecs...the list goes

on and on. These are all regarded as sacraments; that is, sacred medicine substances of great power. They are gifts of the Gods (some even say "flesh of the Gods"), meant to be used only with reverence, and in a sacred matter. The power of these sacraments lies in their ability to temporarily obliterate (or at least radically alter) mundane consciousness and allow communion with, and even divine possession by, the Gods. In traditional Pagan cultures, "profaning the sacraments" (using them in a non-sacred context) is considered blasphemy, leading to the destruction of the soul and psyche of any who would be so stupid as to do so. If such sacraments are to be used at all, it seems to be the unanimous collective wisdom of the Ancient Elders that they should be used in a sacred way.

Here at CAW, we try very carefully to avoid "advocating" anything other than responsible freedom. We follow "The Prime Directive" of non-interference, feeling that whatever a person wishes to do with their own body is nobody else's business.

Q: What is the CAW position regarding war and conscientious objection?

A: The CAW categorically supports the right of all who honor Mother Earth to nonviolently oppose war in any and all forms. War is deacide, for it is destructive of the Goddess embodied in all living beings. War results from various human communities having forgotten their collective origin in the sacred Earth, and managing to demonize each other. War is the basic tool by which the patriarchal takeover and suppression of the Goddess was originally achieved, and subsequently maintained.

We also support the right to choose the path of the Sacred Warrior, to embody an ancient archetype who serves to protect the oppressed, the weak, the innocent, and holy places. Sacred Warriors revere life, even the life of their adversaries, preferring nonviolence to fighting. Martin Luther King and Gandhi were Sacred Warriors. They did not demonize their opponents, but sought to transform them by awakening the sacred within them.

We are all fragments of Gaea; to kill each other is to kill Her. Even our enemies are sacred.

Q: Where did the rituals used in this new religion originate?

A: Some are reconstructed from scraps of history that have survived through arch¾ological research, translation of texts, and direct lineage through families. Many are derived from the legends, songs, customs and folklore that have been embedded so deeply in our cultural heritage that even centuries of Christianity could not dislodge them. Most rituals in the CAW are created by the participants for the purpose at hand. There are many, many rituals. They are countless in their variety, and new ones are being created everyday.

Q: How do CAW Waterkin practice their religion?

A: For Pagans, there is no demarcation between the sacred and the secular, and every activity is essentially a religious activity. Unlike the many people who practice their religion only for an hour on Sunday mornings, we Pagans live our religion 24 hours a day, every day of our lives. For us, taking our cans and bottles to the recycling center is as much a religious duty as prayer and ritual. And so are composting our garbage, protecting animals and children, growing organic vegetables, practicing birth-control and safe sex, using bio-degradable materials, physical exercise, psychic training, study and celebration of the seasons. In our Nests we hold religious services, sensitivity sessions, council meetings, study-discussion seminars, campouts, pot-luck dinners, salons, "magical mystery tours," group "field trips" to concerts, plays and movies, and just plain good time parties. We celebrate the eight seasonal Pagan festivals with feasting, sharing, music and sacred drama. We come together for work parties to plant trees, fix roofs, maintain roads, work on the land, harvest our gardens and orchards, or whatever is needed. Our families, clans and tribe constitute our best friends and lovers, whom we would rather hang out with than anybody else. Many of us travel around the country, speaking to other interested people and groups on request. In all, we recognize that the essence of a religion is in the living of it.

Q: Is modern Paganism part of the New Age movement?

A: The term "New Age" covers a wide range of spiritual practices, religions, and philosophies. In regard to a new movement toward a renewed respect and care for the Earth and environment; an increased awareness of one's psychic skills, yes. However, that is where the similarity ends.

The New Age community derives much of its inspiration from Eastern mystical traditions, such as Hinduism and Buddhism – which place a great emphasis on aestheticism, celibacy, meditation and a rejection of materiality. Pagans tend to derive their inspiration from Western customs, folklore, mythology and traditions. While the New Age community seeks purpose and direction from "above," that is, Ascended Masters and the world of Spirit, Pagans tend to find their inspiration in the Earth and the coexistence of the Spiritual and the Physical.

Perhaps a more useful discussion would be to what extent Paganism is old religion vs. new religion. Many "new religious movements" tend to center around the teachings of a prophet or central teacher. Paganism goes beyond the teaching of any one leader, and it tends to be Nature-centered rather than teacher-centered, as well as rooted in folkways that pre-date the 20th century.

Q: Simply, why should I join CAW? What will it do for my spiritual well-being?

A: CAW is a network of individuals who share a concern for the Earth, a love of the Gods in Their many forms, a sense of community, an enjoyment of good ritual and intellectual banter, and our common love and reverence for our Mother, the Living Earth. We hang out together largely because this is our favorite company, composed of our best friends, family and lovers, who have more fun together than with anyone else. If CAW appeals to you, you are welcome to join our company for as long as you wish. We exist as a tribe of people who find kinship, support, and inspiration with each other. As a group entity, we hope to create an atmosphere that will inspire all of us in our growth and evolution. Your spiritual well-being, however, is your own responsibility. We do not promise eternal salvation or an end to all your troubles. We are not cult leaders, gurus, or mothers telling children what to do, but cohorts on an exciting journey of discovery. "Enter freely and of your own will!"

Witchcraft, Paganism and the Occult
A Basic Glossary of Common Terms and Symbols
by Oberon and Morning Glory Zell *(3rd Edition—1991)*

[Note: When the note (PEIB) appears in this Glossary, it refers to P.E.I. Bonewits, and definitions so designated are quoted verbatim from his 1970 book, Real Magic. *The note (WNWD) refers to Webster's New World Dictionary of the American Language, 1972.]*

Abracadabra— A corruption of the sacred Gnostic term *Abraxas,* a magic formula meaning 'hurt me not.' It was inscribed on an amulet and worn on the breast.

Abyss— In Egyptian religion, a descriptive name for the Underworld. In Babylonian thought, it was the primal chaos from which the universe evolved. In Gnosticism it was personified as the first principle of the infinite deity.

Abuse— Wrong, bad, or excessive use. Mistreatment; injury. A bad, unjust, or corrupt custom or practice. Insulting or coarse language. *(WNWD)*

Adept—One who is very skilled in magic or mysticism.

Agnostic— Greek, "without knowledge." One who claims to have no certain knowledge of metaphysical matters.

Alchemy— The forerunner of chemistry, originating in Alexandria during the first century CE, when Egyptian metallurgy was fused with Greek philosophy and middle eastern mysticism. Stated goals were the transmutation of base metals into gold and the discovery of the Philosopher's Stone. These are regarded as metaphors for personal enlightenment.

Alcheringa— Native Australian for "dreamtime." A realm of archetypal myth and astral experience.

Altar—A table, shelf or platform set apart from the mundane and used exclusively for religious rites and the ceremonial arrangement of sacred paraphernalia.

Amargi— Ancient Sumerian word meaning "freedom" and "return to the Mother," equating both concepts.

Amulet— An object charged with power for protection or to turn aside ill luck. Amulets are usually found and are natural objects.

Anachronism— Something that appears to be from a time period other than the one in which it is perceived.

Society for Creative Anachronism— An historical reconstructionist organization of medieval scholars and speculative fantasy buffs. Founded in Berkeley, CA on May 1, 1966 by Diana Paxson, the SCA holds medieval reconstructionist events, such as tournaments and feasts, and participates in Renaissance Faires around the country.

Anahita— A Persian Goddess of the Fertilizing Waters. Her name means 'the unsullied.' Identified with Anatolian *Cybele* and Greek *Artemis.*

Angakok— A shaman of the Inuit, or polar Eskimos.

Angels— In Judaism, divine messengers. In most denominations of Christianity, inhabitants of Heaven.

Animism—The belief that all things have souls or spirits (Greek "anima").

Ankh— Egyptian hieroglyphic symbol meaning "Life." Often used to signify immortality.

Anthropomorphize— To ascribe human characteristics to that which is not human.

Anthropomorphic personification—Archetypal concepts depicted in human form, such as Death, Destiny, Dream, Desire, Destruction, Despair and Delirium (The Endless). Also Gods and Goddesses, Mother Nature, Father Time, the Seasons, the Fates, the Graces, the Furies, the 7 Deadly Sins, Santa Claus, Jack Frost, etc.

Aphrodite— Greek Goddess of love, beauty and pleasure. The Romans called her Venus. She is always shown naked, and doves and roses are sacred to Her. She says: "All acts of love and pleasure are my rituals."

Apocalypse— Prophetic revelation of the end of the world.

Apotheosis— Deification. Becoming God.

Apotheasis— Becoming Goddess.

Aquarius— The Water Bearer. Eleventh sign of the Zodiac, covering the period from Jan. 21—Feb. 19. Aquarius is an Air sign, and ruled by the planet Uranus, indicating changeability. Its Tarot trump is The Star. Aquarius is the sign of humanitarianism, liberalism, intelligence, progressivism, unconventionality, independence and dreaminess.

Aquarius, Age of— A slight wobble in the Earth's axis of rotation causes a slow precession of the equinoxes, whereby every 2,000 years or so, the position of the Vernal (Spring) Equinox enters a new sign. Each sign stamps its characteristic imprint on the age, as well as contributing basic symbolism to the dominant religion of that age. The 2,000-year Christian Era now concluding has coincided with the Age of Pisces, the Fish, the sign of Faith. The next 2,000 years will be the Age of Aquarius, in which the prophecies envision a utopian era. Space travel and the perfection of the social order are predicted, with water becoming a universal religious sacrament.

Aradia— Daughter and Avatar of the Moon Goddess Diana, and matron of Italian Witchcraf. Her teachings are collected in the book *Aradia, the Gospel of Witches,* by Charles Godfrey Leland.

Arcane— Secret, mysterious.

Archetype— The basic pattern, or idea, in the collective unconscious from which all things of the same class are representations.

Arianrhod— Celtic Goddess of the maiden-moon; often referred to as "Arianrhod of the Silvery Wheel."

Asherah— Canaanite Goddess of vegetation and fertility, equiv. to *Astarte.* Worshipped in sacred groves by the women of the "holy land," many of whom became captive brides of Hebrew men after the genocidal invasion of their country by the Tribes of Israel. The prophets Isaiah and Jeremiah in particular inveigh heavily against the worship of this "Queen of Heaven."

Aspecting— Allowing a God or Goddess to take over one's presence and speak and act through the aspector.

Asperge— Sprinkle with holy water for purification.

Astarte— Goddess of love and fertility among the ancient Phoenicians, derived from the Babylonian *Ishtar.* In the Hebrew Qabalah, she is transformed into the male demon, *Ashtorath.*

Astral— Of or pertaining to the shadowy universe in between the Dreamtime and ordinary consciousness. Any of the alternative realities in which magickal practitioners operate. Various consensual Dreamtimes.

Astral Projection— Extension of one's subjective point of reference beyond the limits of the physical body, usually with an accompanying image of the body as a vehicle.

Astrology— Divination through the correlation of Earthly events with celestial patterns. *(PEIB)*

Athame— A consecrated ceremonial knife used by Witches and magicians; usually black-hilted. In Witchcraft the athame is *almost never* used for drawing blood. Satanists profane it by using it for blood sacrifices.

Atheist— Greek, "no god." One who believes that deities do not exist.

Augury— Divination by means of whatever is most handy. *(PEIB)*

Aura— Biomagnetic field surrounding all living things.

Avatar— A deity incarnate in human form, such as Christ or Krishna. An entity regarded as an extreme or notably complete manifestation of its kind. Exemplar; archetype; embodiment.

Banish— To demand the departure of unwanted entities. To exorcise.

Baphomet— Goat-headed god of carnal lust and materiality; said to have been worshipped by the Knights Templars. Depicted in the Tarot as "The Devil" trump card. Popular deity for modern Satanists and some Witches.

Beltane— The Grand Sabbat, or cross-quarter festival, occurring midway between Spring Equinox and Summer Solstice. Traditionally celebrated on May 1, it occurs astrologically at 15° Taurus. Beltane is the Pagan Celtic festival of the beginning of Summer, named for Belenos or Bilé, a solar god of flocks and the Underworld. It is celebrated with the Maypole, games, fertility rites, sacred marriage, May baskets;

selection of May Queen and King. The night before is called *Walpurgisnacht,* when the door between the worlds is opened. Christianized as May Day.

Bible— From Greek, "Book." Holy scriptures of the Christian religion, containing the Old and New Testaments, and regarded as the official "Word of God."

Bind— To restrain magickally.

Biocurrents— Electrochemical energy currents generated by living cells. *(PEIB)*

Biorhythms— Rhythmic cycles of various types occurring in living organisms.

Black Book— A Witch's personal workbook, containing records and rules of her tradition, seasonal rituals, spells, invocations and magickal notes. A magickal diary. (Often called "Book of Shadows.")

Black Mass— The ritual most commonly associated with Satanism, wherein the Roman Catholic Mass is reversed and profaned. A nude woman forms the altar; blood is drunk instead of wine; flesh is eaten instead of bread; and the Lord's Prayer is recited backwards.

Blessing— The use of psychic energy to benefit an organism.

Blighting— The use of psychic energy to harm or destroy an organism.

Bon— The native Tibetan Pagan religion that was later merged with Buddhism and Tantrism. *(PEIB)*

Book of Shadows— The collection of liturgical and canonical material that is passed down through a tradition. *(Don Frew)*

Botanica— Occult shop serving the magickal needs of the Afro-Catholic communities of Voudoun, Macumba, Santeria, etc. Botanicas sell herbs, spells, charms, votive candles, images of saints, etc.

Brigit— Great Celtic Triple Goddess. She is matron of: the forge and smithcraft; poetry and inspiration; healing and medicine. Christianized as St. Brigit, Her festival is Candlemas or Oimelc, Feb. 1.

Brujeria— A Mexican magical system that is an amalgamation of Catholicism and Native Indian lore; a sort of syncretic mestizo-shamanism. A male practitioner is called a *Brujo,* a female is a *Bruja.* These people are apt to be urban dwellers who burn candles to both saints and demons with equal

facility, they gain their magickal powers through self-initiation, sometimes with training. Though they often claim the more benign title of *Curandero* (a healer) their practices may run the gamut from love spells to curses.

Brutch— An area of psychic distortion in local space/time. (e.g., the "Bermuda Triangle")

Burning Times— The period from around 1000 CE through the 17th century, when as many as nine million people, 90% of them women, were tortured and burned alive by the Catholic and Protestant churches on charges of Witchcraft. The 800-year holocaust of European Pagans. (see **Inquisition**)

Caduceus— The serpent-entwined herald's staff of Hermes/Mercury. As it was also the wizard's staff of the Greek physician Asculepius, it has become the symbol of the medical profession.

Cantrip— A written spell or charm that reads the same forwards or backwards.

Cargo Cult— A religion resulting from the cultural impact of the brief visitation of representatives of a vastly superior technology. Cultists use sympathetic magick in hopes of inducing the return of the visitors bringing their material benefits.

Cartomancy— Divination through the use of cards, especially Tarot cards. *(PEIB)*

Ceremonial Magick— Schools or methods of magick that place their emphasis upon long and complex rituals, especially of the Medieval and later European and Qabalistic traditions; often degenerates into mere ritualism. *(PEIB)* Primarily theurgical.

Cernunnos— Latin "horned one." Ancient Celtic version of the Horned God, shown with stag antlers. Collective spirit of the wild animals. Equated with *Faunus,* the Red Man.

Chakra— One of seven major centers of biomagnetic energy *(prana)* in the human body.

Chalice— A consecrated ceremonial cup, representing the Element Water, and containing the liquid sacrament of communion, usually wine.

Channeling— Serving as a conduit for communications from discarnate entities. Mediumship.

Charm— Spoken or written magickal words. Also, objects carried for their magickal powers or properties.

Christ— From Greek, *christos,* "The Anointed." A title for the Messiah whose appearance is prophesied in the Old Testament. Jesus of Nazareth, regarded by Christians as the realization of the Messianic prophecies. *(WNWD)* The death of the Christ is regarded as a sacrifice to redeem humanity from original sin.

Christianity— That religion based on acceptance of Jesus of Nazareth as Messiah and Son of God, following the account rendered in the New Testament.

Church— A body of adherents to the same religion.

Church of All Worlds— A Neo-Pagan religion founded in 1962 and incorporated Mar. 4, 1968. CAW is inspired by science fiction as mythology, and is dedicated to the celebration of Life, the maximal actualization of human potential, and the realization of ultimate individual freedom and personal responsibility in harmonious eco-psychic relationship with the total biosphere of Holy Mother Earth. A catalyst for the coalescence of consciousness. Ecosophical worldview.

Church of the Eternal Source— A Neo-Pagan religion founded by Don Harrison in 1970 and based on a reconstruction of the Mysteries of ancient Egypt and the worship of the Egyptian gods and goddesses.

Church of Satan— Founded in San Francisco in 1966 by Anton LaVey, who taught that Satan is a symbol of the material world and the carnal nature of man, embodying "the life, joy, pleasure, and particularity intimate and important to man." Their scripture is LaVey's *Satanic Bible.* Legally incorporated in California, the church split into several factions in 1975.

Cingulum— A magickal cord worn around the waist and used for binding, measuring and counting.

Clairvoyance— A psychic vision of events remote in space and/or time.

Coincidence— An accidental and remarkable occurrence of events, ideas, etc. at the same time, suggesting but lacking a causal relationship. *(WNWD)*

Collective Consciousness— A group mind manifesting synergically as a single conscious awareness.

Collective Unconscious— The subconscious aspect of a group mind manifesting synergically. The repository of the memories of all the individuals ever comprising the group.

Cone of Power— The combined psychic energy of a group mind, focused through a magick circle, directed by a single will (usually that of the Priestess) and sent forth to work outside the circle.

Conjuration— The act of summoning up non-physical entities, or spirits.

Consciousness— Negative entropy manifesting in individuated awareness.

Consecration— Sanctification or blessing. The act of setting apart the sacred.

Contagion, Law of— "Objects or beings in physical or psychic contact with one another continue to interact after spacial or temporal separation." *(PEIB)*

Coven— A congregation of thirteen or fewer Witches working together in a circle and sharing a common tradition

Covenant of the Goddess— An international, legally incorporated, ecumenical umbrella organization of Witchcraft covens, providing legal corporate status for otherwise unincorporated groups.

Cowan— One who is not a Witch. Outsider.

Crime— Violation of the social contract. Infringement upon the rights of another.

Cross— Symbol of the Crucifixion of Christ. Generic symbol of Christianity.

Cross, Inverted— Generic symbol of Satanism. Represents the rejection of all that Christianity stands for.

Cult— A group of people slavishly following the dictates of a single leader. A system of worship. The rites of a religion.

Curse— The use of magic to harm an object or being. *(PEIB)* To magickally direct or wish misfortune upon another. A spell of blighting.

Cusp— An intersection in time and space. In astrology, the intersection of two signs or houses.

Death— That condition in which a living system (organism) becomes entropic.

Deity— A spirit of great power. A God or Goddess.

Demeter— Greek Goddess of Grain and Harvest, mother of Persephone. Equated with the Roman Goddess *Ceres,* who gives Her name to cereal.

Demons— Spirits evoked from the human Id.

Deosil— Latin "sunwise." Clockwise in N. hemisphere. Normal direction for movements within a magick circle.

  Widdershins— German "against the way." Counterclockwise in northern hemisphere.

Devil— From Sanskrit *devi,* "little god" (or from Greek *Diabolos).* In Christianity, an evil spirit (also known as demon, from Greek *daemon,* meaning "spirit").

  The Devil— Christian personification of evil; chief of the demons. (see **Satan.**)

Dharma— In Buddhism, a religious precept.

Diana— Roman Goddess of the Moon and the hunt, equiv. to Greek *Artemis.* Most widely worshipped deity of Witchcraft.

Discarnate— "Without a body."

Discordian Society— Erisian sect devoted to universal principles of disorder.

Divination— The magickal arts of finding out hidden information about past, present or future events.

Divinity— The fullest level of aware consciousness accessible to any living being, manifesting itself in the self-actualization of that being.

Drawing Down the Moon— A Wiccan rite of invoking the Moon Goddess. A book by Margot Adler about the Neo-Pagan religious movement, widely regarded as the best study of Neo-Paganism ever written.

Druid— "Oak-knower." A member of an ancient Celtic Pagan priesthood and magickal Order whose social and political power was destroyed by the Romans. Druids worshipped in oak groves and held mistletoe to be sacred. Also a member of any of a number of modern reconstructions of that order.

Dryad— A tree spirit, generally seen as feminine.

Dualism— The doctrine that for every principle there is an opposing, separate, and ultimately irreconcilable counter-principle. Such opposing forces are conventionally arrayed along a good-evil dichotomy.

"Dungeons and Dragons" (© TSR, Inc.)— "D & D" has become a generic term for popular role-playing games, in which players assume personas of adventurers in fantasy scenarios, encountering various monsters and pitfalls in quest of treasure. Magick is an essential component of play, which often draws heavily from authentic myths and traditions of Pagan origin.

Earth-Mother— Female personification of the Life force, fertility of the Earth and its inhabitants. One of the most widespread deity concepts in the world. *(PEIB)* The ancient Greeks called Her *Gaia,* and equated Her with both Mother Earth and Mother Nature.

Eco-Psychic— Of or pertaining to relationships on the psychic level between human consciousness and various individual and collective consciousness of Nature. Presumes a pantheistic world-view. (Term coined by Fred Adams)

Ecosophy— Greek, "wisdom of the home." A holistic, pantheistic, metaphysical world-view based on emergent evolution, immanent divinity, and the Gaea Thesis. (Term coined in 1972 by Norwegian philosopher Arne Naess.)

Ecstatic— Latin, "out of the body."

Elements, Four— The four states of matter: solid (Earth), liquid (Water), gas (Air) and plasma (Fire).

Elemental— A localized focus of the collective spirit of any of the four Elements.

Eleusinian Mysteries— An ancient Greek annual rite enacting the abduction of Persephone by Hades, Lord of the Underworld; the quest of her Mother, Demeter; and her eventual return. These Mysteries conveyed metaphorically both the sacred round of the seasons and the cycles of death and rebirth of humans.

Elves— From Norse *Aelfar.* Originally the *Tuatha de Danaan* (Children of the Goddess Danu); early bronze-age Celts, also known as the *Sidhe.* Later mythologized and amalgamated with **Faeries.**

Emergent Evolution— The unfolding of consciousness in increasingly complex manifestations as a synergic property of biological evolution.

Empathy— Sensing of another's emotions as one's own. "Grokking." *(Robert Heinlein)*

Entity— A being, spirit, living creature or personification. *(PEIB)*

Entropy— A measure of the degree of disorder and loss of energy in a closed system of the physical universe. In physics, entropy always increases; energy dissipates and order deteriorates into disorder.

> **Negative Entropy**— The phenomenon of increasing energy and order manifest in and characteristic of living systems.

Eris— Greek Goddess of chaos and disorder.

Esbat— A full moon meeting of a Witches' coven.

Ethics— Personal propriety. Intrinsic behavioral principles of right conduct.

Evil—Negativity out of balance. The single minded obsession to generate destruction, pain and cruelty, often for the purpose of gaining power over others. Anti-life; anti-evolution; anti-consciousness.

Evil Eye— A penetrating glare, usually with malicious intent to harm or bewitch the object of the gaze.

Evocation— Calling something out from within.

> **Invocation**— Calling something in from without.

Exorcism— A formal ritual of magickal banishment. Involves invoking the authority of a higher power to banish an unwanted entity.

Extrasensory Perception (ESP)— The reception of data from outside of the body by other than normal sensory means. *(PEIB)*

Eye of Horus— According to myth, Horus lost an eye in battle with his rival, Set. A charm in the stylized shape of this eye was regarded as potent protection against evil forces.

Faeries— "Fair Folk:" originally the pre-Celtic Pictish ("Pixie") people of the British Isles. Later applied to all diminutive nature spirits.

Familiar— A non-human being, especially an animal, with whom one has an empathic psychic bond.

Fam-Trad— Family tradition. Psychic training and/or magickal traditions identified with Witchcraft and handed down as hereditary or family lore.

Faun— A minor Roman spirit of the wilderness. Humanoid, but with goat's horns, legs, hooves and tail. May be male or female.

Fauna— Latin, "animals." The "Red Woman," Goddess of animals. Female collective spirit of the animal kingdom.

Faunus— Brother/lover of Fauna. The "Red Man." Male collective spirit of the animal kingdom.

Feraferia— A Neo-Pagan religion founded by Fred Adams and incorporated Aug. 2, 1967. Meaning "Wild Festival," Feraferia was based on a reconstruction of Samothracian and Eleusinian Mysteries. Primary devotion is to the Kore, or "Magic Maiden" archetype.

Fetch— The collective astral projection of a coven or other magickal group. May be used by an individual as a sort of "astral familiar." *(Don Frew)*

Flora— Latin, "plants." The "Green Woman," Goddess of vegetation. Female collective spirit of the vegetable kingdom.

Florus— Brother/lover of Flora. The "Green Man." Male collective spirit of vegetable kingdom.

Flying Ointment— A hallucinogenic salve concocted of belladonna, henbane, aconite and other psychoactive herbs and rubbed on the body to induce astral travel.

Freya— Norse Goddess of fertility and love.

Gaea (or **Gaia**)— Greek Goddess of the Earth. Mother Earth. In current usage, the organic, unified, living entity that is our planetary biosphere; i.e., our living planet. The prime deity of most Neo-Pagans.

Gardner, Gerald— (1884-1964) Founder of modern Witchcraft, author of *Witchcraft Today* (1954) and other books. Gardnerian Wicca remains his legacy.

Glyph— A written or drawn symbol.

Gnome— An Earth Elemental.

God— Divinity manifesting to the perceiver as of masculine gender.

Goddess— Divinity manifesting to the perceiver as of feminine gender.

Golden Dawn, Order of the— Ceremonial magickal lodge founded in 1887 by a trio of English Freemasons. Its prominent members included S.L. MacGregor Mathers, W.B. Yeats, Israel Regardie, Dion Fortune, A.E. Waite, and Aleister Crowley, who was eventually expelled. Its purpose was "to prosecute the Great Work: which is to obtain control of the nature and power of my own being."

Great Mother— The single universal deity of the ancient pre-Judeo-Christian world. Mother Nature. The collective feminine spirit of the universe. Creatrix; Mother of All.

Great Rite— Ritual sex within the magick circle.

Gris-gris— ("Grey-grey") Medicine power sometimes in the form of herbal pouches. Used in New Orleans Cajun-style "Voodoo."

Grimoire— A magickal compendium of spells, herb lore, charms, recipes, etc.

Grotto— A Satanic congregation.

Group Mind— A collective awareness that can be either conscious or unconscious.

Hand-Fasting— A Medieval term for a wedding ritual not sanctified by the Church; now used by Witches and Neo-Pagans for their weddings. Handfastings are not "til death do us part," but "for as long as love shall last."

Hand of Glory— The severed hand of a hanged man. With a lighted candle inserted between the fingers, it was used by burglars as a spell to keep the household asleep while they burgled.

Heathen— Literally, someone who lives on the heath (i.e., where the heather grows). Applied specifically to rural Pagans in the British Isles.

Heavy Metal— The adrenalin/testosterone frenzied music of adolescent rebellion featuring a glorification of sex, drugs and violence with a strong flavor of black leather/studs, sado-masochism and nihilism. Though Heavy Metal music has been cited in teen-age Satanic practices including human sacrifice, much is harmless and it is important to distinguish between the different bands. Some, like *Metallica, Judas Priest, White Snake* and *Motley Crue* currently feature lyrics of rape and rampage. Other more moderate bands like *Dio, Kiss* and *Ozzy Osborne* feature quasi-occult themes strong on raw power and ceremonial magic. Bands like *Van Halen* and *Def Leppard* have safely mellowed.

Hechiceria— The surviving remnants of true Native Indian magical religion in Mexico. Practitioners are most often male and are called *Hechiceros,* or *Naguals* (in Nahuatl), or sometimes even *Bruho Naturaleza.* They believe that those born to be Hechiceros are called by the Gods from a hereditary line. They worship the old pre-Columbian divinities with fragments of surviving rites and indigenous folk rituals.

Hekate— Greek Goddess of the Dark Moon. A popular deity for modern feminist Witches.

Henotheism— Belief in or worship of one god without denying the existence of others. *(WNWD)*

Heresy— A religious belief opposed to the orthodox doctrines of a church; esp. such a belief specifically denounced by the church.

Heretic— A church member who holds beliefs opposed to church dogma. *(WNWD)*

Hermes— Greek psychopomp deity, serving as messenger between the gods and mortals. Patron god of thieves and wizards, Hermes was identified with the Egyptian *Thoth* and called *Mercury* by the Romans.

Herne— British equivalent of Cernunnos, the Horned God. Leader of the Wild Hunt and a protective father.

Horoscope— In astrology, a chart of the positions of the planets and zodiacal constellations as plotted from a particular time and location, especially that of birth.

Horus— Egyptian Solar-Falcon God, of whom the current pharaoh was believed to be an avatar. Horus was an emanation of Ra, the Sun-God.

Hypnosis— An altered state of consciousness of lowered brain-wave frequency (alpha-theta) and heightened suggestibility. Equivalent to state of dreaming, but induced rather than spontaneous. Reasoning under hypnosis operates by induction rather than deduction.

Icon— A sacred image or representation.

Immanent Divinity— The theological position that Nature includes Divinity; that Divinity is a quality, not a quantity, and may be found within, not without.

Impossible— Unlikely, difficult, implausible, uncomfortable, new. *(PEIB)*

Inanna— Ancient Sumerian Goddess of love and battle. Known as "Queen of Heaven and Earth," She is the prototype of all Goddesses of love and sex.

Incantation— A hypnotic and sometimes rhyming chant used in spell casting.

Incarnate— Latin, "to enter into flesh." To take on a body. Having a body.

Incense— Any of various substances, such as gums, resins or herbs, producing a pleasant odor when burned and used in religious ceremonies for purifications and offerings.

Incubus— Demon in male form that seduces women in their sleep, causing erotic dreams.

Initiation— A magickal metamorphosis. A ritualized transformation experience that introduces one to a new level of reality. A rite of passage into a mystical society or religion.

Inquisition— The general tribunal of the Roman Catholic church established in the 13th century for the discovery and suppression of heresy and the punishment of heretics. *(WNWD)* All later trials, secular and ecclesiastical, Protestant and Catholic, stem from early inquisitorial patterns. The accused were presumed guilty until proven innocent, and torture was routinely used to extract confessions.

Ishtar— Babylonian Goddess of love and fertility; derived from the Sumerian *Inanna*. Called *Eostre* in Europe, She gives Her name to Easter.

Isis— Egyptian Goddess; Mother Nature, Queen of Heaven; wife of Osiris, mother of Horus. Isis was adopted by Greeks and Romans, and became the most widely-worshipped deity of the Mediterranean world.

Kachina (plural **Kahinam**)— "Living Spirits" of the Hopi and other Native American Pueblo people. As with the Vodoun Loa, Kachina dancers are possessed by the Kachinam and are considered to be the messengers of the Pantheon.

Kahuna— A native Hawaiian shaman.

Kali—Hindu Goddess of Time, Destruction, Death and Rebirth. The Great Initiator, Portal Between Worlds.

Karma— In many eastern religions, the load of guilt or innocence carried from one incarnation to the next, determining one's lot in the next life; often used by American occultists as a general term for moral responsibility. *(PEIB)*

Krishna— 8th incarnation and avatar of Vishnu, the Preserver God, He has been the most celebrated and revered of all Hindu gods for over 2,000 years.

Labyrinth— A maze design of Bronze-Age Crete, found throughout the world, and symbolizing the path of initiation. Also the underground complex of burial chambers and passages in ancient Knossos, at the heart of which dwelt the monstrous Minotaur—half man, half bull.

Lakshmi— Hindu Goddess of love, beauty and prosperity. Most widely worshipped Hindu Goddess.

Left-Hand Path— Occultists who spend their time being destructive, manipulative and "evil." (PEIB)

Right-Hand Path— Occultists who spend their time being constructive, manipulative and "good." *(PEIB)* Both are patriarchal terms that have grown out of medieval ceremonial magick and Qabalism.

Ley Lines— Straight tracks on the earth connecting sacred points, or "power spots," such as stone circles.

Life— A system exhibiting negative entropy.

Loa— Term used in Vodoun for spirit entities. The Loa are 'fed' by tending their altars, and worshipped by being allowed to possess the bodies of devotees in trance, whereupon they take on specific attributes.

Love— "That condition in which the happiness of another person is essential to your own." *(Robert A. Heinlein)* Devotion with commitment.

Lilith— Ancient Sumerian Owl Goddess. In Hebrew mythology, She was Adam's first wife. Divorced for insubordination, She became the mother of demons.

Litany— A repetitive hypnotic prayer.

Litha— Festival of Summer Solstice. Named for Grain Goddess, cognate to Ceres/Demeter.

Lughnasad— A Grand Sabbat, or cross-quarter festival, occurring midway between Summer Solstice and Autumn Equinox. Traditionally celebrated on Aug. 2, it occurs astrologically at 15° Leo. The festival of first fruits, it is named for Lugh, a Celtic solar god of ritual warfare. Celebrated with competitive games among men and boys. Christianized as Lammas.

Mabon— Festival of Autumn Equinox, named for son of Modron ("mothers"), Celtic God of the Harvest. (Aiden Kelly)

Macrocosm— The large-scale world beyond ones personal boundaries.

    Microcosm— The small-scale world within one's personal boundaries. Macrocosm and microcosm are magickally linked in the principle, "as above, so below."

Macumba— A religion similar to Vodoun, Macumba was started by African slaves in an attempt to continue their ancestral tribal religion after being captured by the Portuguese. Although now heavily overladen with Catholic symbolism, Macumbat is still persecuted by the Church and the Brazilian government.

Mage— A general term for anyone doing magic, especially of the active kinds; often used as a synonym for "magus." (PEIB)

Magi— Zoroastrian priests. Later used for powerful magicians of any sort (singular "magus").

Magician— A practitioner of magick.

Magick— (Spelled with a 'k' to distinguish from stage magic.) Probability enhancement. Coincidence control through manipulation of probabilities. The ability to transform or shape subjective or objective reality in accordance with will, by methods that cannot be explained by the current scientific paradigm. Manipulation of psychic phenomena. Magick is morally neutral, the purpose for which it is used being determined by the ethics of the practitioner. Rainbow magick is color-coded for spells:

    Black Magick— Used for blighting or binding. Popularly, magick done for "evil" purposes.

    Blue Magick— Used for emotional work, love, etc. Peace and protection.

    Green Magick— Used for working with vegetation, as in gardening. Fertility and prosperity.

    Orange Magick— Used for pride and courage. Heroism and attraction.

    Purple Magick— Used for wealth and good fortune. Prosperity, domination and command.

    Red Magick— Used for physical work, as in healing of people and animals. Passion and sex.

    White Magick— Used for blessing, or anything! Popularly, magick done for "good" purposes.

    Yellow Magick— Used for mental work, meditation, etc. Intellect.

Magick Circle— A circle drawn in astral flames with a sword or athame. Its astral shape is a conical vortex. Used as a focus of power for rituals, it is visualized as a doorway between dimensions.

Mana— Psychic energy (Polynesia). One's personal power, charisma, strength, force, etc.

Mandala— A visual image used as an associational device, particularly when drawn in a circular design.

Mantra— Words or sounds used primarily as associational devices.

Mary— From Egyptian, "Beloved." Identified in Christian tradition as the virgin mother of Jesus, Mary became equated with Isis, taking on titles such as "Mother of God" and "Queen of Heaven." Widely worshipped by Catholics, Mary is famed for Her many apparitions.

Maya— Sanskrit "illusion." Reality viewed as but a dream of the gods.

Medicine Wheel— The Native American religious analog to the Magick Circle of Witchcraft. Also used as a mandala. The same symbol is known as a "Sunwheel" in Europe, and is the astronomical sigil for planet Earth.

Medium— A person acting as a vehicle for non-corporeal entities by entering into a trance state or *seance* and allowing her/his mind/body to be possessed.

Messiah— A prophesied savior or deliverer of a people or country. (WNWD) Applied by Christians to Jesus.

Metamorphosis— Change of form, shape, structure or substance; transformation by magic or sorcery (e.g. werewolves). Also called "shape-shifting."

Metaphor— Any description of reality. Metaphors may be poetic, artistic, musical, religious, scientific, etc. All are merely descriptions; none is the reality itself. The map is not the territory.

Metaphysics— Philosophy of the relations between "underlying reality" and its manifestations. (PEIB)

Metokwiosi— Ogalala Sioux ritual expression meaning "All my relations," and implying an acknowledgement of the interconnectedness of all life.

Miracle— A favorable paranormal act or occurrence usually credited to divine intervention.

Mojo— Magickal power from the lower chakras, especially equated with Love and Power in Voodoo spells.

Monotheism— The belief that there is only one deity, who created and rules the universe. Such deity is generally characterized as being omnipotent, omniscient, omnipresent, pre-existent and eternal.

Morals— Social customs. Extrinsic behavioral principles of right conduct.

Motif— A common pattern running through stories, folktales or myths.

Mudra— Physical gestures used primarily as associational devices. *(PEIB)*

Mundane— Latin, "worldly." Commonplace, ordinary. Non-sacred.

Mysteries— Mystical metaphors revealed only to the initiated. Must be experienced.

Mysticism— The passive, theurgical, religious side of magick. *(PEIB)*

Myth— Metaphor, particularly one with a plot and a cast of characters.

Mytheology— A gestalt composed of myth and theology that forms the religious world-view of a people. (word coined by Samm Dickens)

Mythos— System of metaphors and motifs within a society or culture. *(PEIB)*

Necromancy— Greek, "corpse divination." The ritual of raising spirits of the dead, particularly for purposes of divination. (As when Saul went to the Witch of Endor to consult the spirit of Samuel.) Seances.

Numerology— Divination by means of numbers and numerical "values" assigned to letters of the alphabet.

Object Link— An object, such as a lock of hair, that through application of the magickal Law of Association becomes a link between the magician and the person for or against whom the magick is being worked.

Occult— Latin for "hidden." Refers to practices and knowledge unpopular with modern science and religion. Phenomena for which science has no theories or explanations. Arts and sciences based on a different world-view than Christianity.

Odin— Norse Father-God, husband of Frigga. Patron of shamans and wizards, He is one-eyed, having given His other eye as a sacrifice to gain wisdom.

Oimelc (also **Imbolc**)— A Grand Sabbat, or cross-quarter festival, occurring midway between Winter Solstice and Spring Equinox. Traditionally celebrated on Feb. 2, it occurs astrologically at 15° Aquarius The ancient Celtic festival of waxing light, it is dedicated to the Goddess Brigid. Celebrated with women's mysteries of birth and menstruation and initiation into womanhood. Oimelc has been Christianized as Candlemas.

Omega Point— That point in time when the individual consciousnesses of all the living beings of a planet coalesce into a single collective consciousness. Planetary apotheasis. (From Teilhard de Chardin)

Omen— An occurrence or phenomenon portending a future event.

Orishas— Yoruban term used in Santeria for African nature spirits or deities called "Loa" in Vodoun.

Osiris— Egyptian "green man;" God of Vegetation who dies and rules in the underworld as Lord of the Dead. Identified with the recently deceased Pharoah. Husband to Isis and father of Horus, his reincarnation.

Ostara— Festival of Spring Equinox, named for Saxon Fertility Goddess Eostra, cognate with Ishtar/Astarte, whose symbols are fertile eggs and prolific rabbits. Christianized as Easter.

Pagan— From Latin *paganus,* "peasant" or "country dweller." Of or pertaining to indigenous (native) pantheistic folk religions and peoples. A person who worships Nature, considers life to be sacred, and identifies with others who accept the label of Pagan.

Paganism— Pantheistic folk religion. Nature religions in general.

> **Neo-Paganism**— Non-indigenous pantheistic folk religion. New nature religions, emerging only in the past 25 years, but rooted in ancient traditions and attitudes.

Palmistry— Divination by reading the lines in hands.

Palo Mayombe— A Cuban sect of Santeria followed by many Latin American drug gangs. Sort of a "magickal mafia," leaders engage in human sacrifice and other terror tacts to keep followers in line and enemies at bay.

Pan— Pre-Christian Greek God of Wild Nature. Lusty and bawdy, Pan is a favorite God among many Witches and Neo-Pagans. Goat-horned and goat-hoofed, the image of Pan was appropriated to form the physical basis for the depiction of the Christian Devil.

Pantheism— Greek "all divine." The belief that divinity is a quality inherent in and manifesting through Nature; thus all Nature is seen as divine and holy.

Pantheon— The assemblage of deities and other spirits in any given religion.

Paranormal— Unusual or "supernatural." *(PEIB)* Not explainable by the current scientific paradigm.

Path— A method, system or approach to magickal or mystical knowledge.

Pendulum— A device consisting of a weight depending from a cord. The resultant swinging motion is used in divination.

Pentacle— A disk inscribed with a pentagram. It represents the Element Earth and is often used in Witchcraft as a plate to hold communion cakes or bread.

Pentagram— A five-pointed star used as a mandala for magickal conjurations. Represents human figure, with head, arms, legs. Generic religious symbol of Witchcraft.

Pentagram, Inverted— Within a circle, a primary symbol of Satanism. Represents goat's head, with horns, ears, beard. As the inverted cross represents the antithesis of Christianity, the inverted pentagram in a circle represents the antithesis of all that Witchcraft stands for. (Note: some traditional Witches also use the inverted pentagram *with or without a circle* to indicate the Horned God, as Pan.)

Philtre— A spell in which a charm is woven into a potion, for the purpose of transferring ones powers to the object of the spell.

Poltergeist— German, "noisy ghost." Recurrent spontaneous psychokinesis.

Polytheism— The belief that there are many deities.

Possession— An ecstatic occurrence in which the personality is overwhelmed and replaced by a non-corporeal entity.

Potion— An herbal brew used as an auxiliary homeopathic remedy with psychic healing.

Precognition— Latin, "foreknowledge." The ability to perceive events before they happen in contemporary time and space

.Priestess— A woman dedicated to the service of a deity. Her tasks include maintenance of temples and altars, administering of sacraments, conducting and presiding over rites and rituals, pastoral counseling, etc. She may also serve as a direct channel for the spirit of the Goddess.

> **Priest**— A male priestess. May channel the spirit of the God.

Prophet— A person who "speaks out for" a deity or other powerful spirit, usually about future events.

Prophecy— Visions and predictions of the future.

Psychic— Of or pertaining to mental powers or talents which can affect or alter reality by apparently non-physical means. Commonly contracted to "psi."

Psychic Attack— The use of magick or psi to harm or destroy a being.

Psychokinesis— Movement of matter and energy by the mind without any known physical connection.

Psycho-Symbiosis— Intimate and mutually interdependent association of two or more living beings on the psychic level. Specifically applied to the relationship between humans and plants cultivated for their psychotropic properties. *(Tom Williams)*

Psychopomp— The role of spiritual guide, especially between the worlds of life and after-life. Hermes, Anubis, Hecate and Vanthe were divine psychopomps who either brought the newborn into the world or escorted the dead into the afterworld.

Qaballah— (Also spelled Caballa and Kaballa) Originally a compendium of Hebrew mystical lore. It has been translated, Christianized and expanded upon from ancient times through the Middle Ages to become the major source of Western mainstream occultism.

Ra— Egyptian God of the blazing Sun.

Rainbow— An arc of refracted light displaying all the colors of the spectrum. As a symbol it is shared by Christians and Jews, recalling Jahveh's promise to Noah never to destroy the world by flood again. Neo-Pagans and New Agers regard the rainbow as a spontaneous miracle of natural magick and a symbol of beauty in diversity.

Reality— The perceptual field.

Subjective Reality— One's personal sensory experience, verifiable only to the one experiencing it.

Objective Reality— The inferred hypothetical field underlying our perception, verifiable only by apparent consistency of experiential or observational data.

Consensual Reality— An agreed-upon shared group metaphor.

Reincarnation— The survival of some part of the individual nonphysical metapattern beyond the death experience, which subsequently becomes incorporated into some other living being. Psychic recycling.

Religion— From Latin *religio,* "re-linking." A body of expressions of sacred myths, metaphors, observances and practices in a given cultural context designed to connect individuals with Divinity.

Rhiannon— Celtic Goddess of the full moon. Horses and birds are sacred to Her

Rite— A ceremonial act or series of acts.

Rites of Passage— Ritual commemoration of life's transitions. Such passages include:

Being Born— becoming an incarnate being.

Onset of Puberty— becoming sexually fertile.

Marriage— becoming bonded to a partner.

Giving Birth— becoming a Mother or Father.

Menopause— becoming a wise Crone.

Death— going to the Underworld to await rebirth.

Ritual— A magickal psycho-drama.

Ritual Abuse— Abuse that involves a series of repeated physical, emotional and/or sexual assaults combined with the systematic use of symbols, ceremonies or machinations. *(CSER)*

Runes— Any of various magickal alphabets, each letter of which contains an esoteric as well as an exoteric meaning.

Runestones— Magickally charged stones marked with letters of a runic alphabet and used for divination by "casting the runes."

Sabbat— One of the eight annual festivals of the seasonal round celebrated by nearly all Pagans, including Witches. The solstices and equinoxes are known as *quarters,* and the others are *cross-quarters,* also known as **Grand Sabbats** by Witches. Several are also celebrated by both Christians and Satanists. See *Wheel of the Year:*

Ostara— Spring Equinox, Mar. 21 (Easter)

Beltane— May 1 (May Day)

Litha— Summer Solstice, June 21 (St. John's)

Lughnasad— August 2 (Lammas)

Mabon— Autumn Equinox, Sep. 21 (Harvest)

Samhain— Nov. 1 (All Saints' Day)

Yule— Winter Solstice, Dec. 21 (Christmas)

Oimelc— Feb. 2 (Imbolc, Brigit, Candlemas)

Sacrament— An act or substance regarded as inherently holy. Sacramental rites commonly include: seining (baby blessing), rites of passage, communion, marriage, purification, confession, and rites of the dead. Sacramental substances include the wine and bread used in Christian and Wiccan communion, water shared by Neo-Pagans, and blood drunk by Satanists.

Sacred— Especially imbued with essence of Divinity.

Sacrifice— The act of offering the life of a person or animal, or of some object, in propitiation or homage to a deity. Something so offered. *(WNWD)*

Salamander— A Fire Elemental.

Samhain— (pronounced "*sô*-ahn")The Great Sabbat, or cross-quarter festival, occurring midway between Autumn Equinox and Winter Solstice. Traditionally celebrated on Nov. 1, it occurs astrologically at 15° Scorpio. It is the Celtic festival of the dead and the beginning of Winter, and its name means "Summer's End." It is celebrated with a "dumb supper;" a meal of "underworld foods" (mushrooms, nuts, black olives, pork, beans, etc.) shared in total silence, wherein the spirits of the beloved dead are invited to join the feast and be remembered in honor. Samhain has been Christianized as All Saints Day, with the night before being called Hallowmas or Halloween.

Santeria— One of the African diasporic faiths. A religion similar to Vodun and Macumba, which was an attempt for the Spanish-enslaved Africans of the Yoruba nation to continue their tribal religions in Spanish-speaking Cuba. Includes sacrifice of chickens, doves, goats, etc.

Satan— Hebrew for "adversary." During the Middle Ages a full Satanic theology was developed, in which Satan as the Devil became the God of evil and ruler of the Christian underworld, Hell. The collective Christian Id; the Antithesis of Yahveh.

Satanism— An anti-religion developed in reaction to and as an opposition to Christianity. It is the mirror image, the dark side, of Christianity, and shares the same history, mythology, and world-view as Christianity. Satanists regard Satan as equal in power to the Judeo-Christian God Jahveh, and base much of their mythology on Milton's *Paradise Lost,* wherein Satan was the loser in a civil war fought in heaven before the Creation. Satanists believe that Jahveh was not necessarily the more noble of the antagonists; merely the winner, and, disaffected from Christianity, they choose to side with its opponent, reversing all Christian rites and symbols, especially those of Catholicism. Distinctions should be made between religious Satanists, Satanic cults, and self-styled Satanists.

Satyr— A minor Greek spirit of the wilderness, always male, and attendant on Dionysos, God of madness and altered states. Originally depicted as human, with pointed ears, immense phallus and horse-like tail, they later acquired the goat's horns, legs, hooves and tail of Pan.

Science— Accumulated and accepted knowledge that has been systematized and formulated with reference to the discovery of general truths or the operation of general laws, especially knowledge obtained and tested through the use of the scientific method.

Science Fiction— Mythology based on scientific metaphor. Usually future-oriented, making it unique among mythologies, all others of which look to the past.

Scrying— Divination by gazing, as in a crystal, mirror, water, etc.

Seasonal Round— Mythic cycle of the natural year. Also a song about it.

Sect— A denomination. A subdivision of a larger religious system.

Seer— One who can see the hidden; a diviner. *(PEIB)*

Set— Egyptian adversary God, murderer of Osiris and usurper of his throne. Set was defeated and castrated by Osiris' son, Horus, who lost an eye in the battle. Some Satanists equate Set with Satan.

Shakti— The Female Principle in Hinduism.

Shaman— A medicine man or woman. A role in a tribal Pagan culture which is a combination of healer, priest(ess), diviner, magician, teacher and psychopomp (spirit guide). The shaman utilizes altered states of consciousness to produce and control psychic phenomena and travel to and from the spirit realm, or Dreamtime.

Shamanism— The practice of the arts of the shaman in a tribal cultural context.

Shrine— A place of worship, usually centered around a sacred relic. May take the form of a small display or diorama depicting a holy scene or objects.

Sigil— A magickal sign or cryptic device used to identify an entity.

Sign— A pattern of sensory stimuli which is intended to communicate data.

Sin— Specifically, conscious violation of the will of the deity one worships. Generally, hypocrisy; betrayal of one's own commitment.

Skyclad— Wiccan term for ritual nudity. In *Aradia, the Gospel of Witches,* the Goddess says: "And as a sign that you be truly free, you shall be naked in your rites."

Sorcery— Thaumaturgical arts.

Soul— Continuity of personal identity and memory. The spirit of a person or animal.

Spell— Complex interwoven set of mudras, mantras & mandalas, designed to achieve a magickal purpose.

Spiral— Ancient Goddess symbol of emergence.

Spiral Dance— A Wiccan greeting dance celebrating spiral symbolism. Also a book by Starhawk.

Spirit— A discrete consciousness, especially when manifesting in apparent isolation from an obvious physical body.

Spiritualism— A religion based upon the belief in life after death and communication through mediums with the spirits of the departed.

Sprite— A nature spirit, usually the collective consciousness of the life-forms inhabiting a very small but defined area, such as a glade or waterfall.

Staff— A Wizard's main implement. Made the same height as the Wizard, it serves to contain, direct and focus magickal energy. A Wizard's staff embodies his personal *mana,* and may not be used by anyone else.

Strega— Witchcraft of Italian or Sicilian tradition. An Italian or Sicilian Witch.

Supernatural— Ascribed to supposed agencies existing above, beyond or outside of Nature. In pantheistic theology, a null term.

Superstition— Fixed irrational notions held stubbornly in the face of contrary evidence. Any religious or philosophical beliefs you do not share.

Succubus— Demon in female form that seduces men in their sleep, causing wet dreams.

Swastika— An ancient pre-Indo-European symbol of the Sun and of the four directions. It represents the path of life and is virtually universal among ancient traditional peoples from Tibetan Bon-Po to the Hopi Indians of N. America, who depict it turning in either direction. Used as a symbol of the Aryan invasion by the Nazis in Germany and by contemporary Neo-Nazis, who *always* have it turning counter-clockwise. As such it is imbued with the ancient aura of power but is misunderstood and perverted.

Swiving— The ancient rite of copulating in the plowed fields to increase their fertility by sympathetic magick.

Sword— In magick, a consecrated ritual weapon used for concentration and direction of energy, and as an emblem either of Air or Fire, depending on the tradition.

Sylph— An Air Elemental.

Sympathetic Magick— Magick by association or imitation. The Laws of Sympathetic Magick state that the effect resembles the cause, and that which is done in the microcosm is reflected in the macrocosm.

Synchronicity— Simultaneous occurrence.
> **Synchronicity Principle**— Things happening at the same time are somehow connected and mutually influence each other. *(C.G. Jung)*

Synchronicity Wave— A cascading series of synchronicities leading to a significant transformational event. (Oberon Zell)

Synergy— The combined effect of several agencies such that the whole is greater than the sum of its parts. A synthesis in which new properties emerge that were not contained in any of the original components.

Talent— An unusual natural ability, particularly a psychic ability.

Talisman— A manufactured object or mandala carried on one's person for the purpose of attracting good luck.

Tantra— A Tibetan system of theurgical methods and training that particularly utilizes techniques for the control and direction of sexual energy.

Tarot— A set of 78 cards with illustrations into which are incorporated a vast amount of arcane symbolism. Considered by many to contain the sum total of all occult knowledge. The ancestor of our modern playing cards, the Tarot is today used primarily for divination (cartomancy).

Telepathy— Direct communication of thoughts from mind-to-mind.

Teleportation— Instantaneous movement of a person or object from one place to another without going through normal space-time.

Thaumaturgy— The use of magick to effect changes in the reality outside of the magician. The scientific and technical aspects of such workings. Also known as **Sorcery.**

TheaGenesis— Greek, "birth of the Goddess." A description of the process of emergent evolution of planetary consciousness as an aspect of the Gaea Thesis. Equates Teilhard de Chardin's "Omega Point" with the conscious awakening of Mother Earth. *(Term coined in 1970 by Otter G'Zell)*

Thealogy— Intellectual speculations concerning the nature of Goddess and Her relations to the world in general and humans in particular.

Theology— Intellectual speculations concerning the nature of God and His relations to the world in general and humans in particular.

Theurgy— The use of magick to effect changes in the magician's own internal reality. Magick used for self-actualization or personal apotheosis. Focus is on prayers, invocations, meditations.

Thor— Norse God of lightning and thunderstorms, giving his name to "Thursday."

Thurible— A consecrated ritual incense-burner.

Totem— A species of plant or animal regarded as having an ancestral or affinitive relationship to a specific tribe, family, or individual.

Trance— A mental state of disassociation and withdrawal during which the brain wave activity is slowed down to 8 cycles per second or less. Hypnosis.

Transcendent Divinity— The theological position that Divinity exists apart from or outside of Nature; that there is a "supernatural" realm. That Divinity is a quantity, not a quality, and may be found without, not within. "The Divine Forever Other."

Tree of Life— Symbolic representation of the emergent evolution of lifeforms. Represents the umbilical cord of Mother Earth.

Triskelion— A three-part symbol used by the Celtic Druids to signify all the Sacred Triads, such as the Triple Goddess.

Undine— A Water Elemental.

Veve— Drawn designs used in Vodun to summon the various *Loa.*

Vortex— A helical flow of energy about an axis, drawing into its center all that surrounds it.

Vodoun (Voodoo)— A transplanted tribal religious tradition brought to the West Indies and the Americas by enslaved Africans. Its rites involve ecstatic possession by ancestor archetypes *(loa)* and raising power to do magickal workings. Includes bird and animal sacrifices.

Wand— A consecrated short rod used ritually for concentration and direction of energy in circumstances where it would be inappropriate to use a blade. Emblem for Fire or Air, depending on one's tradition.

Walpurgisnacht— Beltane Eve.

Warlock— From either Anglo-Saxon *waerloga,* "oath-breaker, or Old Norse *varð-lokkur,* "caller of spirits." During the Burning Times, "warlock" was the word used for a Witch who betrayed others to the Inquisition. Erroneously used by cowans to refer to male Witches. Contemporary Wiccans use the term for an initiated Witch who turns against the Craft.

Weather-Working— The application of psychokinesis to effect meteorological change.

Web, the— The total pattern formed by all the interactions of all matter and all energy. *(PEIB)*

Wheel of the Year— The Seasonal Round of 8 annual festivals, or Sabbats, equated with the macrocosmic Magick Circle.

Widdershins— Counterclockwise. (see **Deosil**)

Witch— From Anglo-Saxon *wicce* (f.), "sorceress," from root *weik,* "to bend." A magickal shaper of reality. A shaman of Celtic or Saxon pre-Christian European tradition. A trained and initiated practitioner of Witchcraft. In medieval and renaissance times, Witches specialized in herbalism and midwifery, and were mostly women. Modern Witches may be both men and women, and workings are directed primarily towards healing, both of people and the Earth. The single most common ethical statement acknowledged by Witches is *The Wiccan Rede:* "An it harm none, do as you will."

Witchcraft (Wicca; The Craft)— The practice of shamanism in the context of a European heritage. Currently, the major faction of the Neo-Pagan religious movement. Organized in autonomous *covens* of up to 13 members. Various denominations, known as *traditions,* include: Gardnerians, Alexandrians & Georgians (named after their late founders); Dianics (mostly all-women, worshipping the Goddess exclusively); Faeries (mostly all-men); Shamanics, who seek to function in the original tribal medicine way; various ethnic traditions, such as Welsh, Celtic, Norse, Saxon, Strega, etc.; and Eclectics, who assimilate whatever they find useful or appropriate among all other traditions.

Witches Anti-Discrimination Lobby— Contemporary organization for the purpose of legally combatting slander and libel against Witchcraft.

Wizard— From Anglo-Saxon *wysard,* "wise one." A solitary practitioner of magick and repository of arcane knowledge. A loremaster. Commonly a specifically masculine term, but this is not necessarily so, as women have been and are now also sometimes called wizards..

Working— A thaumaturgical act.

Worship— Communion with Divinity, however that is defined by the worshippers.

Wortcunning— Herbal lore. *Worts* are herbs.

Wraith— Projected astral body.

Xenophilia— A fascination for that which is new, different or strange.

Xenophobia— A morbid fear of that which is new, different or strange. *(PEIB)*

Yin & Yang— In Taoism, yin is the female, negative, dark, passive principle in the universe, and yang is the male, positive, light, active principle. This dualism underlies much of Chinese philosophy, religion, medicine, science and magic.

Yoga— In Hinduism, mental discipline directed toward the identification of consciousness with its object.

Yule— Norse, "Wheel" for turning of the year. Festival of Winter Solstice, longest night of the year; celebrating birth of the Sun-God. Christianized as Christmas.

Zodiac— The band of twelve constellations along the plane of the ecliptic through which pass the sun, moon and planets across the sky. Each constellation, or sign, is attributed symbolic significances and associations that affect various aspects of life on Earth.

Zombi— In Vodoun, a reanimated corpse whose soul has been possessed by another through magic and whose body is at the disposal of the magician. In actuality, one who has apparently died, then been revived in a disoriented state, due to deliberate poisoning with puffer fish venom and subsequent forced ingestion of jimson weed combined with hypnosis.

Online Writings About CAW

"Robert A. Heinlein's *Stranger in a Strange Land* and the Church of All Worlds," by Carole Cusack, September 2008. https://www.researchgate.net/publication/344084782_Robert_A_Heinlein's_Stranger_in_a_Strange_Land_and_the_Church_of_All_Worlds

"The Production of Ritual in a Modern Pagan Religion: The Church of All Worlds," by Carole Cusack, July 2011. https://www.researchgate.net/publication/344084756_Ritual_in_the_Church_of_All_Worlds

"Science Fiction as Scripture: Robert A. Heinlein's *Stranger in a Strange Land* and the Church of All Worlds," by Carole Cusack, September 2011. https://www.researchgate.net/publication/277740535_Science_Fiction_as_Scripture_Robert_A_Heinlein's_Stranger_in_a_Strange_Land_and_the_Church_of_All_Worlds

"Church of All Worlds," by Isaac Nash & Jacob Holbrook, May 9, 2014. https://prezi.com/wbvsbhh-czbh/church-of-all-worlds/

"The Church of All Worlds, a Brief History," Sacred Texts, https://archive.sacred-texts.com/bos/bos572.htm

"Atompunk Spirituality: The Church of All Worlds," July 18, 2014. https://steampunkopera.wordpress.com/2014/07/18/atompunk-spirituality-the-church-of-all-worlds/

"Church of All Worlds," by Lux Ferre, July 25, 2017: https://occult-world.com/church-of-all-worlds/

"Church of All Worlds, A Brief History." The Pagan Library, August 19, 2018. https://www.paganlibrary.com/reference/church_of_all_worlds.php

"The Church of All Worlds: From an Invented Religion to a Religion of Invention," by Damian Lanahan-Kalish. A Thesis submitted in partial satisfaction of the requirements for the degree Master of Arts in Religious Studies. June 2019. https://escholarship.org/uc/item/9m54h81q

"Church of All Worlds." Wikipedia. https://en.wikipedia.org/wiki/Church_of_All_Worlds

"Oberon Zell and the Church of All Worlds," Neo-Paganism.org. https://neo-paganism.org/oberon-zell-and-morning-glory-zell/

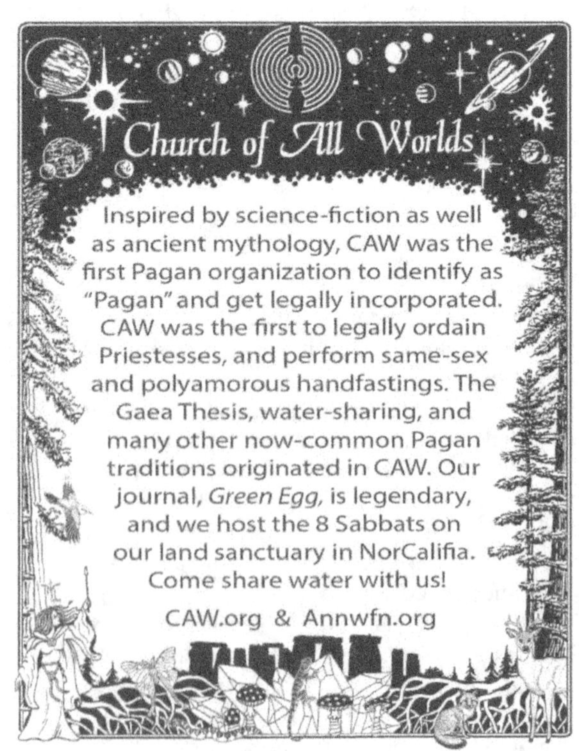

Essential CAW books. Available on Amazon.com